LES BROWNLEE

THE AUTOBIOGRAPHY OF A PIONEERING
AFRICAN-AMERICAN JOURNALIST

LES BROWNLEE

THE AUTOBIOGRAPHY OF A PIONEERING AFRICAN-AMERICAN JOURNALIST

Marion Street Press, Inc.
www.marionstreetpress.com
Oak Park, Illinois

Cover design by Gloria Chantell
Cover photo by A.G.R. Photography, Arlington Heights, IL
Edited by Susan S. Stevens

ISBN 1-933338-10-5
ISBN 13: 978-1-933338-10-1

Marion Street Press, Inc.
PO Box 2249
Oak Park, IL 60303
866-443-7987
www.marionstreetpress.com

Foreword

As a reporter, Les Brownlee helped break the color line in Chicago journalism, once as rigid and unyielding in big city newsrooms as it had been in major league baseball.

Les did this as gracefully as Jackie Robinson of the Dodgers, and stayed a reporter to the end, writing this memoir of an extraordinary life, even with death pressing down upon him.

After one of the many journalism award banquets and tributes to him before he passed away, we sat together off to the side, teacher and student. There was an urgency to these awards and ceremonies of recognition, and he knew it, and we knew it.

Guests at these dinners approached him, old friends and colleagues, former students, and folks he'd never met, taking one last snapshot, offering what they must have figured would be their last congratulations. He enjoyed it, and was also amused.

"How many people get to see their obituaries before they're dead?" he said with a chuckle.

Obituaries involve words often written by strangers, and these can be puny things when used to measure a human life. It's difficult enough to measure one's own life, at night, at difficult times, in those hours before dawn when the house is silent and the earth is cold and you're alone with quiet demands of honesty. That's difficult enough, as it must have been for Les.

Yet in the hands of strangers who end up doing much of the measuring, obituaries can be particularly clumsy and limiting. Through no fault of their own, the dead are put into someone else's context, shaped and molded to fit the requirements of the living. That's where the sin of it comes in.

If you've lived long enough, you've come to understand this. Les Brownlee, my teacher, was a journalist who lived long life, so he'd seen it, too.

But he solved the problem the way a good reporter would solve it, by refusing to be scooped on his own story, by writing this book. And what a story it is.

He lost a father to racism, because the local hospital wouldn't accept a black man in the emergency room. He was almost denied an education, but wanted to learn so badly that he left home as a teenager and lived in a caddy shack at a golf club. He slept without heat at night, and ate where he could, and walked miles so that he could attend a superb North Shore high school.

Those chapters in this book could inspire so many families, this story of a young man, alone, so desperate to learn, and read and understand.

He made his mark as a reporter, but he was also a teacher, always encouraging, always supportive to his journalism students at Columbia College. And though he has a fine professional legacy, stories reported in print and broadcast, there is nothing older than old news. It becomes brittle and yellowed and crumbly.

Les Brownlee left more than clippings and memories behind him. He left a family and his dear wife, and another legacy as well.

It is found in newsrooms, in the generations of news reporters he nurtured and trained in his classroom, kids that wouldn't have much of a chance in this business without his kindness and encouragement. And I'm one of them.

Brownlee's students didn't have much money, or fancy journalism pedigrees, or family connections to publishers and news executives.

We were mostly of two types, city kids who scraped by out of high school, and suburbanites who'd failed at other colleges. Many of us had come to college late, some of us had dropped out of other schools, finally taking another stab at education at Columbia College, if not wiser then at least older, somewhat desperate and hungry, ready to focus and learn and work.

We didn't come for theory or lectures from people who taught because they couldn't report. We were aware of time passing, and needed to find jobs. We'd heard they had pros at Columbia, teachers who'd actually worked in Chicago newsrooms and knew others who still worked in those newsrooms.

And what we required were pros to teach us, to show us the way. Many of us found that pro in Les Brownlee.

Though he's celebrated as an African-American pioneer who opened doors for African-American journalists, I'm not one of them. I was a child of Chicago's white flight of the 1960s, whole neighborhoods running from parts of town that would become ghettos overnight, the same neighborhoods that news organizations ignored.

And he helped me, and he helped others, regardless of race or ethnicity, always patient, always interested, always encouraging as long as we understood that reporting wasn't about attitude.

For Les, reporting was about accuracy, gathering facts and questioning assumptions. And about treating folks with respect.

Unfortunately, many young reporters demonstrate just the opposite each time they walk up to someone, flick open their reporter's notebook, and with pen poised and ready, prepare to measure a stranger's life.

They didn't have Les Brownlee to teach them. He would tell us about the power of that reporter's notebook, how intimidating it could be to folks who'd been minding their own business until they were hit with something that an editor deemed newsworthy.

The last thing they needed was some reporter descending upon them, notebook ready, a stranger eager to fix their lives in print and judge them with a stranger's words, as butterfly collectors fix insects with pins on a board.

Les would tell us: Keep the notebook in your pocket for a while. Get to know the people. Talk to them. Treat them like human beings. Don't ever treat them a subjects of some study.

If you wait, and treat them with respect and let them fill in the blank spaces in a conversation, they're more apt to tell you what they're thinking.

Another one of Les Brownlee's rules for young reporters was "Be kind to the secretaries." This was especially apt for reporters who would end up doing the heavy lifting, covering the building beats, from police headquarters to the statehouse.

The secretaries, Les would say, have families, and if they don't have families they have other special interests. Get to know what those interests are. Get to know them. Remember their birthdays with a card, or a phone call.

"They're the non-commissioned officers who run things," he'd say. "Be nice to them. They know where stories come from."

I can't tell you how many times I've used his advice, in beat reporting and later in writing a column here for the Chicago Tribune.

Of course, he was right, as he was about so much, and now he's gone. But unlike so many who are gone, unremembered, Les Brownlee left his mark.

He left behind his wife and family, his colleagues, and his students.

And he left us this book — in which he measured himself — to remember him by.

John Kass
Oct. 8, 2006

Introduction

A couple years ago — I think it was the winter of 2004 — Les and I joined our artist friends Tom Seagard and Brigitte Kozma at an Italian restaurant.

Tom, though in his 50s, is the perennial 60s fellow, always sporting a ponytail and beard. Brigitte is the archetypical beautiful and vivacious painter with long wavy hair.

They were already seated, with drinks, water glasses and menus. We sat down and waited for service. And waited. Tom, annoyed, fetched a waitress, demanding service. After a long wait, someone brought us empty glasses but no water or menus.

Tom, this time angry, dragged a waitress to the table. She went to get a pitcher of water and then proceeded — literally — to throw water and ice cubes into Les's glass, causing the water and cubes to spill over onto the table and Les's and my laps.

Tom began to fume. He tried to get the busboy to bring rolls, to no avail.

After a while our orders were taken and Tom and Brigitte were served, but not Les or me. Tom started to rant. A few minutes later someone brought me part of my meal, but nothing for Les.

That was it. We all got up to walk out. While I was negotiating what we would not pay, Tom was verbally blasting the owner and pledging to blackball the restaurant to anyone who came into his Mill Road Gallery in Door County, Wisconsin.

Les had sat calmly during the whole affair, chatting and chuckling with Brigitte and me. We all walked out, Les's holding my hand with one hand and his Kenya made cane with the other. We all met at another restaurant.

Tom was still fuming and devising ways to do the restaurant in. Les sat back, then forward, looked gently at Tom, and, with his characteristically soothing baritone voice, said:

"Tom, it was your ponytail!"

Later Les would say that the incident reminded him of the Jim Crow days. His immediate objective, however, was to get Tom to feel better. Les had to fly to Tom's defense, as he did whenever he witnessed injustice.

Naturally, racism was an issue Les faced throughout his life. "Over the years I was able to go beyond his always-present good humor and discover the African-American whose good nature and warm friendship masked a deep and ongoing anger against the prejudices and mistreatment he had suffered at the hands of bigots," wrote our friend Herb Kraus in the Headline Club Bulletin. Our friend Studs Terkel said, "His remarkable and unique thoughts on race had an exhilarating effect on all readers, especially this one."

How does one describe and explain the Wonderful, the Magic, and the Joy, that was Les Brownlee? Les would frequently say, in casual conversation or when interviewed, "I have lived the life of a fairy tale." Or, he would say he had lived a "charmed" life.

In this book, most of his autobiography (many stories were cut for space), Les relates his "fairy tale" life in his own words.

I knew Les almost my entire life, from when I was two, three or four. He was close to my late father, Curtis D. MacDougall, Les's professor at the Medill School of Journalism at Northwestern University. Les referred to Dad as his "adopted father." Les and his first wife Vera, a popular Evanston schoolteacher, were frequently at our house while I was growing up. It was always a treat to see them. Sometimes they brought their cute and brilliant son Laird, seven years younger than I (and now my stepson).

Les and Vera were both always interested in and encouraging of whatever I was up to. I realized many years later that I had been privileged to have been given the influence of Les's magic even as a child.

Thus, when I asked my nieces Jennifer Cottrell (Miller) and Stephanie Cottrell (Bryant) in 1986 if it was OK with them if I married Les, I told them that it was important to both of us that they accepted him even though it would mean fewer trips with me to Europe and elsewhere. Stephanie, after joking about wanting the trips, asked me "Do you love him?" I told her "I've always loved Les."

When we married, in 1987, I knew that Les had done just about everything in journalism, and was considered the African-American pioneer in his field. But, I had no idea just how much he had done. When he was on the Daily News, the Chicago Defender, the Chicago American, etc., in the '40s and '50s I wasn't reading newspapers. The journalism arena I knew him in was TV — I can still envision and hear him signing off, "Les Brownlee, Channel 7, Eye-Witness News." He told us how he thought up the term "eye-witness news" on the spot after actually witnessing the aftermath of a savings and loan robbery that day.

Les's great niece Jennifer Frances, granddaughter of his sister Agnes, frequently tells about how her family would rush to the TV every night to see Uncle Les on TV. "It's Uncle Les, it's Uncle Les!" someone would excitedly yell and Jennifer's siblings Lisa, Donna and Bruce would come running. People often came up to us on the street to tell us they used "to go to bed" with Les, or that he had been in their living room many times.

In 1987, when I married Les, I also did not know much about his New Trier High School friends or his family and how close he was to them despite physical distances (his mother and two sisters had moved to California in the '50s). By 1986, when I finally took Les's years of marriage proposals seriously, Les had lost his mother and sisters Gladys, who had introduced him to the world of books and poetry; Agnes who used to get him in free to the movies where she played the piano for the silent movies, and Elizabeth (Itsy) who could out dance anyone — "Gads, could that girl dance!" Les frequently ruminated.

Les's nieces Carole Brewer and Marletta Martenia, his sister Lejeune (June) and his brother Ray and son Laird, and Les's brother and sister in law, Carl and Louise (sister of June's husband Monroe) Hutt became my family after my mother died in 1992 soon after my sister had married someone my mother disdained, and had gone her own way with the nieces. On my mother's side we still had my mother's dear friend Germaine Asbury, and my grandmother's sister Opal Uzzell for a few years. Aunt Opal just loved Les and introducing him in redneck southern Illinois territory as "my nephew." Les and Aunt Opal would sing hymns together. Germaine would accompany Les singing opera.

While Les referred to his life as a "fairy tale" he also characterized all the family, and some professional, turmoil we faced in our lives together as a "soap opera." He deeply grieved the deaths of his brother Ray in March, 1999 and sister June in February, 2000, and the estrangement of my nieces and his beloved sons from his second marriage.

But, you go on, he would say. Like in football, when you are tackled, you get up and say, "Now, on the next play..."

When Les's life-long friend Art Nielsen — who, in 2002, seeded the funding for the annual Les Brownlee Journalism Series — visited Les when he was in intensive care last November 2005, Les opened his eyes, looked up at Art and softly said, "It must be Christmas." He could not say much more at that time or when several of his New Trier group of friends, Bud Riley, Mary Evelyn Sundloff and Mary Frances Badger Bridewell, visited him shortly thereafter.

Les's sister Maxine Hickman of California survives all the siblings. After Les was diagnosed with non small cell lung cancer on April 19, 2005, days after we returned from our annual trip to the Hotel Glavjc in Torno, Italy, she and her daughter Charlene Hickman came to Evanston for a family reunion and open house for all of Les's friends, students and colleagues. "I had the best conversation I have ever had with my brother!" Maxine happily exclaimed.

When we married in 1987, Les had been teaching at Columbia College since the late '70s. I grew up used to students and former students idolizing my late father, who built the School of Journalism at Northwestern, and also my mother, who taught in the Winnetka Public Schools. But, the adoration, the devotion and love I saw (and still see) coming from Les's Columbia College students, colleagues and friends was something so extraordinary, so unprecedented, it was and is truly "beyond words." Les deeply believed in the mission of Columbia College, to give the opportunity of a college education to anyone with a high school degree or equivalent.

In an interview with Professor Louis Silverstein respecting an oral history of Columbia College, Les referred to Columbia students as "swimming upstream" with all their financial and other obligations. "What I found in my experience in teaching goes back to the same thing that I learned coaching junior high and teens: Not only do you have to show them how but you have to brainwash them into the feeling that they can do it."

Scott Fosdick, Les's colleague at Columbia in the 1990s, sent a tribute for Les's Emeritus ceremony in October 2004:

"I will miss hearing about the countless students who have been inspired and rescued by his patient attention, his continual recognition that character drives performance...All I really know about Les is what it is like to share an academic foxhole with him. But that is enough. When memos from deans and provosts are flying over your head, when committees converge and needy students spread across the carpet like landmines, when collegiality becomes the last casualty in a war of attrition, there is no better company than Les Brownlee. His smile heals all wounds. His handshake confers power. All he has to do is wag his head and chuckle to let you know that he has seen far worse and survived, that the present crisis — whatever it is, and there always is one — will not last, that in any case, come what may, he is your comrade in arms until the last dog stops barking."

Another Columbia educator and Chicago Tribune journalist, Wilma Jean Randal, wrote of Les: "When I learned that he was on faculty I made a point to seek him out, this legend in Chicago Journalism history and in the history of African-American journalists ... Les was one of the people I really needed to talk with, touch base with, when I decided to quite the Tribune in Feb. 1988 and accept a job in West Africa. He was so encouraging ... I hope it gives you comfort to know how his talent and kindness touched the hearts and lives of so many people — I am one of them, and for that I am truly grateful."

I often told people that I "shared" my husband. Knowing what a remarkable influence he had on people, I wanted everyone to have the advantage of knowing him. Les would be in a grocery line and, by the time he had his groceries bagged up, he would have inspired the salesperson to go back to school and come to our party that night.

After Les's death I received a phone call from a military charity. Devastated to learn of Les's death, the representative told me that they had spoken about once a year for years, that he had encouraged her to go back to school for her degree and that she had done so. She had hoped to tell him about it. She had never met Les.

"Les was always helping people, even people who had done bad things, always talking to them in a way to make them feel good about themselves and their abilities and to encourage them to do their best," said our friend Lorraine Fishman, Les and Vera's neighbor on Skokie in the '50s and '60s.

Poetry was always a part of Les' life, and some of his friends wrote poems in his honor. Dr. Aaron and Joyce Hilkevitch wrote this poem for Les' 90th birthday:

Here's the story
He transcends each category
A man for all seasons
Who consorts with logic and reasons

Martha Urban, a student and a swimming pal of Les', wrote him a cinquain for his emeritus:

NU
Photo lab mate
Y pool swimming pal,
The coed with the 'cute knees' sends
Her best.

And close friend Blair Laden wrote the following for Les' Memorial Celebration:

Miz Brownlee's Child

When Rosa's child Les was born,
he bellowed loud and clear, "I am here."
Miz Brownlee's child had much to say,
Miz Brownlee's child made his mark in his own way.
With recipes for apple pie,
With Rosa's Rolls and muffins too.
He earned his way through Ivy's halls.
One helping hand along the way,
Named MacDougall claimed him for his clan.
Whether cook or football star,
He worked with fun and vigor.
Throughout his life the feasts increased,
To all our nurture and delight.
As husband father, family, friend,
Love remained the main ingredient.
As soldier and reporter he challenged barriers of color
and spoke for all to hear.
Whether to presidents or prisoners,
His message was loud and clear:

Fear not the bellringer!

With passion he passed on his skills
As teacher and role model.
As Torch Bearer for future bellringers
He lights the way

Les himself wrote poetry, and he had a poem or saying for almost any situation, often made up on the spot. A favorite:

Inevitable is the nearing day
When small impellencies shall supercede
The high illusions, and a lesser creed
Shall blanch horizons which were scarlet gay
Into a sober mistiness of gray.

Although I could go on for pages citing accolades upon accolades about Les,
I will conclude with part of Leslie McClellan's presentation at Les's Memorial,
one of the last letters he wrote to his friend Art Nielsen, and a segment of one
of the poems Les recited most frequently.

Leslie McClellan wrote: "I learned the most amazing lesson about genuine-
ly caring for people just being in Les Brownlee's hospital room.... It seemed as
if until the very end, Les was still bringing us together. Still making us laugh.
Still reaching out to us. Still caring for us even though we were there to care
for and support him."

After Les retired from Columbia College on July 1, 2004 we traveled — to
Alaska, California, Utah and New York. Upon our return Les wrote to Art
Nielsen, inviting him to Thanksgiving.

Precious Little Brother—
My fingers are strangers to the keyboard, so I'll just hunt and
peck.
When yellow leaves or none, or few do hang upon the boughs that
shake against the cold. Bare ruined choirs where late the sweet birds
sang. (Shakespeare)
I know we are reaching that time in our lives "when yellow leaves
or none or few..." and perhaps we should plan to see each other more
often before we are unable to see at all.
I suspect that you and Patti have plans for Thanksgiving, but we
would be pleased if you two could share turkey-day with us (I make
terrific dish of candied sweet potatoes).

Actually, the last thing Les cooked was candied sweet potatoes, for his former student Cynthia Rodriquez Pelayo. (She and her husband had joined us in
Italy a few weeks before Les's diagnosis). Les just had no energy, so he sat in

the breakfast room and I brought him the ingredients.

Les was admitted to the hospital on October 18, 2005 with pulmonary emboli. He eventually caught the inevitable hospital infection before he was stabilized well enough to go to a near-by nursing home where I could stay with him. When he was taken to the ICU, on Veteran's Day, Wisconsin friends Della Tesch and Dawn Masbruch, with her son Cody, drove down in the middle of the night to be with me, with us.

With Della and me by his sides, my holding him behind his neck with my left hand, asleep with my head on his right shoulder, and holding his right hand, Les died in his sleep around 3:30 a.m. on November 21, 2005.

A book of verses, underneath the bough,
A jug of wine, a loaf of bread — and thou!
Beside me singing in the wilderness-
Ah, Wilderness, were paradise enow!

Love Poem by Omar Khayyam

—Priscilla Ruth MacDougall, December 2006

Chapter 1

"Daddy's Dead!"

Dr. Rudolph Abelard Penn sat in the living room of a crowded apartment in Evanston, Illinois. Tears rolled down his light brown cheeks as he spoke to Rosa Brownlee and the two eldest of her seven children.

"The doctors at Cook County Hospital said they could have saved Reverend Brownlee's life if they had received him 15 minutes earlier," the family physician told them.

My mother and my sisters, Gladys, 22, and Agnes, 20, began sobbing.

I was eavesdropping in one of the two bedrooms shared by our family of nine.

"Daddy's dead! Daddy's dead!" I screamed to my three youngest sisters, Elizabeth (Itsy) 4, LeJeune, 2, and Maxime, 10 months, and my brother, Raymond, 5.

Everyone in our home soon started crying, rejecting Mother's efforts to comfort us.

Leonidas Brownlee's death of a burst appendix on December 31, 1922 occurred when he was 46 and I was seven years old.

Because of my father's skin color, Evanston Hospital was not open to him, and no ambulance would transport him to another hospital. Dr. Penn had taken Daddy by Yellow Cab on a two-hour ride from our home at 1720 Emerson St. in north suburban Evanston's African-American ghetto to Cook County Hospital on Chicago's West Side.

Locations for Daddy's burial also were limited. Daddy was laid to rest in Sunset Memorial Cemetery — a "colored" graveyard.

This was an inglorious ending for Reverend Brownlee, a dedicated pastor who had been building a congregation at Evanston's Church of God.

In terms of health care and many other things, doors were still closed as if we were slaves. During my life, I never set out to open any doors, but managed to break down some of those barriers anyway.

Mother told me that, although we were sorry that Daddy was no longer with us, we should be glad that Daddy was in Heaven with God and all the angels. When outside, I kept looking for Daddy, Bible in hand, preaching to an old white man with a long, flowing beard, seated on a golden throne and surrounded by white angels with long white wings. Now and then the angels would exclaim: "Amen, amen!" There were colored angels, too, with long, black wings, on their hands and knees polishing the streets of gold while they hummed Negro spirituals.

The family

Daddy was the youngest of three brothers who grew up around Anderson, South Carolina. Their parents had been slaves, but he had been born free in 1877. It had been illegal to teach a slave to read, but Daddy's mother, Alicia, was a "house slave" charged with looking after a 10-year-old girl. When the tutor taught the girl to read, Daddy's mother also learned. She later taught her sons to read, making them much better prepared than the offspring of most slaves.

I was given Daddy's brothers' names, Harrison and Pierce, as middle names on my birth certificate.

My parents wanted their children to be proud of their heritage and stand out from the crowd, so embellished on our names. I believed my first name was "Lestre" until I was well into adulthood. When I learned my birth certificate read "Lester," I would have changed my byline but had already been using "Les." My sister Maxime still thinks her name is Maxine. Her birth certificate actually reads "Mabel Josephine," but no one ever called her that. I remember Daddy saying that she would be Maxime with an "m" and that is how I have always referred to her.

Daddy's two older brothers had gone north and established a dry cleaning business in Wakefield, Rhode Island.

Daddy, who had remained in the South, got a job driving for a livery stable in Anderson. He met Mother when he took a fare to the small hotel where Mother was working as a cook. Mother was 16 when she met and married Daddy in 1899.

Gladys Lorena, their first child, was born in 1900. Mother told me that after their second child, Agnes Marie, was born in 1902, Daddy wrote to his brothers to complain about how difficult it was to make ends meet. The brothers invited him to Rhode Island to help them with their business, which had grown. He went, learned the cleaning business, sent money home to his wife and two daughters, and saved so that he could move his family to join him. Mother, Gladys and Agnes arrived in Rhode Island 12 years later, in 1914. I was born there in 1915.

Daddy had been studying for the ministry by correspondence with the

The only known photo of Rev. Leonidas Brownlee, Les' father.

headquarters of the Church of God in Marion, Indiana. He was ordained in 1916, and in 1917 he was assigned to a small congregation in Pittsburgh.

Mother's family

My mother had many more years to tell me about her childhood than Daddy did. As a girl, she had attended a rural school near Belton, South Carolina, for three months out of the year for four years. She had learned basic arithmetic and had learned to read from the one book the school owned: the Holy Bible.

Mother was the seventh of eleven children. Her parents had been slaves on a plantation near Belton, and they stayed on the plantation after slavery was abolished. Everyone worked in the fields, mostly picking cotton. Everyone was expected to pick 200 pounds of cotton a day — except mother. While very young, she developed an uncanny ability to cook. From the time she was eight years old, she was sent home from the fields at about four o'clock in the after-noon to prepare supper for the family, and to take care of younger siblings.

Cooking dinner meant that first mother gathered wood, built a fire in the range and put on a big kettle of water to boil while she picked the mustard, col-lard greens or other vegetables that grew in the garden next to the house. She would put a large piece of "fat back" into the water and add the greens. She would cook potatoes, and while these items were cooking, she would stir up a big batch of corn-bread or biscuits.

Not much had changed for the family when slavery was abolished. They were introduced to a new economic concept called "share-cropping." This meant that they were supposed to get some of the profits from the crops they harvested. No one knows if they got their fair share of the proceeds. They got what "the man" said they earned, but they didn't go hungry.

They had a garden behind their house and grew much of the food they ate. They had chickens, several hogs, but no cows. Sometimes "the man" gave her father some money, and they would buy cloth to make clothes for the family. Also, they got money enough for shoes. They saved those for Sundays. The rest of the time they went barefoot.

Of the four boys and seven girls in the family, none had much education. As adults they drifted apart, rarely keeping in touch with one another. Mother learned many years later that her oldest brother, Henry Latimer, had moved to Columbus, Ohio. She attempted to get in touch with him, but was told by his family that he was very ill. Later, she learned that he had died. His offspring seemed uninterested in following up the contact.

I inherited Mother's talent in the kitchen. When I was 10, she began teaching me to cook for the family while she was at work. My cooking skill stood me in good stead repeatedly through my early years.

My parents' lives consisted of two principal goals — survival and heaven after death.

*

In Rhode Island we had a bulldog named "Trouble." I am told that he was so well trained that he could be sent to the store with a market basket and a note. The store owner would fill the order, place the food in the basket, and Trouble would return with the order.

I know nothing of that, but I do recall one episode vividly. Trouble was sent to watch me when I went onto the sidewalk to play. I saw a dime about two feet off the curb in the street. When I tried to step off the curb to get it, Trouble grabbed my coat in his teeth and would not let go. I pounded him on his head, but still he would not let go. I went home crying, but got no sympathy.

Daddy worked with his brothers in the cleaning shop each day. When I was about a year and a half old, Mother went to work in the shop cleaning ladies gloves.

Agnes later told me she and Gladys were responsible for me while Mother was at work. She told me that the two of them locked me in a room with a piece of bread and jelly while they went out to play. They would return in time to clean me up before Mother came from the shop.

My brother, Raymond, was born in 1917 and my sister, Olive Elizabeth (whom we called Itsy, because she thought she was "It") in 1918.

Daddy's Church of God transferred him to Sharon, Pennsylvania, then to Evanston in 1919, when I was four years old. The Church of God in Evanston was a storefront in the 1800 block of Ridge Avenue near Emerson Street. The congregation numbered fewer than 50.

The small flock greeted the new pastor with enthusiasm, but without housing or salary. Daddy's expertise in cleaning silks and other fine fabrics, as taught him by his brothers, won him a job with the 619 Cleaners on Benson Avenue.

Our family lived in a large room in the rear of the storefront church. We smaller children were bedded down on a pallet made of a folded quilt for a mattress, with a blanket for cover. It was difficult to sleep on Wednesday and Sunday nights because of the noise from services in the front of the store.

As finances improved, we moved to an apartment, then managed to rent what we considered a fine house at 1720 Emerson St.

Daddy's Big Boy

After Daddy's death, I cried myself to sleep night after night. I remembered well how he would park his bicycle on the front porch when he came home for supper. He would enter the front door and pick me up in his arms and ask, his mustache tickling my face: "How's Daddy's big boy?" Mother, too, called me her "big boy." Every time I heard someone on the front porch, I expected Daddy to come in. I could not accept the idea that he was gone.

He used to sit me on the handlebars of his bicycle. With the admonition, "Hold on tight, son," he would take me to the many places he went.

I remember one episode in which he had gone to a barber shop for a haircut. Some man challenged him: "Ain't it true, Pastor, that the Bible says, 'You can fall in sin, but you don't have to wallow?' " Back on the bicycle we went to the house. He picked up a Bible and we rode back to the barber shop. He held everyone there — and some who came in from the street — spellbound while he preached a sermon. This was not an unusual practice for him.

*

After Daddy died, there was no money at all. The "saints," as members of the church were called when they were "saved and sanctified," brought food and a great deal of consolation to the family. But Mother and my two older sisters had to make a living.

Mother went to work as a laundress in Kenilworth for two days a week and Gladys got a part-time domestic job on the east side of Evanston. Agnes stayed at home to look after the children and play the big player piano Daddy had bought her.

We moved to a less expensive place, paying $20 a month at 1520 Sherman Ave., an ancient, one-story frame house that was heated by a large coal stove in the dining room and a coal-burning stove in the kitchen. We had a boarder occupying one of the three bedrooms.

Presents for Mother

It was in February, right after Maxime's first birthday, when I heard Gladys and Agnes whispering that Mother's birthday was May 1. They were wondering what they could get her. They wanted it to be something special since Daddy had died so recently.

I thought of what I could get mother. I received some money for my birthday, April 25, and I had it with me when I saw a beautiful pink blouse in a store window on Davis Street. I had to get it for Mother's birthday. I took my money to the man clerking the store and asked: "How much more do I need?" He smiled and said, "I think you've just about put up enough." To this day I've wondered if he didn't take pity on a kid who was trying desperately to buy his mother a birthday present. He told me to come back on April 30 and he would have it wrapped for me.

I was there bright and early to pick up my prize package. When I handed it to mother on her birthday, she opened it, her face lit up, and tears rolled down her cheeks. "Son, it is the prettiest blouse I ever saw," she said. She picked me up and began kissing me on the cheek. I was proud, but felt that her affection had overpaid me for what I had done. Years later, I realized that no one is too small or powerless who is driven by dedication.

Later that year, as Christmas approached, I had saved a total of $2 that I was going to use to buy mother a present. I went shopping in several stores but didn't find anything that I thought was worthwhile. I was sauntering through the toy section when the bargain of bargains hit my eyes. There it was! A genuine leather football — and only $2. I bought it immediately and gloried in the fact that I had such a bargain. It wasn't until I got home that realized I had spent all my money on a football, and hadn't any left to buy mother a present. There was only one thing to do. I wrapped it up neatly and placed it under the Christmas tree with all the other presents — with her name on it, of course.

Christmas morning was always special in our house. First, mother insisted that we eat breakfast because she knew that it could be hours before we were through admiring our presents. Then, we lined up behind her and — being careful not to bump into the coal-burning stove in the dining room — we marched into the living room singing "Joy to the world, the Lord is come. Let earth receive her King."

We took our places on the floor around the tree. Agnes lit all the candles (a bucket of water handy, in case the tree caught fire) and then began reading off the names on the presents. I had received two, but couldn't open them until I knew mother's reaction when she opened the one I had for her. Finally, she opened it, and everyone in the room burst into laughter. But mother, much to my surprise and delight, exclaimed: "A football! Just what I wanted!" I was relieved.

Two months later, she gave it to me, saying: "I don't think I'm going to have enough time to learn how to play this game. Why don't you keep it for me?"

*

During the summer after Daddy's death, mother heard I could get a scholarship to St. Benedict's Moor Mission in Milwaukee and removed me from Foster Elementary School in Evanston.

At St. Benedict's we spent a great deal of time either learning Catholic prayers or reciting them. For example, someone made a donation to the school and requested 100 prayers to be said for a relative who had died. We spent all of a sunny Saturday afternoon going in and out of sanctuary reciting the same prayer over and over again. I wondered if God was so dumb that He did not hear us the first few times.

Also, there were classes that taught us that the only true religion was the Catholic religion. After I wrote a letter to mother to tell her that, it was not long before I was on my way back to Evanston, to start third grade at Miller School.

*

Gladys had decided she wanted to go to high school. She and Agnes had finished elementary school in Rhode Island. So, at age 22, she enrolled in Evanston Township High School as a freshman. The house was too noisy for her to study, so she went to the public library, two blocks away. She took me with her for company.

I attribute my love for the English language to this period, when I spent nights in the library reading. Soon, I was going to the library with or without Gladys.

A smiling librarian brought me a copy of "Robin Hood." I cannot count the number of times I donned the Lincoln green and became part of the merry band of outlaws in Sherwood Forest. And there were other heroes, too, including King Arthur and his Knights of the Round Table, who made a place at the table for "Sir Lestre."

Rosa's Rolls

In those early years, I didn't know we were poor. Everybody we knew had a hard time putting food on the table. Mother, with her unflagging faith in God, assured us we would have enough to eat. I don't remember going hungry.

Dinnertime had ritual. We would seat ourselves at the table. Mother would say grace, thanking God for bringing us through the day and for putting food on the table. Then each of us would have to recite a Bible verse we had memorized. Most of us recited a verse that had a special meaning to us. But Raymond always recited John 11:35 – "Jesus wept." Mother chided him, but he stood by his conviction that it was a biblical verse. The repartee usually made us laugh. Meals, sparse as they may have been, were times of great merriment.

When we gathered at the supper table, we joked, laughed and teased one another. The meal was rarely sumptuous. Not infrequently there were fried potatoes, cabbage, mustard or collard greens, and, of course, cornbread. The meat was "fat back," the salt pork used to season the cabbage or greens. On Sundays chicken was usually the main meal.

Also, there were mother's famous rolls. She developed the recipe in 1900 when she was 17 and cooking for the small Southern hotel.

I have recreated mother's roll recipe with only a few changes. Here is the recipe for "Rosa's Rolls":

In a very large bowl, mix together:
3/4 cup sugar
1-1/2 teaspoon salt

1 cup shortening
1 cup potato water (hot if you are using a solid shortening)

In another, smaller bowl, mix:
1 cup potato water (115 - 120 degrees)
2 packages of dry yeast (1 tablespoon and 1 teaspoon of dry yeast)

Allow yeast to "work" about an hour and a half, and then add two large or extra large eggs. Beat this mixture until smooth and add to shortening mixture. Add 7-1/2 cups flour to the combined mixtures and knead until smooth. Form rolls, place in a greased muffin tin.

Allow rolls to rise for 1 to 2 hours under a damp cloth (or overnight in refrigerator). Bake in a preheated oven at 400 degrees for 15 to 20 minutes, or until golden brown. Serve immediately with butter (and smile as you receive the compliments, but remember to credit Rosa!).

As Mother's reputation for rolls spread, more and more people placed orders for them — especially for Sunday morning breakfasts. Mother, who charged 15 cents a dozen, spent Saturday evenings putting together the dough and forming as many as ten dozen rolls to rise overnight. Then, as they rolled out of the oven on Sunday morning, Ray and I would be sent running around the neighborhood delivering hot rolls — before we could get any to eat.

We had to finish the errands in time to get ready for Sunday School. Somehow it seemed like punishment, but those coins meant we could eat other food during the rest of the week.

Maybe it was because we were poor, but we thought of money only as an agent to buy food and shelter. We never thought of accumulating it as some people do. I suppose that this concept keeps many people penny-pinching.

Each of us learned to wash, iron and mend our clothes. When we returned home from school each day, we took off our school clothes and put on work clothes. Our school clothes were also our "Sunday-go-to-meetin'" clothes.

Leaving Evanston

When our boarder announced that she was moving back to the South, we had to find a less expensive home. We chose to move to Chicago's black belt on the South Side. We had heard all the horror stories about the crime and violence in Chicago. Would moving there place our lives in jeopardy? This thought crossed our minds many times as we packed, but the cheaper rent won over our reluctance.

On the night before we moved Mother's prayer was the same as every other night, but somehow this night was special. She prayed: "We thank Thee, Lord, for having brought us safely through this day. And we thank Thee for giving us health, food to eat, and a roof over our heads..."

After all the other things she thanked God for, tears streamed down her pretty face as she implored: "Dear God, you have given me all these wonderful children, and you know that I'm a poor widow woman with little education.

Please show me how I'm going to raise these children as good Christians." All the children cried while Mother prayed. I thought God must be awfully cruel to make Mother cry. She would assure us: "God will show us the way. He has shown us the way all these years. And as He has shown Christians before us, He will not forsake us now." Mother and her family had placed their trust in God to help them survive in an alien and unfriendly land.

When it came time to move to Chicago, some of the "brothers" from the church brought a horse and wagon and helped us settle at 3415 S. Giles Ave.

In Chicago, I attended the world's largest grammar school, Douglas, with 3,200 classmates. We went in shifts. One shift went from 8 a.m. to 10 a.m.; the next from 10 a.m. to noon. Then our shift returned from noon to 2 p.m., and the second shift from 2 p.m. to 4 p.m.

*

We moved from Giles to a still-cheaper apartment on Calumet Avenue. We had been there less than a week when a drunk who had seen Agnes at a store followed her home. He came to the door and exclaimed: "Let me in, you black bitch! I'm gonna fuck you 'til you drop!"

He was pushing against the door, and Agnes was trying to keep him from coming in. She called to me: "Bring me the kettle off the stove!" I took it to her. When the drunk inserted his leg in the door, she poured boiling water on it. He yelled a string of curses, and pulled his leg back from the door. She banged the door and locked it. After a while, he left, still cursing.

When mother came home that night and was told what had happened, she decided that we had to move again. Within a week we had moved to the second floor at 4331 S. Dearborn Place.

I attended Colman School on 46th Street. Each day I had to run home down the alley to keep Willie Flowers from beating me. My trouble with Willie started in the classroom when he was unable to answer a question. I raised my hand and gave the correct answer when the teacher called on me. I didn't know that no one was supposed to answer a question Willie didn't know.

I was nine years old and Willie was 12 — and large for his age. One day he chased me into the house and into the living room. He pushed me down on the sofa and was beating me when Agnes began pouring a kettle of hot water on him. He fled the house screaming.

After that, he was going to give it to me. One day as I arrived at the back gate, I found it locked and he caught me. I decided that I was going to fight him this time. My brother, Raymond, saw what was happening. He ran down from the second floor porch and climbed on the fence. As Willie came near to him, Ray hit him on the head with a broom. Willie grabbed his head and ran.

The next encounter we had with Willie may have been fatal for him. Ray and I were on the roof of a two-story building that faced State Street. We were dropping roofing pebbles on passersby. We would drop a pebble, and pull back so that person on the street wouldn't know who had done it. We had been doing this for about a half hour when I looked up and saw Willie coming toward us, his face contorted with anger. When he reached to grab me with both arms, I ducked under his grasp. His momentum kept him moving forward, his knees hitting the foot-high brick barrier, and over the edge of the building he went. We heard a scream. When we looked over the edge of the roof, we saw Willie lying still on the sidewalk, blood oozing from his mouth. We ran home and told Agnes. She said he had earned his injury. We never saw him again.

*

Our next door neighbor was a notorious whorehouse and bootleg joint. We spent many an hour watching the people come and go.

We saw men fighting and shooting at each other. Two were shot, and a third was stabbed to death. One night, about three weeks after the first killing, a well-dressed man came around the side of the house from the front. He seemed to be in good spirits, judging from his lively step and the tune he was whistling. A woman emerged from the rear door and started toward the front of the house. She stopped and drew herself close to the wall just behind the bay window. As the man approached her, we saw the silvery flash of a large knife blade, and she said: "You won't fuck my daughter no more, you two-timin' bastard." The knife passed through his throat. He grabbed his throat, made a gurgling sound as blood gushed through his fingers. He fell on his face and was still. She wiped the blade clean on his coat, put it back in her purse and sauntered into the street. The body was there for two days.

One night about three months later, I had finished washing the dishes and was taking the garbage out to put in the can on the back porch. A man ran past me breathing hard. A shot rang out from the street below. The man gasped, reached for his back and fell down the stairs and crashed into the garbage can. I stood there, too scared to move. Finally, I dropped the garbage and ran into the house to tell Mother and Agnes.

Mother said: "We just can't let him lie there. I'm goin' to the corner store and call the police." "Let me go, Mother," Agnes said. She took a nickel from her purse and waddled down the stairs. She was big with child. When she returned in about 20 minutes, she said: "The police sure didn't seem to care. I heard him tell someone there in the station that somebody was always gettin' killed in this neighborhood."

The police did remove the body about five hours later. I was prepared to tell them what happened, but they didn't ask a thing. Mother shook her head and said: "Come, children. Let's pray that God will keep us alive until we can get out of this vile neighborhood."

Another day I was returning from a store at 43rd and State streets, and I saw a man standing near the curb. He had been cut in at least a dozen places, and was bleeding so badly on his face that he couldn't see. "Please, help me somebody," he begged. "Please help me somebody!" He was holding a blood-soaked handkerchief under his elbow to catch the dripping blood. I walked over to him and took his arm and led him to the drug store on the corner. At least a dozen people had been watching and nobody moved to help him. As we approached the drug store, the manager saw us coming and yelled to me: "Don't bring him in here. I'll call for an ambulance." I waited with the man until the ambulance came, and took him away.

Each night before we went to bed, all the family knelt and listened while Mother poured out her heart to God. It went something like this: "Dear Lord, we come before thee in prayer, thanking you for having seen us through this day, and having looked out for us so that no harm came to us. You know, dear God, that I am thankful that you gave me these wonderful children and that you have kept us well and free from peril. I don't ask much from you, Lord. Just that you give me strength to work and provide for my children. Some days I feel so tired and my bones ache so much that I feel as if I can't make it. But if you will just give me strength to keep going, I will be grateful and praise your name forever."

I'm not sure that I believed in God at that time. But I know I believed in Mother. If she said everything was going to be all right, I knew that everything was OK.

Some mornings I heard Mother pleading with God to give her strength to make it through that day. She had to get up at 5 a.m. to take the "L" to Davis Street in Evanston. There she boarded the North Shore Line to take her to Kenilworth. After she got off at Kenilworth, she walked six blocks to the Ketcham's house, where she washed clothes on Monday and ironed on Tuesday and Wednesday. She cleaned other people's houses on Thursday and Friday — and sometimes on Saturdays. She got $5 a day and carfare. With that money she had to pay rent, buy food and try to keep us in clothing. We went to the Salvation Army store most of the time to buy what few clothes we had.

One Sunday night we attended a revival at church. The choir was there until after midnight. The next morning Mother couldn't get out of bed to go to work. She was little better on Tuesday. So she missed that day, too. Each day, Agnes went to the corner store to telephone the Ketchams about Mother's condition.

Wednesday, she dragged herself out of bed and took that long ride to Kenilworth. Somehow, she was able to work one more day that week. She didn't get paid for the days she hadn't worked. So we were looking at a bare cupboard. Mother said: "Children, let's ask God to help us!" We got on knees and Mother started praying. She was well into her prayer when there was a knock on the kitchen door.

When I answered the door, there was the man I had met six weeks earlier at 43rd and State. His face bore the scars of that night, but he was smiling. "Boy, you saved my life. Nobody else would help me and I couldn't see."

He had a bushel basket and it was crammed with food. In addition to such staples as flour, corn meal, salt pork, coffee and such, he had two chickens, a pot roast, potatoes, and candy for us children. "I didn't know who you were or where you lived, but the druggist told me."

"Thank the Lord," Mother exclaimed. "We were completely out of food and were praying for some help. God answered our prayers. You must kneel with us and thank God!" The man, Mr. Carter, looked somewhat bewildered as Mother forced him to his knees. As she started her prayer of thanksgiving, Mr. Carter reached up and took off his hat. When she had finished, she thanked Mr. Carter, who got out in a hurry, and she turned to us: "Children, God answers a Christian's prayers, and I am a Christian."

*

During the following week, Agnes had a baby. The father was an Evanston man Mother had refused to let her marry and had thrown out of the house because he had "whiskey on his breath." When Agnes went into labor, she called a cab and was taken to Cook County Hospital on Chicago's West Side, the same hospital where our father had died a little more than two years previously. This time, the hospital helped a new life into existence. Agnes's daughter, Carole, grew up with us — more like a sister than a niece.

Hoboing

Another of Mother's prayers was answered when the Ketchams decided to give her a raise and an extra day's work. Now we could return to Evanston. Agnes, with a talent for locating inexpensive housing, found a house at 1911 Ridge Ave. and we moved in.

The house was adjacent to a railroad siding, and we were awakened one morning by the clamor of a circus coming to town. It was about 3 a.m., but there was no more sleep for us. I crossed Ridge Avenue and watched as the huge elephants were shepherded out of box cars. It was the most exciting experience I could remember. Later that day I got a job lugging buckets of water for the elephants. They seemed never to get enough. I was given two tickets for my reward, and my brother Raymond and I went to see the circus. I was dazzled by the acrobats, and electrified by the animal trainer's act. I never got over my love for the circus.

One day Ray and I came across a hobo jungle along the railroad tracks just east of Ridge Avenue. We watched as one hobo squeezed the alcohol from Sterno, canned heat, through a handkerchief into a pint whiskey bottle half-filled with water. After he got as much alcohol as possible, two other hobos joined him in drinking the brew. They launched into telling lies about their narrow escapes from railroad "dicks," the security cops hired by the railroad to keep hobos off the trains.

One hobo told us how to catch a train. We were to wait until it had just started, then run to catch onto the coal car. Once on the car, we were to sit behind the barrier that held the coal until we got to our destination. However, we were to be sure to get off before the train got into the station. Otherwise, the railroad dicks would be there with their big clubs to beat us before they took us to jail.

At home that night, we decided we would hobo to Milwaukee and back, a trip of about 80 miles. We slept in an unfinished attic and could climb down over the front porch roof. We made it to the Davis Street train station just in time to see a train pulling into the station. We got near the coal car and as the train pulled out, grabbed on and grinned at each other, happy in our success.

We were, however, not prepared for how cold we would be. We huddled together for the ride. We hadn't been to Milwaukee before, so didn't know when to get off. Suddenly, the train pulled into the station, so we rushed to get off. Just then we heard a man shout: "Hey, you black bastards, come here!"

We jumped from the moving train and ran. The fat man was no match for the speed of us young boys.

Now, we had to figure how to get back. We assumed the detective would be in the station watching for us, so we went south of the station about two blocks, crossed the tracks and came back on the other side, staying far enough away so that he wouldn't see us. Our ploy worked and we were able to board a southbound train less than an hour after we had arrived. The trip back was colder and we were dog-tired when we climbed back over the porch and into bed around 2 a.m.

We didn't feel like getting up that morning. Mother used her favorite trick. She soaked a washcloth in cold water and laid it across our faces. She made both of us howl as we bounded out of bed, bleary-eyed. The next time we took the trip, we started earlier, wore heavier clothes, and got off the train sooner. After the third trip, the glamour was gone. Or maybe it was just the loss of challenge.

"Now on this next play..."

Agnes had discovered a bigger house, at 1716 Payne Street near the North Shore Channel of the Chicago River. This latest move would introduce me to two new experiences. One, football, was a love that would last a lifetime. The other experience was institutionalized racial discrimination.

Our new house was less than two blocks from Foster Field, a one block square recreational area adjacent to Foster School. When I had left Foster in the second grade, "coloreds" were in the minority. When I returned for fifth grade, there was only one white boy left — Felix Kujuwinski. His father had refused to transfer his son to a white school when whites were given the opportunity, saying: "All his friends are here. My friends live here, too." Felix was to grow up as if he were colored, and would marry a black girl from the community.

My fifth grade teacher — Mrs. McCallum — was an attractive lady who loved music. She and the District 75 music teacher decided to produce a musical. I was selected as the lead male singer, and promptly fell in love with the female lead, Marianne Hutchison, a neat, light-skinned girl, rather pretty, who dressed immaculately. I bought her a box of chocolates at the neighborhood sweet shop. Some classmates got their hands on it and dumped it upside-down on the top of my desk. Marianne laughed at this; the romance ended.

My second love, football, has been true to me all the years of my life. My brother, Ray, and I watched older boys playing the game in Foster Field. The game had all the magic and derring-do that a 10-year-old could ask. We started playing in a field across the alley from our house and behind Lark's Laundry — a black-owned business.

I learned one of life's most valuable lessons. That lesson was that each time a man got tackled, he didn't quit. He huddled with his teammates to discuss "this next play." I would be tackled many more times in life. Each time I would go into a huddle with myself and say, "Now on this next play ..."

*

In the sixth grade, the class was given the Stanford-Binet Achievement Test. Thomas Brunson and I scored high, and we were told that we would be permitted to go to Haven Junior High School. All the rest of the class had to finish seventh and eighth grades at Foster School. Foster was the only school in the district that had seventh and eighth grades. In all other schools, as soon as the pupil successfully passed sixth grade, he or she went automatically to junior high school — either Nichols or Haven. Foster was the only almost all black school in the district.

Apparently this was the first time this test had been administered. As a result, the district superintendent, Dr. James Roy Skiles, wanted to talk to the two boys who had done so well. Our teacher, Mrs. Goodman, escorted us to the district headquarters.

Dr. Skiles began: "Congratulations, you boys did very well. Let me explain my philosophy. I don't believe in educating people into disappointment. This city needs some good domestics, and that's what most of your classmates will end up doing. However, that community is going to need doctors, dentists, and lawyers. You boys have shown that you have the capability of becoming professional men. That's why you are being sent to Haven Junior High School."

I interrupted: "Dr. Skiles, don't you think things are changing and that Negroes will want to become engineers and the like?" He responded, "When conditions change, we will change our educational practices." Then I asked, "But shouldn't you start educating them now so that they will be ready when the change comes?" He replied, "They won't change in our lifetime."

Mrs. Goodman became uneasy, and she interrupted: "Thank you, Dr. Skiles. Back to school, boys, it's time we got going." Once outside, she tore into me: "You should be ashamed. After all, he called you in to congratulate you, not to be cross examined about educational philosophy." I was so angry I said nothing.

My next unhappiness in sixth grade was with my former fifth grade teacher. I brought a golf club to school, and as I walked down the hall past her room, Mrs. McCallum said: "I think you should leave that club with me until after school so that it doesn't get you into any trouble." I forgot about the club and left school without going into Mrs. McCallum's room. She went to Mrs. Goodman, my teacher, the next afternoon and told her that I was supposed to go to her room. Mrs. Goodman told me to report to the fifth grade room after school.

When I went into the room, four or five of her own pupils were being kept after school and made a great deal of noise teasing me. When Mrs. McCallum returned, she was livid. She told everyone to take readers out of their desks and turn to a certain page. I complied, and remarked: "Oh, I've read that story already." Mrs. McCallum strode swiftly back to where I was seated and slapped me hard across the cheek; she grabbed both my wrists to be sure that I didn't strike back.

I stood up and glared at her, and said nothing. After a while, she let the other pupils go but kept me there, glaring at her silently. She spoke: "I know I shouldn't have struck you, but you aggravated me so with the smart-alecky remark. You shouldn't have done that. You can go now."

I didn't move. I sat there glaring at her. She seemed uncomfortable, maybe a little frightened. I was aware that I was making her uneasy. I sat and glared at her. She stuttered when she asked: "Don't you wish to apologize?" I said nothing. I kept glaring at her. She puttered around with things on her desk and finally said: "You have to leave now. I have to lock the room." I arose from my seat, walked slowly to the door, glaring at her all the while.

I told no one when I went home. I was too embarrassed. I knew also that I would be the laughingstock the next day at school. I made up my mind. I wasn't going to school. But where could I go? The public library.

During my 17th day at the library, a kindly looking man sat next to me and began asking questions. I learned that he was a truant officer, and I was taken back to school. School officials thought there was something odd about me, so they sent me to Northwestern University's psychology department for an examination. The report came back that there was nothing wrong with me, that I was very intelligent, that perhaps the school assignments weren't challenging enough.

When I returned to class, I was a hero. I had gotten away with ditching school for 17 days.

*

My mother and older sisters were part of the black and mostly female corps that cooked, cleaned, washed and ironed in the better North Shore homes to pay the rent and grocers' bills.

No one seemed to talk about anything beyond survival — except Gladys, who had graduated from high school and gave poetry recitations in churches. Gladys had gone to high school when she was 22 and became the family's first high school graduate. Her diploma hangs proudly in our Evanston home. So does her correspondence with Helen Keller.

Gladys spoke of her employers as if they were literary people. I pictured them sitting around their living rooms after dinner reciting Shakespeare, Keats, Shelly and Wordsworth to each other. I thought learning about literature could help me escape from the depressing ghetto of western Evanston. So, I began to read anything and everything I thought was good literature.

Les with his mother and sisters.
Top row: LeJeune, Les, Elizabeth. Bottom row: Agnes, Rosa, Gladys.

*

One afternoon Mrs. Goodman was reading to the class. I was seated behind Freddie Mae McCarthy, a big-bosomed girl of 12. In the next row to my right and one seat behind me sat Wardell Sutton. He tapped me on the shoulder and gestured for me to give a note to Freddie Mae. I took the note, tapped her on the shoulder and gave her the note. She read it, bounced out of her seat, and laid it on the teacher's desk.

Mrs. Goodman asked, "Where did you get this note?" She pointed directly at me. I knew the code of honor. You didn't squeal on anybody. Mrs. Goodman said to me. "Let's go to the principal's office." The principal, Mrs. Rowley, looked at the note, scowled, looked up at me and said: "You're expelled until you bring your parent to see me."

I was angry — angry at Wardell for not admitting that he sent the note, angry also because I had no idea what was in the note. I waited for Wardell to leave school. When he emerged, I asked him: "What was in the note?" He began laughing, and I didn't wait for another word. I began beating him until he fell to the ground. Then I dragged him by the heels until his face was bleeding from the scratches he received from the gravel on the playground. He went home bawling.

This incident had repercussions years later after World War II in Italy.

Haven School

Haven School was the first school I attended with so many white pupils. I was not entirely welcome. White boys shouted "nigger" at me more than once. One day early in the school year they tried to goad me into fighting. They knocked me down, getting the knee of my new trousers dirty and tearing the sleeve in my new shirt. When I got up, I swung a hard left into one boy's face. He ran away crying. The second boy also ran, screaming "Help!"

Some subjects at Haven pleased me very much. I liked Music Appreciation and Art Appreciation. Instructors asked for students to try out for parts in the play, "A Midsummer's Nights Dream." I went for an audition. I was ignored completely. I suspected that was the instructor's way of telling me that he had no part for a black student.

I was barred from bringing my marbles to school after I cleaned up on the playground. And I got into trouble for playing with another boy's marbles. I was told to bring my mother to school the following day. "Each time Mother misses a day at work, she doesn't get paid, and that means we don't eat," I told the teacher. "Perhaps that will teach you to obey me when I speak," she said. I started out of her office, and she called me back. "I'm going to forget about this incident this time. I hope it never happens again. If so you'll really be in trouble."

Barely two weeks later, I was seated behind June Thrall when June let out a scream: "My purse is missing!" The teacher made me come to the front of the room and empty my pockets. I didn't have the purse. She asked me what I had done with it. I replied that I did not take the girl's purse. She replied: "When this class is over, you and I are going to the principal's office."

About 15 minutes later, a girl came into the room with a purse she said she had found in the girl's washroom. "That's my purse!" June screamed. June and the teacher both thanked the girl for bringing the purse.

No one said anything to me. I was relieved and angry. I was thankful that I didn't have to face the principal again and that Mother wouldn't lose a day's pay, but angry at being falsely accused of a theft and that no one apologized to me for having accused me.

When I told Mother, she said: "Son, some people have bigotry so deep in their hearts that they don't even know they are hurting others. But think how bad they must feel with all that hatred running through their minds. They must feel terribly sick. We have to pray for sick people to get well, don't we? Besides, what else can we do in a situation like this?" Mother's answer to problems was prayer; I wanted to hit somebody. It would be years before I could accept the wisdom of her reasoning.

Horse business

I met Tom Logan at Northwestern Golf Course, where we both were caddies. I liked his swagger, his ability to run off a series of swear words. I even liked the way he spit through his teeth. He seemed to like me, and soon we were inseparable. When one of the boys at the caddy shack was giving me a hard time, Tom stepped in and punched the boy in the face, saying, "Don't ever fuck with a friend of mine!"

One day when it was raining and we were not going to caddy, Tom turned to me and asked, "Did y'ever fuck a horse?" I thought he was joking, but I followed him to a barn on the corner of Church and Oak streets where a dairy kept its horses.

Tom took the handle of a broom and poked a mare in the vagina. She moved her tail to one side. He took a milk crate and stood up on it and began to fuck the horse. I was too startled to do anything but stare.

Suddenly, a man came through the door we had left open and yelled. Tom jumped down and ducked under the man's grasp and ran out the door. I was paralyzed. The man grabbed me by the arm and hauled me outside. He saw a policeman and told him what he had witnessed. I was hauled off to jail.

A policeman said that if I told him who my companion was, he would let us both go. I told him and asked about going home.

He gave me a wry grin and said: "Niggers are so stupid! Why should I let you go?" Shortly after that, Tom joined me in the cell. I told him what had occurred. He told me: "You can't ever trust a cop. They're the biggest liars in the world."

I was a very frightened 12-year-old. Not because I was locked in jail but because I was going to have to tell Mother what happened. She always warned me to be careful about the guys I ran with. I always thought I could tell the good guys from the bad. How was I going to tell her? It finally occurred to me that she didn't even know where I was.

After I had not come home for two days, she went to the police. They told her they had forgotten to inform her.

Tom and I were taken to the Juvenile Detention Home on Chicago's West Side. My "friend" was sent to the Parental Home, a place on Chicago's West Side where boys were incarcerated; I was sent to the state operated School for Boys near St. Charles, Ill., on acres of wind-swept prairie miles from anything that looked like civilization.

I had to learn dismounted drill. I soon learned to march in step and a series of commands. Each cottage had a first sergeant and corporals who had the authority to punch us if we didn't learn rapidly enough, or if we disobeyed them.

We went to school a half day, and worked the rest of the day. The job I remember most was waxing a floor with a bar of wax, and then, on knees, polishing it until it was smooth.

After I graduated from eighth grade, I was transferred to Polk Farm, which had an apple orchard. The house mother learned that I knew my way around the kitchen, and I was assigned to do kitchen chores. I told the house mother about Mother's rolls and she let me make some for the 22 boys on the farm. Soon, I was cooking many of the dishes that were served. My reward was that I got to pick the choicest pieces of meat or other goodies.

My sentence was for one year, but I didn't get out for 13 months. I finished eighth grade there and was ready to enter Evanston Township High School as a freshman in 1930.

My mother had tears in her eyes as she welcomed home a young man who had left her as a boy. I can't remember being happier. I was glad to accompany her to church on Sundays — delighted to hear the songs and voices with which I had grown up. I wept with joy as we sang "That Old Rugged Cross."

Hoops

At Evanston High, we were permitted to play football and run track, but we were not permitted to play basketball — because the coach didn't like colored players. We couldn't be on the swim team because the team held its meets at the Grove Street YMCA — which didn't admit blacks. Most of us didn't mind the restrictions. After all, we had the Emerson Street YMCA, which was set aside for blacks. It was not a pretentious structure, but it had a large gymnasium, a swimming pool, recreation areas, and a dormitory for residents.

We also played basketball there. One of our Emerson Y teams played the Harlem Globetrotters once each year. We didn't beat them (few teams could ever boast of that accomplishment) but they knew they had been in a ball game. The first black allowed to play on the ETHS basketball team was a tall skinny kid named Jesse Peaks. He became a star on that team, even though he wasn't able to make our YMCA team.

Gang

In those days youths in a neighborhood formed gangs. All of us were students at Evanston Township High School, and we prided ourselves on being able to use our fists in any brawl. We believed it was cowardly to use a weapon.

Our gang was as wholesome as a Boy Scout troop, not like anything now called a gang. Our religion was athleticism. Our heroes were athletes. Our bibles were the sports pages of newspapers, and we could quote athletic statistics with as much authority as a preacher quotes from the Holy Bible.

I can't remember that we ever actually fought together as a gang, except for one occasion. We had moved our football practice from Foster Field to Mason Park, about two miles away, where black and white neighborhoods joined; blacks living on the north side of the park, and whites living on the south side. We moved at the invitation of Willie Marinelli, the only white boy on our team and from the white neighborhood. We had moved because the older black youths in their early 20s, "The Wolverines," had commandeered the football field at Foster Field and kicked us out.

As we were leaving practice one day, a group of white boys started throwing stones from the nearby railroad tracks. Because this park separated the white residential area from ours, the boys were trying to chase us away. Several of us were hit before we took cover behind a nearby building. I don't know whose idea it was, but we decided to go around the rear of the building and take the gang by surprise.

Before the half dozen white boys knew it, we had come up on their rear and began flailing them with fists. They soon took to their heels, wearing black eyes and bloody noses. We had bruise marks from stones they had thrown earlier. They never attacked us after that, and I don't remember that we ever fought another "gang."

*

The seats in my home room were arranged so that two seats were joined side by side, and the class was seated alphabetically. That placed me with blue-eyed blonde Elaine Bernstorff as a seat partner. We became friends during home room, and she invited me to her birthday party.

Edgar Leach, the teacher, called me into his office, and said, "I understand that you are invited to Elaine's birthday party." I nodded "yes." He told me, "If I were you, I wouldn't plan to go. None of your friends will be there, and you'd feel very uncomfortable." I replied that I couldn't go anyway. The party was being held at the same time that I was delivering for the Noyes Street Pharmacy, I said. He smiled and excused me.

I told Elaine about the session with Leach. She was angry. She wanted to confront him. I begged her not to do that. However, she had a plan that she didn't tell me about.

On the day of her party, she telephoned the store where I worked and ordered a case of Coca-Cola to be delivered to her home at 1216 Judson Ave. When I arrived at the back door, the maid got Elaine. She took me by the hand and led me into the room where all her party guests were and introduced me as her friend. She offered me a piece of cake. I declined, saying that I had to get back to work.

The following day Leach called me into his office. He was livid. "I thought we had agreed that you were not to attend Elaine's party," he growled. I replied, "I was ordered to deliver a case of Coca-Cola to that address. I didn't have a choice." He continued, "You didn't have to go into where the party was going on." I answered, "Elaine took me by the hand and led me into the room." He shot back, "You two think you are very clever, don't you? I think that you may live to regret your actions. You may go now." I had no way of knowing the extent to which he would go to get his revenge.

*

During my sophomore year the high school conducted a speech contest. Each student studying English had to write and deliver a three-minute speech.

Mine was a pretense of a radio broadcast that was jumbled up to be humorous. I won in my class, in the division room, among all sophomores, and I won in the finals.

I thought I might qualify for the Forensic Club. I was not welcome. I tried the debate team; they had all they needed. The school newspaper. "No thanks!" I tried for the Latin Club; the same reply.

When I tried for the Art Club, members rejected my application. Their rejection angered Miss Goff, the art teacher and faculty sponsor of the club. Most art projects displayed in the school were done by members of the Art Club. Miss Goff began to give them to me, ignoring members of the club in many instances. Suddenly, she stopped giving me assignments. She never told me, but I learned later that she was warned to stop ignoring the Art Club.

I was so bitter I refused to play football with the school team, and stuck with my Foster Field sandlot team, "Pikey's Pals."

*

We formed an intramural basketball team made up of members of our colored YMCA team. Not only did we not lose a game before the finals, but we beat most teams by such scores as 82-5, 69-3, 75-7, etc. When we came to the finals, we were up against a team composed of all whites except Cornelius Champion, the school's black football hero.

The referee, who was also the school's basketball coach, took our star player, Fred Brooks, aside and demanded that he show a sales slip for gym shoes that he had owned for three years. The ref stated that the shoes looked like ones that had been reported stolen. Since he could not produce a sales slip, he was not permitted to play.

The game became a joke. Every time we made a move, the ref called a foul. The other team figured out what was going on and took sympathy on us; they refused to make the free shots. Instead, each would slam the ball against the backboard.

When the game ended, we were leading 12-11. The referee called some technical foul and gave their team captain the ball. He didn't try to make it. Whereupon, the ref kept giving him shots. After the eighth time, he accidentally made it. The game was tied 12 apiece.

In the overtime, the ref called a foul just after the jump ball opener. Again, he had the team captain shoot several shots. We finally began to plead with the team captain to please make the shot. He did. They won 13-12.

There was no way the white basketball coach was going to permit an all-black team to be intramural champions.

Edgar Leach's revenge

It would be many years before I recognized the white man's dilemma. After all, he had been steeped in the lore of white supremacy and buttressed by the divine right of superior firepower, so why should he waste money educating a group of fugitives from slavery? What would they do with an education? They certainly didn't need to know how to read to clean toilets, scrub floors, or follow the mule. They hadn't shown enough ability to master the alien tongue of English. And to quote Edwin Markham, "What to him are Plato, or the swing of Pleiades?"

Edgar Leach's revenge came during the last week of my sophomore year.

I had been in the boy's gym and had gone into the washroom. There I found a book on top of a urinal. I tried to get into the school building to turn it into the lost and found, but the janitor would not let me in.

Out on the corner of Emerson and Dodge I met Robert "Curly" Clark, who asked: "What are you doing with that Modern History book? Ours is the only class studying the subject and you are not in our class." I explained how I came to have it and asked him to take it to his class the following day. He agreed reluctantly.

The following day I was called from a class and ordered to report to the principal's office. When I arrived, I found Leach and Francis Leonard Bacon together. Leach spoke: "You are accused of stealing a Modern History book. You had better go home and bring your mother to meet with us." I denied that I had stolen the book, but left for home.

Mother and I returned the following day. This meant that she would have to miss a day's work — and a day's pay. Bacon spoke: "Mrs. Brownlee, we know it isn't only the colored who steal. Some of the whites do, too. We can't tolerate this kind of behavior."

Mother interrupted him to ask him to explain what I wanted with a book for a course I was not taking, and for the one week remaining in the school year. Also, why would I have sent it back by way of a friend? Leach and Bacon ignored her. The principal continued: "Mrs. Brownlee, Lester has more education than most coloreds get, so we are prepared to give him a work permit so that he can help a widow like you." Leach grinned as I was expelled.

Not a muscle moved in my mother's face, but tears rolled down her cheeks and her voice trembled as she spoke: "As long as my boy wants an education, and as long as God gives me strength to move a muscle, he will get an education. Come on, son." We started out of the office, but Mother turned around and returned, saying: "I'm going to pray for both of your souls. Heaven knows you need it." We walked out of Evanston Township High School in 1932, our heads held high, hand in hand.

For days — better say weeks — after our encounter with Principal Bacon and Edgar Leach, anger took over my entire consciousness. I was not particularly angry that I had been kicked out of school. I was seething because two white men had made my mother cry. They had called her from work — which meant that she lost a day's pay. My anger was so intense that there were days when I would not eat. I had frequent fantasies of meeting either or both on the street. I would beat them into a bloody pulp. There were nights when I would lie awake and fantasize about what I was going to do to them. Then mother intervened.

One night at dinner, Mother watched as I stabbed at the food on my plate. After dinner, she called me into her bedroom and said: "Son, I know you're upset about being expelled from school, but being angry really punishes you — and not them." I replied: "I'm angry because of the way they treated you. They asked you to give up a day's pay to come to hear them pronounce a sentence they had already decided. They didn't listen to you at all."

She answered: "Don't be angry, son. You're just punishing yourself when you're angry. You're the one who is punished. You should feel sorry for those men. Can't you imagine how that prejudice is boiling inside their minds? They know they are wrong, and they are really suffering from it. You don't want to go through your life hating people who are sick, do you? All we can do is pray that God will heal the sickness in their minds and souls. God will punish them in His own way and in His own time. No evil deed goes unpunished. Maybe this is God's way of moving you to a better school. Who knows?"

I would recall this conversation a few years later when I was riding the crest of popularity at New Trier High School. Once again, I would marvel at Mother's wisdom. Some people say they have a guardian angel. I don't remember any such person — except times when I felt Mother's presence so strongly that I turned around expecting to see her. On occasions I was sure that I saw her smiling face, nodding as if to assure me that I could do whatever task was before me. I'm sure that my dogged determination was because Mother's presence gave me the courage to stick it out.

It was not only during the difficult times that I felt mother's presence. Sometimes, when I have had an opportunity to do a good deed and been divided about whether to do it, I'm sure it has been Mother's smile that assured me that I should do it — and not expect any pay for doing it. If this is what is meant by the term, "guardian angel," then I'm grateful to be so fortunately endowed.

A real good time

Early in my 15th year, I had mumps. My testicles swelled up to the size of 16-inch softballs. There was no pain, but in my panic I called Mother. She called a doctor. He came and gave me an injection of sodium iodide. In the next few days my testicles returned to normal. He had me go to his office about a week later. He massaged my prostate, took some fluid which emerged from my penis, and examined it under a microscope. He came back to me smiling. "Well," he said, "you'll have a real good time, but you won't have children."

The thought of not having children didn't particularly bother me at 15. What he said about my having a real good time started a short time later, with a 24-year-old model who was a regular at Al's gas station where I worked. I had asked her out on a date, on a bet with a co-worker, and she accepted. Things moved along quickly, though at first she was just helping me out.

The lovely woman told me: "If you are going to be my lover, you are going to have to know a few things. First, you never make love to a woman unless you plan to please her. And I intend to show you how. You have to be patient, and be sure she's ready. And this is what you do." After that lesson, and the practical demonstration, I looked forward to each additional lesson. And there were many. We were together frequently until I moved to Glencoe and New Trier.

Serious money

After I left ETHS at the end of my sophomore year, I worked for three years at a number of small jobs. I was a sign painter until my employer could no longer afford to pay me the pittance he had given me — perhaps out of pity. Then I worked as janitor, Arabian rug cleaner, delivery boy and dishwasher at Walgreens. I also shined shoes. On a good day at that job, I made $1.50.

I worked for a while as second cook at a small lunchroom at 1231 Emerson St. It was called "The Coffee Pot" and was run by a man named Herbert Laffoon. It didn't pay much, but it gave me a chance to refine the cooking skills Mother had taught me. When business was bad, he had to let me go.

In good weather, I caddied a great deal at Skokie Country Club in Glencoe. I made serious money as a caddy — up to $12 a week. I couldn't earn that much anywhere else. Grown (colored) men were lucky if they could make $18 a week. When the weather turned cold, I had to look for something else.

A dollar a drill

Around 1933, I learned I could join the Illinois National Guard and get paid a dollar for each drill. I was motivated by money — not by any feeling of patriotism.

The 8th Infantry of the Illinois National Guard was composed completely of African-American officers and enlisted men. The outfit had a distinguished history, having served on the Mexican border and later in France in World War I. No white American officers had wanted anything to do with these "colored" soldiers. So, the regiment was attached to the French Army. This unit helped break the famed Von Hindenberg line, which started the defeat of Germany.

I was placed in Company D, a machine gun company under Lt. Marcus Ray, who would figure prominently in my future. He was always very smartly dressed, almost as if he were a model. He was tall, handsome, and very articulate. Because I had learned some dismounted drill during my sentence at St. Charles School for Boys, I showed aptitude, and the company's non-commissioned officers liked me at once.

The whole battalion was sent to Ft. Custer, Michigan, to wage a mock war. I was not prepared for the forced marches in this mock war. One time, I fell asleep while marching down a road, and kept going in the same direction after the column had made a half-left turn. A corporal raced up to me and brought me back to the column.

We know what we are doing, lady

I can facetiously thank harassment by the Evanston Police Department for whatever success I have had in life.

My first personal encounter with the police had occurred when I was about 12 years old. There were about 20 of us black youths playing baseball in Foster Field when two "Black Mariahs," the name we gave paddy wagons, pulled to the curb near our game. About six uniformed police alighted and ordered us into the vans. We cried, "What did we do?" and "I didn't do anything!" To no avail.

We were placed in several cells. One policeman said to another as they left: "We'll ask her to come down here and pick out the guilty one." After about six hours, when a policeman brought us our dinner of a lunch meat sandwich apiece, someone asked: "When are you gonna let us outta here?" Came the snarling rely: "As soon as the guilty one confesses, or when the lady comes down to pick out the guilty one." His remark was followed by a chorus of protestations. "What are we supposed to have done?"

After awhile we settled down to sleep on the concrete floor. About midnight, parents began to arrive.

They had learned about our situation from an eight-year-old girl who had witnessed the arrests. She did not know all the boys' names, but when she told her father, he began to get in touch with others. Parents were allowed to come in singly to the cells and talk briefly to their children.

Tears came to my eyes when I saw my mother's gentle face. I was angry at the police, but doubly angry because they were causing the distress I could see on my mother's face. As I touched her hand through the bars, she smiled at me and said: "Have courage, son. I'm praying for you and God will make everything work out all right." Her brief words of encouragement made me feel better. I was no longer afraid of the police. I just wanted vengeance.

Three days later, the "lady from Sheridan Road" came to view us. She said she couldn't have come sooner because she had been preparing for a big dinner party. As we were paraded before her, she kept protesting: "It was dark outside, and as I came from my dining room into my living room, I saw someone on my porch. I couldn't see who it was."

As I was paraded in front of her, she asked the police detective in charge: "Don't you people have the third degree, or some other way to get niggers to confess?" After she had gone, without identifying any of us, we were let go, with the warnings, "Behave yourselves. You were lucky this time. We'll get you next time."

The next time I was in a police roundup was about a year later. This time some youths saw the police coming and ran. They caught only 12 of us. We were taken to a home just east of Evanston Hospital.

At the house, a woman told the police that on the previous night she had heard a noise on her back porch. When she raised the shade in the back door window, a man ran down her back stairs and along the walk, and vaulted over the back fence.

One by one, the police ordered us to run down the walk and vault over the back gate. She protested that she was not able to identify any of us by this exercise.

"Besides," she added, "you have only colored boys here. There are some white boys in the neighborhood who have been pestering me. Why haven't you picked up any of them?" A policeman replied, "We know what we are doing, lady." She refused to participate any more, and the police let us go.

Another day after carrying "doubles" — caddying for two players — all one Saturday, I returned home $5 richer and dog-tired. I went to bed. I was awakened in the morning by the sound of men's shouts. I walked out of my bedroom, and saw my mother talking to two policemen.

She was saying: "My boy could not be the one you want. He was here in bed all night." One policeman asked, "How do we know you're not lying?" Mother replied, "I'm a good Christian woman, and I don't lie." His response: "All niggers lie."

I was angry and started for him, and Mother held me back. "Don't stop him," the cop said. "Let him come and taste some of this billy club." I got dressed and went with them down to the police station. By the time I got there, other policemen had got a confession out of some poor boy, whether or not he was guilty. "You can go home now, boy," I was told, and I walked out into Evanston's clean but segregated air.

What did he steal?

I got a job as a yard and house man at 620 Foster Street, just off the Northwestern University campus. I got the same salary as at Walgreens, but I also got my meals and my room. I had to work only nine hours a day. I liked the job and the lady who was my boss.

One night as I walked back to my job from the Valencia theater downtown, a police car pulled up beside me and an officer yelled at me: "Get in!" I protested, "I haven't done anything wrong." He shouted again, "Get in." I was taken to the police station and locked up overnight. I was told: "If nobody reports anything stolen tomorrow, you can go home."

About 10 a.m. the following day, I was let go with the warning: "Stay out of trouble and you won't get locked up." I walked back to my job only to find an irate boss. "Where have you been? Why weren't you here to do your chores? Your bed wasn't slept in last night." I told her what had happened. She didn't believe me. She telephoned the police. She reported that they asked her: "What did he steal? We just let him go, but we can pick him up again."

She turned to me, full of apologies. Now she had a cause celebre. She was back on the phone. "How dare you pick up innocent people and put them in jail? This is not Communist Russia. You say he's been picked up before. For what? Was he found guilty? You mean you just pick up people on suspicion and keep them in jail? Don't tell me I don't know nig - colored people. They have worked for me for more than 20 years and never took anything that didn't belong to them."

About a week later, another police squad car picked me up as I was walking from the theater. My protests were to no avail, and I was locked up again. It was shortly before midnight when the next sergeant came on duty and saw my name. I was brought upstairs and told to go home. As I left, I heard the sergeant remark: "I don't want that woman cussin' me out again about that nigger."

When I told my police episodes later to a long-time resident of the community, he said: "Man, you were lucky! You didn't get your head split open or any of your teeth knocked out."

Pack your clothes

We had just finished the nightly prayers. My sisters and my brother were hurrying to listen to a radio program. My mother said to me: "Wait a minute, son. I want to talk to you." Her tone was so serious I wondered what I had done that she was going to scold me about.

Instead, she said: "How much have you saved?" I replied, "I think I got about $10, Mama." She came back with: "Ten dollars in two years. What happened to the rest of money you made? You've been working all along … no, you don't have to answer. I know. Every time some little emergency came up in the family, you dipped into your savings. You'll never get an education as long as you stay here and let us bleed you. You're a strong boy and an intelligent boy, and God knows I love you and I'm proud of you. So, I want you to listen to me and understand. I want you to pack your clothes and get out!"

I started, "But, Mama." She interrupted, "Shush, son. I've thought it over a long time. You can take care of yourself, and heaven knows this is one of the worst communities you could possibly live in. The white people here are so bigoted that they will go out of their way to keep you down. And the police will make a criminal out of you if you remain here. The colored people here have just given up. Very few of them have a dream that goes beyond Saturday night's pay. You've got to get out of this town, son, or they'll drag you down with them — and you've got too much promise to let that happen to you."

I cried when she finished her speech because I knew that mother was demonstrating very deep love for me, crying because I was going to have to leave my home and family. Plus, I was a little frightened. We were sitting on her bed, and Mother placed her hand on my thigh and said in comforting tones: "You are my big boy, and I am proud of you. Don't worry about us. God has taken care of us before, and He will again. Also, I'll be praying for you, and I know He'll take care of you too. Don't give up. Keep on trying, no matter how dark the future may seem at times. And remember, with God on your side, what might appear to be a misfortune can often be a blessing in disguise."

I went to my room, but there was little sleep for me that night. It was July and the weather was warm, and I was still caddying at Skokie Country Club every day. Some of the white boys who hitch-hiked in from Chicago would spend nights in the caddy shack when they wanted to be among the first to get jobs the following day. Andy, the caddy master, sold half pint bottles of milk, candy bars, and apple slices, so his crew didn't have to go hungry the next morning. There was a restaurant on Park Street in downtown Glencoe where we could get a decent meal, if it seemed important. Mostly, we would buy some lunch meat and a loaf of bread and make sandwiches. And, there was the ubiquitous and nutritious peanut butter.

So, I made the caddy shack my home.

Chapter 2

New Trier

In the fall of 1935, at age 20, I decided that I was going to enroll in New Trier High School, a great college-prep school in the North Shore community of Winnetka.

But I needed an address in the community to give. After I talked over my plans with Bill Seabron, an older guy who caddied sometimes, he volunteered: "I've gotta give it to you man. You're one helluva dude. If you need an address to enroll, why not use ours?" So, it was settled for the time being. I had an address at 358 Adams. However, while registering for school, I accidentally listed my mother's address in Evanston, rather than Seabron's address.

The dean of boys called me in and said: "The state law requires a student to go to school in the township in which his parents' reside. So, you are not eligible to be enrolled here." My spirits sank. I left his office and sat on the front stairs of the school, my chin in my hands.

I sat there for hours and was deep in self pity when I heard a voice: "Can I help you?" I looked up and saw a man smiling at me. So was the lady who was accompanying him. "They won't let me enroll in school," I said. "Who are they?" In a voice that was trembling in frustration, I told him the story. He smiled and turned to the lady. "I don't believe that the state Legislature meant the law to be used to keep someone from getting an education, do you?" She replied, "No, I don't." "Let's take the matter up in the board meeting this noon."

He turned to me and said: "I'm the principal, Matthew Gaffney. What's your name?" I told him and he said: "Come see me tomorrow. I think we can help you."

Another sleepless night. I was at the school door long before anyone else arrived. Gaffney came about an hour and a half after I arrived. He saw me on the steps and came over to me smiling, and said: "You may register today. I've told the dean of boys that it's all right." I thanked him and could hardly contain my emotion.

Now, I had to do good for Gaffney as well as for Mother. The memory of Mother's tears in Bacon's office, and the smile on Gaffney's face as he told me I could enroll inspired me many times.

*

At first it made sense to stay in the caddy shack. I saved every penny I could, eating sparingly. As the weather became colder — especially at night — I had a hard time keeping warm. I had nowhere else to stay, and couldn't even imagine returning home. My efforts to get an education at New Trier seemed doomed.

I had just about made up my mind to give up the effort. Then, in the dark of that caddy shack, I saw Mother's image. She smiled at me and said: "I'm so proud of my big boy. I know you can do it. Don't give up. Just stop and think. I'm praying for you and God will open a way for you."

Suddenly, I was not cold or hungry. I realized that I could go to the Chicago and Northwestern Railway station in Winnetka, which was open and warm all night. I moved to the train station, washed out my underwear and shirt in the men's bathroom at night and hung them on a radiator to dry.

Now, I just had to figure out how to get food, since winter eliminated my caddying income. I started making the rounds of the several restaurants in downtown Winnetka, asking if I could work as a dishwasher or janitor just for meals. I don't know how many turned me down. Finally, a young white man who was the dishwasher at a restaurant whispered to me, "Come back about 10 o'clock and look in the garbage cans." When I returned and lifted the lid on the first garbage can, a piece of cardboard held a delightful array of food — meat, potatoes, vegetable, and even a piece of pie for dessert. Printed on the cardboard was the message "Come back every night."

For several weeks when I returned to the garbage cans, a delicious and ample meal, or meals, waited for me. Often there was enough food for me to save and eat a hearty breakfast.

But about the last week in November, I found no food. I was hungry and I decided to pick over the food that others had not eaten. I took the food back to the station, washed it off, and tried to eat it. Most difficult were attempts to try to wash cigarette ashes from meat where diners had extinguished their smokes. However, it kept me going.

The Gobles

I had been on this diet for about a week when a police officer discovered me asleep in the train station. The Winnetka officer was courteous as he said: "You can't sleep here, son. Where's your home?" I explained that I had no home. "You'll have to come with me, then," he said.

I was taken to the Winnetka police station where I explained my situation to the desk sergeant. He was amazed when I told him that I was a junior at New Trier. I was locked up for the night. In the morning, after a breakfast of sweet rolls and milk, I was brought before the desk sergeant again. "The principal, Mr. Gaffney, said that not only are you a student there, but you are one of their best students. He asked us to take you to the school. Good luck, kid." Once again I was in Mr. Gaffney's office.

"Lester, you amaze me," he said with a wide grin on his face. "Why didn't you tell me that you didn't have a place to live when you enrolled?" I pleaded, "I did have a place when I enrolled, but circumstances change."

He thought, then said, "When we talked before, you told me that you are a cook, right?" I told him, "My mother taught me to cook. I've been cooking for the family since I was 12." He said, "I have an idea. Wait in the outer office until I make a few calls."

It seemed as if I waited hours, but in reality it was just a few minutes. He emerged and beckoned me into his office. "My friend and neighbor, Sherman Goble, and his wife believe that they could use you. They had three sons who were graduated from here some years ago. They live in a big house, and Mrs. Goble could use some help in exchange for room and board. I think you'll like them."

The Gobles seemed like a king and a queen to me. They had had their attic fixed up neatly for their three sons, who were now living and working in New York. So, I had a three-room apartment all to myself.

They seemed solicitous of my well-being, and when I brought my report card for Mr. Goble to sign after I had been there about a week, he grinned: "I've never had the pleasure of signing a report card with grades this good — three A's and a B." I told him, "I promise to do better on my next card." And I did. The next marking period my report card contained four A's.

Poetry

My New Trier experience was heaven on earth to me. My teachers were excellent, and I made friends among the students. I was never more motivated to study, to learn, to excel.

I'm sure students who saw the wide grin on my face as I signed up for classes must have believed that I was about the friendliest boy they had ever seen. One asked me: "Do you play football?" "And basketball, too," I replied. I believe that he looked at my six foot, 173 pound frame and in his eyes I became a hero before I put on a uniform.

Psychologically, I was not prepared for New Trier. Instead of the indifferent or hostile teachers I had known at Evanston High, I found teachers who were friendly, encouraging — even flattering.

I was pleased with all my teachers, but I took a special liking to Stanley "Pete" Peterson, my English teacher. He made language come alive. In his class I discovered my love for language. He wrote a sonnet every day, and I began to fall in love with the iambic pentameter. He was in charge of the school's liter-

ary magazine, "Inklings." He asked me to be on the staff. So, I wrote poems and
short stories for the magazine.

My first offering, a poem which commanded a full page in the magazine,
was titled: "Chicken Breas'."

Here it is:

> Some folks be mighty choicy
> 'bout the kinda food they eat
> Dere vegtibles got to be certin kin'
> "N' they just gott hab this meat.
>
> Me, I ain't that choicy
> I has et rice an greens.
> "N' I membes one day las' week
> when I even stooped to beans.
>
> but when you's 'vitin' me to dine
> "N' feedin' me the bes',
> Remember if ther be chicken,
> I expecs the breas'
>
> You can have yo' legs, yo' gizzauds,
> Yo' drumsticks and all the res'
> Jes remember when you serve,
> I wants the breas'
>
> SO, when you see me smilin',
> Chicken gravy on my ves'
> You can bet yo' bottom dollah
> I jes had chicken breas'

My brother Ray, who later performed vaudeville in New York City, was
particularly adept at reciting this poem, on stage and before private audiences
until his death in 1999.

I was never more flattered than when Mr. Peterson made me editor-in-
chief of the magazine for my senior year. Also on the staff was Connie Clough,
another poet, who caused poems of love to gush from my heart. Now Connie
Ratcliffe, she remains a close friend.

I wrote to Connie regularly during World War II and she read my letters
to her students at Gulf Park College in Mississippi, leaving out the fact I was
black.

My reputation as a poet grew when I started writing sonnets for girls I
liked. Soon, I was being paid $1 each for sonnets I would write for fellow teens'
girlfriends. Not a week went by that I did not make $4 or $5 writing about love.

I produced sonnets to moonbeams, to flowers, to a dove, to just about every girl who attracted my attention at New Trier. One of them was Joy, who invited me to dinner with her family. The whites seemed uncomfortable until a squirrel leaped from the fireplace chimney into the living room. That broke the ice.

When it was time for me to leave, I thanked everyone and Joy walked me to the door. I extended my hand. She took it, pulled me closer and kissed me on the cheek. I stood transfixed for a full minute. Once at home, I turned on the radio and heard the song, "Claire d'Lune." I telephoned Joy and told her to tune in the station. That became "our song."

When my junior year was about half over, Goble informed me that he was due a five-month vacation for time he had accumulated over the years. He and his wife were planning to take it in Mexico. Would I want to join them? I was afraid that if I left school I would never finish. So I thanked them and went to look for another job.

Once again, Gaffney galloped to my rescue. He sent me to work for Mr. and Mrs. Alfred Brittain III in Winnetka.

For the Brittains, who had three sons, my principal job was preparing meals. Shortly before the school year ended, Mrs. Brittain was riding in an auto with a niece of Harold Ickes, secretary of the interior under President Franklin D. Roosevelt, when a Chicago and Northwestern Railway train hit the car. Both women were killed.

Shortly after the death of the two ladies, the railroad began excavating and moved its tracks below grade. Today, the only place in the North Shore community where that train runs below grade level is in Winnetka. Every time I drive north along Green Bay Road, and pass that spot, I am reminded how it figured in my history.

Mr. Brittain took his sons to live with his mother and I looked for another job.

One of my friends, and a fellow track team member, George Murray, asked me what was wrong. I told him. He said, eagerly, "Why not come and live with us and work for us?" I told him I'd be glad to. He went to the phone and called his mother. In about 15 minutes, he bounded back gleefully: "You're gonna live with us, you're gonna live with us!" His twin brother, Bill, came over to where we were celebrating. We told him. There were three of us in a gleeful dance.

Working for and living with the Murrays was an everyday picnic. When my work was done, we tussled just like teenage boys do. We raced through the house and rough-housed. Mrs. Murray, a kindly smiling woman, seemed to tolerate the playing, sometimes cautioning us: "Boys, boys, you're getting out of hand!" That admonition calmed us for a little while, and then we were back at it again.

Each of us had jobs delivering a shopping newspaper on Thursdays after school, starting at $2 a week.

There were the inevitable bull sessions. The one I remember most had to do with what girl each was going to ask to the prom. Each time the boys would make a suggestion for me to ask for a date, they named a white girl. I began to wonder if they saw me as one of them. Finally, I told them that I had someone in mind, a girl who was not in our high school.

I had met a lovely girl while I was competing in a tennis tournament in Waukegan. I had learned some tennis pointers from my dear friend, Arthur C. Nielsen, Jr. Nielsen made himself my friend after I stopped a big bully from picking on him. Art, in fact, called himself my "little brother." He was the Illinois Men's Single champion at the time. I couldn't hold a candle to him, but I could beat his sister, Peg. I could do that largely because I had more power.

I won the tournament, which was sponsored by a black social club, and the trophies were to be awarded that evening at a dance. I invited Helen Edwards, a girl I met just after the tournament ended.

Helen was one year ahead of me in high school, and she chose to go to the University of Illinois in Champaign-Urbana. We exchanged letters all year and I was getting very serious about her. I mustered enough money to make several long distance telephone calls to the sorority house where she lived.

During my freshman year at college, I did a favor for an executive of a small airline, and he gave me a round-trip ticket to Champaign. I telephoned her and asked what she was doing for lunch. She thought I was kidding when I told her I would pick her up for lunch. The girls in the house broke into squeals of delight when I appeared at the door. Helen's stock went up as the girls wondered what she had done to lure her guy to make a plane trip just to take her to lunch.

Eventually, she broke up with me. She said my ambition frightened her. She said she was sure that I was going places and would be a great success. She didn't want to be in that kind of environment. It hurt. I thought my ambition and achievement were something to be proud of, but they had lost me a girl I really cared about.

Distinguished graduate

New Trier High School commencement in 1937 was a stirring event. I was number 16 or 17 in a graduating class of 521. I got a standing ovation when my name was called.

As we turned in our caps and gowns, someone started singing "Auld Lang Syne" — and we burst into tears, and started hugging one another.

I gave my high school diploma to my mother, and she said: "I'm so proud of my big boy!" I felt that I had made a partial payment for all the trouble I had caused her up to that point and had proved that Evanston High School officials had made a major mistake when they expelled me. My picture now hangs in a hallway at New Trier among other "distinguished graduates."

*

Mr. Murray, a woolen goods salesman, brought a guest for dinner the last week of high school in June 1937. The guest, Wallace Meyer, was a vice president of an advertising agency. He claimed the distinction of rescuing the corset

First Row (left to right): M. Harshaw, J. Bignell, R. Goodwin, P. Sheriffs, P. Gooder.
Second Row: M. Tuttle, C. Clough, B. Dodds, J. Macdonald, E. Baughman, F. White, J. Kassner, B. Glenn.
Third Row: B. Barnard, J. Graf, D. Werthimer, B. Mathison, H. Bergman, D. Farwell.

INKLINGS

SPONSORS ....MR. PETERSON, MR. LEHMAN
EDITORS..LESTRE BROWNLEE, ROBERT GOODWIN

BROWNLEE - GOODWIN

In the spring of 1935, "Inklings" made its first appearance. This initial edition was sponsored by the English department to commemorate the tri-centennial of secondary education. The purpose of the magazine was to encourage literary talent in the students. The publication was so successful that it again appeared the following year.

"Inklings" is now published twice a year, in December and in May. It has expanded to include not only the best contributions in literature, but also illustrations by the school's outstanding art students. Any student at New Trier is eligible to enter any short form of literature to be accepted for publication. The "Inklings" staff, headed this year by Lestre Brownlee and Robert Goodwin, co-operated with their faculty sponsors, Mr. Peterson and Mr. Lehman, and selected the best contributions for the magazine.

The student body has profited much by "Inklings." It not only offers recognition for outstanding literary and artistic talent, but it helps those students who have not made contributions to appreciate the fine talent and methods of expression exhibited in the accepted material.

1936

A page from the 1936 New Trier yearbook.

business — which had suffered because women shunned the name — by inventing "the girdle."

There were six for dinner: Mr. and Mrs. Murray, Mr. Meyer, Bill, George and I. For dessert, I baked an apple pie for which I had gained a little fame.

My recipe:

Preheat oven to 425°
Pie crust — Sift together
2 cups flour
1/2 teaspoon baking powder
1/2 teaspoon ground nutmeg
1 teaspoon salt

Cut 3/4 cup of Crisco into the above mixture and refrigerate while rest of pie ingredients are being prepared. Pare and thin slice 6 green or sour apples. Place apples in a bowl and mix with 1-1/2 cup sugar and 2 teaspoons ground cinnamon, and 1 tablespoon lemon juice and 1/2 teaspoon salt.

Divide pie crust mixture in half and return one half to refrigerator. Using a roller that has been stored in the freezer, place pie crust half between two pieces of wax paper and roll into a flat circle to fit a 9-inch pie pan. With tines of a fork, make several punctures in bottom crust after it has been fitted into pie pan.

Place apple mixture in bottom crust, mounding toward the center. Make small dots of 4 ounces of butter and distribute evenly over apple mixture.

Remove balance of pie crust from refrigerator and roll out between two sheets of wax paper. Cut strips about 1/2-inch wide and apply to top of pie in a lattice-like pattern. Into each of the interstices in the top crust, insert one rigatoni pasta (like small chimneys).

Place pie in oven and bake for 15 minutes; turn oven temperature down to 350° and bake for an additional 45 minutes.

ENJOY!

Lake Shore Drive

Murray and Meyer traded stories, as veteran salesmen do, and all of us were kept in stitches with laughter. After we had finished the first apple pie, Meyer said: "I've never had a piece of pie that tasted that good. I'd like another piece, if you don't mind." I told him that we had eaten all of the pie, but if we adjourned the party to the kitchen, I'd make another. We did. I made another. We ate all of that pie. Then, Meyer said: "I just bought a farm outside of Baraboo, Wis. And we just lost the cook we had at our apartment. Would you be interested in working for us?" I jumped at the offer.

I left my New Trier "heaven" with a great deal of trepidation. I had been treated so well — like a favorite son — that I feared returning to the "real" world where people would treat me with the kind of bigotry I lived with in Evanston.

Les greets New Trier classmates Art Nielsen and Chuck Percy at their 65th reunion in 2001.

I moved first to the Meyer's apartment at 3750 Lake Shore Drive. It had a dozen rooms, including one off the kitchen, which I occupied. Mrs. Meyer told me: "We don't like fancy food, just good plain cooking. You order the food from this market (and she gave me the name of the store). We do like ample proportions, though."

The two Meyer sons, six and eight, looked at me as if I were a spectacle from the zoo. They did not speak, just stared. Because Mrs. Meyer had suggested meat loaf as an example of the kinds of food they ate, I prepared one for that first meal, along with mashed potatoes, a vegetable and salad. But the main attraction was Mother's rolls. And for dessert — of course the apple pie that had got me the job.

After dinner, Mrs. Meyer came into the kitchen raving about the food. She said, "What did you do to those vegetables? Usually I have a hard time getting the boys to eat vegetables. They gobbled them up like they were ice cream."

She had further praise for me when she received the grocery bill. "How do you manage to cook such delicious meals so inexpensively?" she asked. I replied, "Because we were poor, Mother taught me the way poor people cook."

I received a similarly friendly welcome when we moved to the farm outside Baraboo. I won over the resident farmer and his wife with Mother's rolls.

Most days I had only the four Meyers and the resident farmer and his wife to cook for. However, Mr. Meyer occasionally invited guests to spend the weekend on the farm. That gave me a chance to demonstrate some of my tastiest recipes — like soul cakes for breakfast on Sundays.

Here's the recipe:

Preheat griddle to 450 degrees. Then sift together:
1-1/2 cups flour
1/2 cup yellow corn meal
1 teaspoon salt
1/2 cup sugar

In a large bowl, mix:
1 cup milk
6 ounces cooking oil
yolks of four eggs (place whites in another bowl)
Combine the two mixtures and stir until smooth. Beat egg whites until stiff (adding a bit of cream of tartar before beating).

Fold beaten egg white into batter and cook on hot griddle. Turn cakes after they begin to bubble. If desirable, blueberries may be added after cakes have been turned.

*

I was introduced to the eight horses, including an almost all-black mare, "Lady," who won my adoration. On my days off, I saddled up Lady and we took to the hills. Sometimes, I galloped her for a short distance, but usually I let her have her way to wander and graze while I sat in the saddle writing poetry.

On one such trip I began to realize for the past several years I had met not one single white person who had treated me with less than respect, most with a gesture of friendship. How different from the bigotry I had received from most whites in Evanston. I remembered then what Mother had told me: get out of Evanston to save myself.

I became friends with several teens from neighboring farms. On Saturday afternoons, each would bring his or her favorite horse to the farm. We would race down the half mile to the Ringling Farm, whose owners were kind enough to leave the pasture gate open so that we could finish our race into their pasture.

On one of my days off, Mr. Meyer asked me if I had seen the University of Wisconsin at Madison, his alma mater. When I told him that I had not, he suggested that I take the car and drive down to the university.

I was overwhelmed at first by the beauty of the campus with its many tall trees hugging the south shore of Lake Mendota. (The Indians called it the "lake of the morning.")

Everyone I met seemed happy and friendly, as if they had known me for years. As I walked across the campus, I was greeted by many pleasant "hellos" from summer school students. As I stood gawking, some students seemed to think I was lost and stopped to offer to help me find my way.

I saw one black student and asked him if he knew where black people lived in Madison. He said they lived in a number of places, but the biggest cluster could be found on Washington Street, and he told me how to get there.

When I reached the street, I saw more white people than black. However, I saw a tavern where there were some black people, and I saw a small restaurant that was run by blacks. I entered and was greeted by an attractive young lady who asked my order. I ordered a cup of coffee and told her I was visiting and thinking of enrolling in the fall. In our pleasant but brief conversation, she told me that the black students she had met all seemed pleased with the university and Madison, but complained that there was no night life to speak of. I thanked her and left.

After spending several hours in Madison, I returned to the farm, sold on the idea that the U of W was for me. I knew that I had to go to this university, no matter what sacrifices I had to make.

When I was ready to leave in early September, Mr. Meyer suggested that perhaps I would be better advised to remain as the family cook for another year so I could save more money. I wouldn't hear of it. I was always afraid that if I interrupted my quest for an education I might not get back in school.

I had one heart-rending hesitation. I overheard a man ask Meyer the price for Lady, "my horse." When Meyer told him that he would sell her for $125, I was sorely tempted to buy the horse myself and work another year. I could not decide, so I flipped a coin. The coin came down in favor of the university. I gave Lady a hug, an apple, two lumps of sugar and a promise that I would see her again at the end of the semester in February, which I did.

Chapter 3

University of Wisconsin

When I arrived in Madison in September 1937, I had $130 — my earnings for the summer. I had no job, no place to stay, and knew only the waitress in the restaurant. Tuition for one semester was $28.50, but if one was an out -of-state student (which I was) an additional $100 was assessed. I paid my $128.50 to the bursar, and I still had what was known as Freshman Week before classes started.

I went back to the restaurant and asked the waitress if she knew where I might get a room. She told me that Mrs. Dyer at 219 Park St. used to rent a room to a student. She told me also that Mrs. Dyer cooked for one of the downtown department stores.

As soon as I began to talk to Mrs. Dyer, I began giving her some of my recipes. We were immediate friends, and I her tenant. "Come on in, son. I know you'll pay me." She helped me find a job waiting tables at the Phi Delta Theta house in exchange for meals.

To pay my rent, I got a job at the university Press Bureau. I had to take a written test to get the job. Freshmen were not eligible. So, when I made out the application card, I didn't fill in the blank that asked for class. I passed the test and got the job.

On the way back from getting the job, I ran into a guy who had been in New Trier with me and on the Inklings magazine. He asked me how I was getting along. I told him that I had a meal job, and one that would pay my rent, but that I didn't have any money for books. He knew that I had worked for a classmate's family for three weeks one summer while their chauffeur and yard man was on vacation. The classmate, Peg Stein, was at an eastern college.

The guy I had met telephoned Peg Stein, who called her mother. Two days later I received a check for $50— and my book issue was taken care of. I believe that if people who know you believe in you, they will make sacrifices and contributions to help your cause.

When I told Mother about my good fortune, she responded: "This shows you that God answers my prayers." Once again, my faith in Mother was enhanced. Everything seemed to be falling into place.

The Poet

In my first week in English composition class, the instructor said he wanted to see how well each student wrote. He asked us to turn in a piece of original description. This was just the kind of writing that I knew how to do well.

At the session after we had turned in our papers, he passed all of them back except mine. Then, he said: "I want to read a paper to you." He read mine. "That's what I call writing," he said as he handed me my paper.

He asked me to stay for a minute after class. He asked me about my writing background. I told him that I had been editor-in-chief of the high school literary magazine, and that I wrote poetry. He asked me to bring some to his office. I did. He said he had talked to the English Department chairman and was told that I shouldn't be taking the English composition course. Instead, I should spend the year writing poetry.

I was given to a committee of English teachers and I had to report to them each week with my latest composition. Sometimes I did little but revise a poem to get closer to an idea or image.

During that period I met and became friends with Dean Goodnight, who was also a poet. We would sit and think of words that would provoke the response we wished in a reader. I enjoyed these experiences very much. He once asked me: "Do you plan a career as a poet?" I told him, "I understand that poets have a hard time making a living, and I like to eat regularly."

Sinclair Lewis

When an announcement came that Sinclair Lewis, author of "Main Street" and other best-selling novels of the day, was coming to the university to teach a course in fiction writing, I was enthusiastic. When I learned that about 4,000 manuscripts had been submitted by students who wanted to be in the class, I thought I didn't have a chance. So I did nothing.

I was washing windows for a lady when she came to a window and yelled: "Come quickly. Sinclair Lewis is on the phone!" He asked: "Can you join me for lunch today?" I turned to my employer and asked. She exclaimed: "Yes. Yes. Go. Go."

We were alone in his house except for his manservant, who joined us at the table. Lewis explained: "I don't believe in separatism. I had a hard time convincing him to eat with me at first. Now he's used to it."

Lewis told me that I had been recommended to him by several people on the faculty. He asked me to be in his class. I was overjoyed. I was one of 15 in it. The class met for two hours on Wednesday afternoons. Lewis discussed plotting, character building and a number of other things.

Early on, he gave us an exercise. He took it from the second chapter of St. Luke and the seventh verse: "And she brought forth her first-born Son and wrapped him in swaddling clothes, and laid Him in a manger, for there was no room for them in the inn." He said, "I want you to improve on that verse." None of us could.

On Friday evenings, we met at his house. He provided light refreshments, and we socialized with one another until we met individually with him and discussed the progress each had on his or her project. These were extremely important to me, and I suppose to others, too.

He pointed out how important it was to select the names of our principal characters. He used the example of "Elmer Gantry" to show how a name really fit a character. This name made the character more believable, he said.

A tragic story about an interracial couple that I heard from another student bothered me so greatly that I decided to write an epic poem about the doomed lovers to illustrate the stupidity of anger. I called it, "A Portrait of DeGrewe."

I became so involved in the iambic pentameter verse that I wrote until the poem was finished — about 73 hours later. My body ached from sitting for three days, unaware of anything except my mission. It was the first time I had an "out of body" experience.

What was that poem? I remember only one verse:

They lived together in that spangled blue
So long a time that some affinity
Which started with a friendship mutual
Waxed opulent and blossomed into love

Sinclair Lewis said the poem showed a lot of talent and a lot of promise. He left before the semester ended to help with a Broadway production of his play, "Angela is 22."

A brain named Brownlee

My good grades became a source of embarrassment at football practice. The freshman football coach, Russ Rippe, got the grades of all the freshman football squad. He made the announcement: "We've got a brain here — a brain named Brownlee. His grades are three A's and one B. Can somebody like that play football?" After the round of laughs at my expense, I made up my mind that I would show them what I was made of.

I got the chance on the following day. Rippe said our tackling was sloppy. He selected George Paskvan, an all-state fullback from LaGrange, Illinois, to run the gauntlet to see how we tackled him. I was about sixth in line. Up to that point the players had not been able to stop him. As he came to me, I got squarely in front of him, and drove into him.

"That's the way to tackle," Rippe exclaimed. "Brownlee, do it again to show these guys how it's done." Varsity Coach Harry Stuhldreher (who had

Courtesy of University off Wisconsin Athletic Dept.

**The 1937 University of Wisconsin freshman football team.
See Les at top left.**

been quarterback on Notre Dame's famed Four Horsemen) later asked where I had played football before. I told him, and he said: "You show a lot of promise, kid; a lot of promise!"

I played football the whole time I was at Wisconsin, mostly as a pass receiver. I had to be carried off the field after damaging my knee during our come-from-behind 14-13 victory against Purdue during the 1939 season.

*

After I left my meal job and got home, I was so tired that I couldn't keep my eyes open to study. I started pacing the floor holding the book in front of me. Even that didn't work. I found that I was walking in my sleep, and nothing would go into my tired brain. Then, I hit upon an idea. I would go to bed and set the clock for three or four in the morning. That way I was able to keep up my grades. I needed to do that to be eligible for a scholarship for the second semester.

I did get the scholarship, and had it for the rest of my time at the university.

I sold my first magazine article as a UW sophomore. It was on how inadequate lighting in schools hurts students' eyesight. I made $40 on that Hygiea article in 1938. Before that, writing was merely a class exercise.

Timber Wolf

The first semester gave me little time to be with girls. Besides, I was still in love with Helen, and I thought that she was in love with me. About the same time that I received notice that I had a scholarship for the second semester, I got the note from Helen that we were through. It hurt so badly that I decided

I would fill my life with other women and forget her.

One of the first made me interested in the Youth Committee Against War. I had been reading what Hitler was doing in Germany, and felt that the United States was sliding toward war. I got a 15-minute radio show on Friday mornings on the university station, WHA. The show was dedicated to peace. As a result, I was made the Madison area chairman of the Youth Committee Against War.

A newspaper columnist said my rantings resembled "the howling of a timber wolf." Thus I was nicknamed "Timber Wolf," a nickname I still hold dear.

Also on radio, I did book readings for kids "and older folks, too." I made up my own stories, such as one about a boy whose foot became caught in a rock but beat off wolves.

I composed and staged a musical, "Raising Hell," about the world's best-looking woman selling the Devil on the idea of improving Hell's reputation. It was staged at the UW Union.

My brother Ray was working as a porter in the Greyhound Bus station in Madison, and we took voice lessons from Madame DeVoe, who put on an opera each year. Madame was very much impressed with the quality of our voices. She had two lovely daughters, and I'm sure that I got interested in singing after meeting her daughters. Ray and I ended up in Leo Delibe's opera, "Lakme."

Through contacts made at the DeVoe Institute of Singing, I got a gig with a five-piece band and met Ruth Jean Smith. We were never lovers, although we sang many love duets as the band played in a number of small towns around Madison.

Hot pants

I was not secretive about the fact I was sterile, that I had had the mumps when I was 15 and could not produce viable sperm. The information led to a series of "girlfriends."

I began to pay more attention to the differences women presented. I couldn't remember two who were alike. Sometimes the differences were small, but there were always differences. I learned that most women believed that they were just about the same. Nothing could be further from the truth, and I began to realize that many men did not realize the wide varieties which were presented to them. Maybe because they didn't have enough women to detect the difference. The difference was most pronounced when having three women in succession.

One friend explained my sudden, vast popularity: "Your name is being passed up and down sorority row. First, they know that you are sterile, they know that they will not meet you later in their social set, and you are supposed to be fantastic in bed. So, when one gets hot pants, she arranges to meet you — and you know what happens after that."

I didn't want to believe her, but when four new acquaintances appeared on the scene within the next two weeks, I suspected that what she said was true. That's when I stopped following up on requests. It wasn't that I didn't appreciate the sessions. I just began to feel used. Also, most were just not that good in bed.

I began wondering: What is the significance of an individual sexual encounter? Is it merely an opportunity to have some pleasure? Or, is this the act of two people who are very serious about their relationship, moving toward marriage? Should a couple seek pleasure in the sexual act, or should it be only the encounter necessary for the reproduction of the species? If pleasure is not a goal, or a primary or important goal, then it matters not that some females go through life without ever experiencing orgasm. However, if the sex act is to bring pleasure, then someone ought to teach each partner what brings pleasure.

About this time, my old friend from New Trier, Art Nielsen, got me a job waiting tables in his fraternity house. Sigma Phi was full of millionaires' sons. I became good friends with many of the 20 members of the fraternity.

Art placed my name in nomination to become a member of the fraternity. He told me that I received 19 of the 20 votes of the active members. He said: "If I ever find out who cast that black ball against you, he'll wish he had never lived."

I've often wondered what would have happened if I had been voted in. What would I have done for money? The experience, however, showed me what I meant to Art, and we have grown only closer over the years.

*

As a member of the university's speakers bureau, I traveled throughout Wisconsin, usually speaking on peace and prejudice. Almost invariably, the invitations came from church groups, and often during the period known as Negro History Week.

During these trips, I became aware of the inroads Hitler's anti-Semitism was making in the United States. I remember seeing signs in some restaurant windows that read: "Gentiles Only." In one such town, such a sign was posted in the restaurant several doors from the church where I was to speak. After the speech, I noticed that the sign was gone. I don't know if it was because of my speech.

Oftentimes I would be faced with a ring of smiling faces, people eager to shake my hand. There would be invitations to dinner, invitations to spend a vacation with them, requests that I promise to return to speak again.

In all my talks, I had only one unhappy incident. One man pushed his way through the crowd and yelled at me: "I don't care what you say. You're still a nigger as far as I am concerned!" My response: "I am very glad that I am. I am also glad that I'm not eaten up inside by hatred." The crowd pushed him out of the church, and church members protected me when he and his cronies showed up at the Greyhound bus station to "put me in my place."

One of my rescuers explained: "We figured this would happen. There have been whispers in the community about his parentage, but no one ever discriminated against him. He was always spouting off about what he would do if a Negro came into this community. So, we were ready."

The pastor of the church came to see me weeks later in Madison. He said the attacking group had moved out of the community. He asked when I could return to speak to the church's teenage crowd. We made a date. I was received as a conquering hero when I went back.

My reputation as a speaker spread. I think part of it was due to the fact that I asked no speaker's fee, just expenses. That meant there was no group that could not afford to hear me. Each time I was reimbursed for my expenses, and I was usually given $10 or $15 extra.

*

An English blonde provided a romance that almost led to marriage. One day I got a telephone call from her. There was anxiety in her voice: "I've got to see you right away." We sat on her couch as she almost whispered to me: "My period is late, very late. I think we're going to have to get married."

Several thoughts chased one another through my mind. I was certain that if she were pregnant that it was not mine. If she were pregnant by someone else, should I lose the only chance to have offspring? I knew I could tuck tail and run, but I wouldn't do that.

Two days later I borrowed a car, and we headed to Dubuque, Iowa, where it was possible to get married in one day. All the way there, she seemed to be in a festive mood and joked: "You should be happier on your wedding day."

We were almost to the Wisconsin-Iowa border when she began to laugh, almost hysterically: "I'm not pregnant. I just wanted to see if you were serious about me." I turned the car around and headed back to Madison. I didn't think it was a joke, so I was not smiling. It had cost me money. I had lost time, and it was not the kind of joke one plays on another. I told her so. She was profuse in her apologies, but I made up my mind then that I would not marry her, ever.

I soon left, to work for my rich uncle — Uncle Sam.

Chapter 4

The Army

After I was notified that I was 1-A and knew I would soon be going into the Army, I dropped out of the UW and returned to Evanston. I was devastated because of my years preaching against war.

I took a room in the Emerson Street YMCA (the colored Y), and got a job working for a small restaurant named Restaurant William. I was a dishwasher and bus boy until the owner learned that I knew how to cook.

When the cook became ill I volunteered to stand in. His sickness was a fake, because he was interviewing for another job — which he got. The job gave me an opportunity to display my skill in baking French pastries, which became very popular with the clientele.

Once back in Evanston, my first sexual mentor got in touch, and we began advanced experiments. She was very pleased with how well I had progressed.

But with all this apparent pleasure, a cloud hung over my spirits. There was something wrong with my having to go into the Army. I brooded over that thought night and day.

I became aware of many things that were wrong with our society. In the first place, in the community where I grew up the guy who picked the fight fought his own fight. He was the worst of cowards to expect someone else to fight his battles. I thought then that if the heads of state who engineered the wars had to fight them, there would be many fewer wars.

I'm certain that some of the depression I was experiencing was caused by what was going on in the community. Ever since talk of the draft had started, people began to act as if we were in the war. There were many horror stories from people who had lost lovers, friends and relatives in the "War to End All Wars," World War I.

*

A 15-year-old girl invited me to have sex in the shower room at the Y, saying she wanted my baby in case I didn't return from the war. When I told her I appreciated her offer but didn't want to risk going to jail for having sex with a minor, she replied, "If you went to jail, then you wouldn't have to go to war, would you?" That thought hadn't occurred to me.

I pondered the idea of going to jail, not of having sex with this girl. "Well," she demanded, hands on her hips and displaying substantial pubic hair. "Please go," I pleaded, and left the shower room through the door to the men's locker room. Later I heard that I must be gay because I refused to have sex when it was offered to me.

Evanston's first draftee

About three dozen of us gathered early on March 26, 1941 in an office on an upper floor of one of Evanston's downtown businesses. None of us draftees were smiling. We were sworn in and a doctor began to examine us. I have the questionable distinction of being the first drafted in Evanston because my name was called first at that meeting.

After our physicals, we were marched to the train station and transported to Chicago's Union Station. Later that night, we boarded another train for a slow ride to Battle Creek, Michigan. There we got into army trucks and were taken to Fort Custer, which I was familiar with because of my years with the National Guard.

Came Sunday and a free period, I walked to the other end of the post. There was my old National Guard outfit, but it was no longer infantry; it was the 184th Artillery Regiment. Whom should I see but Marcus Ray, who had been a second lieutenant in charge of my platoon? He remembered me: "Brownlee! Are you down at the reception center?" I nodded "yes." He responded, "We'll have you transferred here tomorrow." And he did. The following day I was in the Second Battalion Headquarters Battery, and I was a clerk for Major Marcus L. Ray.

I was being given more extra duty than any other person. I knew this and I didn't complain primarily because I knew that to complain would invite more duties. Major Ray became angry at a first sergeant who piled on duties, and had me transferred to the Regimental Headquarters Battery.

To ensure that I would not be burdened with chores, I was promoted to sergeant within the week. I have never been richer in my life. My pay was $60 a week and I had no room or board to pay.

When I was being abused by the NCOs at Second Battalion Headquarters Battery, I applied to join the 99th Pursuit Squadron, which was training at a camp in Tuskegee, Ala. When Col. Anderson F. Pitts, our regimental commander, learned that I was being considered, he told Major Ray: "We need new officers, too. Send Brownlee to the Officer Candidate School in Fort Sill, Oklahoma."

Vera

On one leave, I returned home and visited Dorothy, a friend of mine who was a student at Northwestern University. In her circle was a 95-pound woman with a winning smile, lovely legs and no breasts. She had something that was more powerful. She had a wealth of womanhood — a power of femininity. Her manner was so soft and tender that when she spoke I could feel her heart reach out and encircle mine. On occasion she would smile and cast her beautiful eyes downward, almost apologetically, and it made me want to gather her in my arms to offer her comfort from anything that threatened her. I was captivated by her charm, and I was afraid that I would do or say something that would lose her. It was like tiptoeing on eggs.

She was studying for her master's degree in English literature, and loved poetry. We had a common ground. I recited some of my favorite poems by English poets; she responded with some of hers. Also, I recited some of my own poems — which she professed to like. The courtship ran apace like a fairy tale. Everything we touched turned to magic. There were no errors, no medium cool, nothing but superlatives in everything we said and did. I knew that I had to marry Vera Lucile Burr.

A few days later I was engaged to be married. I was never happier in my life. I sang at the top of my voice all the way to the home of Howard Geter, Jr., where I had been spending nights while I was seeing Vera. I asked him to be best man at my wedding — a wedding which had not even been planned.

As I returned to duty, I spent a considerable amount of my time on the train in blissful dreaming. The shock of jim-crowism slapped me awake as I entered Fort Sill. All officer candidates were housed in tents of six. There were three blacks in our tent: Ernest Davenport of Ohio, Albert Briggs and me from the 184th Field Artillery.

All were given identification cards which showed we were members of the "Field Artillery School, Detachment White," which was to cause some confusion at the gates when we tried to enter.

I showed my card to the military policeman on duty, and he asked: "Where did you get this card?" I replied, "I was issued it." He telephoned the Officer Candidate School. He asked: "You got an Officer Candidate named Lester Brownlee?" I didn't hear the answer, but the MP said: "There's a nigger with his card."

Then, the response. "Why in hell didn't you tell us that there were niggers in the OCS?"

There was no evidence of segregation or discrimination in the way the classes were handled.

Who's Pearl Harbor?

The weekend of Dec. 6-7, 1941, I got a pass and went to Tulsa. I had been invited to spend time with a pastor whom I'd met at Fort Sill when he came to meet the Negro officer candidates. We arrived at Sill at midnight or later and went right to bed.

In the morning at breakfast, all the soldiers were talking about Pearl Harbor. I demanded: "Who's Pearl Harbor?" After the guffaws, they told me the Japanese had attacked our base in Hawaii.

The only official reference made to Pearl Harbor by any of the officers who taught us was the change in target identification on the firing range. Targets that were formerly identified as German pill boxes suddenly became Japanese pill boxes. Otherwise, all classes went on as scheduled.

About this time, Col. Jark called me into his office to tell me that my orders to report to Tuskegee for flight training in the 99th Pursuit Squadron had arrived. I was troubled. By this time I had become completely sold on being an artillery officer. Col. Jark apparently noticed my indecision. He said: "You are doing very well here, Sgt. Brownlee, and in another six weeks you should have your commission in artillery. If, at that time you still want to go to the Air Corps, you are at liberty to make application." I'm sure I grinned, because he continued: "I'll just send this order back saying that you are not interested at this time."

I arrived at Fort Sill weighing 188 pounds. Three months later I graduated weighing 173 pounds — sheer muscle. We were called "90-day wonders."

Graduation Day, Feb. 11, 1942, was special. Col. Jark assured us that before the war was over, all of us would be captains and some would be majors.

After I donned my new uniform, I went to the Enlisted Men's Exchange, which was full of black soldiers. Almost to a man, they rushed to line up, grinning, to salute the first black officer they had ever seen. I pushed back tears as I realized what my commission meant to the black soldiers who had been given orders only by white officers — the same whites who had always dominated their lives. Other black officers and I represented hope that things could change.

I knew instantly that my achievements could not ever be mine alone. It meant that every time I took an important step upward, a large group of blacks were in lock-step with me. It made me realize that I had a very deep obligation to the men under me; that I must always think of their well-being. This resolve paid big dividends later in combat as troops I commanded recognized that I was always looking out for their best interests.

Wedding bed

A joy each day at Sill was writing to Vera. It was not that she demanded a daily letter. My heart demanded it. She later reread my letters to me. I decided that some of them were literary gems. Of course, I had equal pleasure in reading her daily missives of love. I had never imagined that one human could be so happy. I dreamed of our reunion.

Now that graduation was over, I could hardly wait to return to my bride-to-be. We set Feb. 14 – Valentine's Day – for our wedding. Vera engaged the intimate Thorndyke-Hilton Chapel on the University of Chicago campus and arranged for a minister. I remember little about the wedding. I was in a daze

Les and Vera's wedding.

thinking only of being married to Vera. Howard Geter, Jr. was my best man. I do not remember how we got the ring. I do remember how erect Mother sat and the pleased smile on her face when Vera and I said, "I do."

Geter took us to dinner at a barbecue joint, and we laughed as we spilled barbecue sauce on our clothes. The three of us went back to Vera's apartment, and the three of us lay across her bed and started recounting the events of the day. The next thing we knew it was morning. After that, Howard told people he slept with us on our wedding night.

"This is the Army, Mr. Jones"

After my 10-day leave for my wedding, the battalion was transferred to Camp Forrest, Tenn. It was our first experience of being Negroes in the Old South. We were to learn some hard lessons — and teach a few.

We were attached to the 80th Division Artillery and that blue-eyed general didn't like it. He told Ray on their first meeting: "Colonel, I don't believe that Negroes will ever make good artillery men." Ray replied, "We hope to prove you wrong, sir." And Ray was clever. He returned, assembled the battalion and reported what the general had said. I could see the looks of determination on the soldiers' faces.

Then came the general's first test. "Your men look like they are out of condition, Colonel. Tomorrow after breakfast I want to see them go through that four-mile hike in 50 minutes."

The following morning the soldiers jumped out of bed to march. One of the sergeants set a pace that was just short of running. We marched out two miles and back two miles. As the sergeant passed the reviewing stand, he broke into song: "This is the army, Mr. Jones" — a popular song of the era. The tune was picked up by every soldier in the battalion. The general's face turned beet red. We had covered the four-mile distance in 37 minutes.

He ordered the men to assemble in the firebreak between buildings. He went through and selected those who looked most tired and made them do 10 push-ups. All performed like champions. I wanted to hug them. After that, and almost every day — and sometimes for hours on end — the general was in our area, finding fault, making us soldier even harder. We took it and proved to be as good as he could have expected from any soldier of any color or background.

Chicago blacks

One of my cooks, a quiet well-disciplined soldier, had invited his wife down to see him, and had arranged a room for her in a pastor's house, next door to the Colored Service Club. The couple had been at a dance in the club and he took his wife back to her room next door. He kissed her goodnight, and as he reached the sidewalk, he was confronted by two white MPs who accused him of being a "Peeping Tom." They beat him so badly that he had to be hospitalized.

I was sent an arrest form and directed to punish him. I took the arrest form and went to the MP company headquarters. "Who made this arrest?" Nobody responded. I persisted. "This form requires the person who made the arrest to sign the form. This one isn't signed."

The lieutenant in charge turned to the men and in a loud voice remarked: "How many times I got to tell you men to sign the arrest slips." I said, "I want to have the arresting man testify at a court martial. How can I punish a man when he can't be faced by his accusers? Maybe I should subpoena the entire company." The lieutenant went pale — as if he had been confronted by a charging bull.

These MPs had never met a group of Chicago blacks before. When I returned to my battery, I assembled all my men and told them what had happened, and ended by saying: "I'm not going to sign any more passes to town unless you go in groups of six or eight and plan to stay together all evening. I'm tired of having my men beaten." Then, as I was leaving, I said in a voice slightly above a whisper: "If they find some of these MPs beaten up with their Jeep turned over on them, this kind of thing would stop."

That evening six of my toughest sergeants came to ask for passes to town. "We plan to stay together all evening, Sir," one said.

The next morning I heard a report that there were two MPs in the hospital with broken arms. Two more were found in a ditch with their Jeep turned over on them.

Now, the angry lieutenant wanted to come to my battery to look at my men. But before he and his wounded men showed up, one of my sergeants came to me and said: "Sir, we need a truck to take some sheets to the laundry." I realized what was afoot. I told him: "Get a truck and take what men you need." I saw the truck leave with the same six sergeants who had asked for passes the evening before. Needless to say, the two men with their arms in slings could not identify their attackers. None of my men was ever beaten again in Tullahoma.

The next episode occurred when a group of 12 officers went to the post movie house and sat in the officer's section. About halfway through the picture, the film was stopped, the lights in the theater were turned on, and six MPs armed with automatic weapons, led by the post commander colonel, ordered the black officers out of the Officer's Row. He commented that this Officer's Row was not meant for "niggers."

Ray made a report to Second Army headquarters under whose command we were. The Second Army commander was Col. Anderson F. Pitts, our former commander at Custer. The post commander was brought up for court martial and quickly sent to combat. He was killed in action.

*

Then came the Second Army's tests of all artillery battalions' efficiency. There were four battalions in the 80th Division, and our battalion, which had been attached for administration and training. After the tests were finished, we learned that one of the 80th Division's battalions had received a grade of 76, another got a grade of 72, and the fourth got a 62 — flunking. Our battalion got a grade of 89. The general had been so busy kicking our butts that he made us good at the expense of one of his own battalions.

We were ordered to be severed from the 80th Division Artillery so that division would not impede our efficiency.

Then the next blow. Our well-trained men were being transferred out, and by the end of 1943, we had only a cadre left. It became apparent that the Army was not eager to send a highly trained black artillery battalion into combat. In fact, Ray was approached with the offer to change us into combat engineers. We fortunately had a friend in Washington who had President Franklin Delano Roosevelt's ear. That combat engineer offer disappeared.

Next, we were given a group of black soldiers who had been table waiters and dishwashers for an aviation command. The new arrivals were a slovenly lot. They had not been required to demonstrate any discipline for months. They were almost as untrained as raw recruits. We had to start all over again.

The first job was to give the men a sense of pride of arms. We used the red piping on their caps to tell them that they were now artillerymen, and they must walk with heads high, walk with pride. The men responded quickly. They wanted to think of themselves as something more than flunkies.

Our biggest nightmare with the area was yet to come. At roll call on a Sunday morning, four of my best sergeants were missing. I was certain that something was wrong because they were too responsible to have gone AWOL.

Some of the men said they had left the evening before to go into Aiken.

A telephone call to the police in that city failed to uncover any information. I feared they had been lynched and were swinging from some trees in a South Carolina swamp. Inquiries at MP headquarters failed to turn up anything. The Augusta Police Department reported that it did not have them.

After four anxious days, I was called to our headquarters. There sat a middle-aged white woman who had been talking to Ray. She repeated her story: "I just told your Colonel that Sunday night, no it was Saturday night early Sunday morning. I was on the bus from Aiken to Augusta and there were four 'Nigrah' soldiers on that bus. The bus was very crowded, and when we got about half way, some white people wanted to get on. The bus driver told the soldiers to get off. They were pleading with him, telling him that they would be AWOL because there was not another bus until sometime Sunday morning. One asked the driver to give him back his fare since they were being put off the bus. The driver got mad and called the sheriff, who was nearby. The sheriff pulled his gun and ordered them to the station. That's the last I saw of them. I've been trying for four days to find out to whom the soldiers belonged. My son is in the service up North somewhere. I wouldn't want him treated that way."

We both thanked her. She continued: "The reason I didn't tell you my name is because if it were ever found out that I helped a Nigrah — especially one that wasn't working for me — I could be in deep trouble. God bless y'all."

Ray got on the telephone and soon located the sheriff. He was told that the sheriff had four nigger soldiers who were doing 60 days on the chain gang for disturbing the peace. When asked what they had done, he was told that "they were giving back-talk to a white bus driver. And after they got off the bus, they refused to shut up when I told them to. They kept on asking to make a telephone call."

He said he got fed up with them, and ordered them put on the chain gang because he didn't have money to feed four niggers until the circuit judge would come next week. Asked how the soldiers could get out of jail, he was told that as soon as they served their time, they could get out.

Ray made a long distance phone call to Truman K. Gibson, Jr., an aide to President Roosevelt. Gibson reached Roosevelt; Roosevelt called the governor of South Carolina, who called the sheriff. The men were immediately returned to our unit in a squad car.

The sheriff complained to us: "Why didn't they tell me they was important niggers? I would have brought them here that night. Now, you done got me in trouble with the governor."

Once back at the battalion, the soldiers recounted the horrors they had experienced, showing the lash marks on their backs because they had not moved fast enough for the overseer of the chain gang. Also, they ate like they had not had food for four days. The gruel they described made me want to vomit. Our soldiers did not want to go to Aiken any more — few even wanted to leave our area.

All of us had learned a lesson that slaves knew all too well. When a white man tells you to do anything in the South, do it without asking any questions.

*

The weather was hot for February in Georgia. During that hot spell, we were ordered to form for a battalion inspection. The sun beat down mercilessly and I watched five of my men faint from exposure. But the white inspecting officers acted as if nothing had happened.

I fell out of ranks to order my men to be taken to the first aid station. I was later reprimanded by the white inspecting officer. I responded: "I was always trained to look out for the well-being of my men. No one else seemed concerned." What I heard back: "Watch your tongue, Captain. You may be on the verge of showing disrespect to a senior officer. What you should have done was to ask permission to fall out of ranks to help the soldiers. I'm sure that I would have given permission."

I had to respond to this: "What would have happened if I had done nothing?" He replied, "You know as well as I that you could have been court-martialed for failure to look out for the well-being of your troops." I could see I was getting nowhere. There was a long silence. Then, I asked: "Request the Colonel's permission to return to my duties in my battery." He waited awhile, then said: "Permission granted." I seethed for many a day after that. Ray finally told me: "Don't waste your emotions trying to understand Army stupidity."

Eventually all our officers were transferred to Fort Huachuca, Ariz. to take over an artillery battalion. I've always suspected that Truman K. Gibson, Jr. had a great deal to do with it. We were to take command of the 600th Field Artillery Battalion of the 92nd Division — the "Buffalo Soldiers" — as our shoulder patches displayed.

The men we had been training for field artillery would be sent to various service units. At the same time that we were sorry to be losing men to whom we had begun to give some feeling of pride of arms, we were also glad that we were to remain artillery officers.

As we approached Fort Huachuca on the Mexican border, I thought about us taking over a battalion that had been commanded by white officers. I suspected that some of the enlisted men, if not a majority, would doubt that Negro officers knew enough about artillery to do a good job. I was certain that some had been brainwashed into believing that we would be less "military."

The first thing I did when I took command of the Headquarters Battery was to assemble all the men in the mess hall and introduce myself. I told them my civilian and military background and concluded: "I am happy to have this opportunity to share with you the military tasks which confront us. I am positive that we will be a great success."

Some men applauded. Some looked disconsolate. I was happy that the first sergeant seemed to be on my side. I overheard him talking to some men outside the orderly room, saying: "You don't know that. Let's give him a chance." One of the things I had learned early was to refer to my men as "gentlemen." Also, the previous command had the lieutenants take over the Reveille formation. I think they were surprised to see me present at the first formation of the day.

The first test of how I would handle troops came early. One of the men missed bed check and reveille the next morning. When the first sergeant, Norman Bailey, hauled him in front of me later that day, I said to him: "You realize that under the 104th Article of War I have the authority to give you battery punishment. That would not do me any good, and I doubt that you would be pleased with it. Suppose we shake hands like gentlemen and say that it won't happen again." He had a look of surprise on his face as he accepted my extended hand and said, "Yes, sir! It won't happen again."

The very next weekend, he did the same thing. When he showed up in my office, I did not talk to him. Instead, I turned to the first sergeant and said: "Take this man to the guardhouse, and make up charges for a court martial of him." He began to try to explain. I said: "You can explain it at the court martial."

Word of what had happened traveled through the battery very rapidly. Bailey came to me and said: "The men are really pleased with the way you handled that man. You never once raised your voice."

About two weeks later, we were given notice that officers from the top command (all of whom were white) were going to inspect the battery. I realized that this was the top brass's chance to show the inadequacy of the new Negro officers. I assembled the men and said: "Gentlemen, there will be an inspection of our battery starting at 8 a.m. tomorrow. That means that we will have to really get busy preparing for it. Perhaps the division wants to see how well we can do."

The men worked assiduously, finishing slightly after 2 a.m. When we fell out for reveille just hours later, the first sergeant told me that there was one soldier who refused to get up.

I went to the barracks with several NCOs. I asked the soldier, "What's wrong? Are you sick?" He responded: "I didn't get enough sleep. I'm not going to get up." My response: "I understand. None of us got much sleep last night. But you can't stay here during inspection. So, two of you get the head of his bed and another two take the foot and carry the bed over and put it in the guardhouse."

I turned and started walking back to my office. When I turned to look back, the soldier was out of bed and putting on his clothes. We passed inspection with flying colors. So did all the other batteries in the battalion under the new regime.

Once our credibility had been established, the enlisted men began to respond to our rigorous demands for excellence. In fact, many were eager to learn and become excellent artillerymen.

Even with all this preparation, the days seemed to drag into weeks of "we're not going anywhere." Then, one day in September 1944, we got the order: "Prepare for overseas deployment."

The training we had been going through took on a more somber meaning. We were being prepared for combat. We did not know if we were being shipped to Europe or to the Pacific. We hoped that it was to Europe. As soon as we were issued our Army Post Office number we knew that we were scheduled for the European theater.

We had a long train ride from Arizona to Hampton Roads, Va. to the staging area where we boarded our ship for Naples, Italy. Then we had a long cruise to Italy.

Once ashore, we were bivouacked in squad tents, and had nothing to do but eat, sleep and wait. The men soon discovered the San Carlo opera house, and would queue up in the afternoons to wait to see and hear opera — an art form new to almost all of them.

To chase women they had one great barrier. The men did not speak Italian; the women did not speak English. The need to talk to a woman found some GIs poring over their language booklets in the evenings. Perhaps that's the best way to teach a foreign language: make a person have to learn in order to satisfy his or her wishes. Each morning at reveille, I gave the men in my battery the same warning: stay together in groups, don't get drunk, and use a prophylactic if you have sex. They seemed to heed my injunctions. In fact, many of them stayed around the area, playing ball or engaging in some other pleasant pastimes.

Along with women selling their bodies, on the streets were women and young boys who seemed always to be asking: "Una sigarreta?" I handed out cigarettes, two or three at a time, not realizing that I was giving away the currency that could buy many things. I learned several days later when a middle-aged woman offered to wash my shirt for "due sigarrette." She grinned, displaying a mouth with many teeth missing. "Multi grazie, multi grazie."

I realized that war had taken away just about everything the country had to offer, and that the real challenge was to stay alive.

It was particularly disturbing to see young children going around with sores from pellagra — evidence of malnutrition. I seemed to be inside a nightmare. My visions of war in the past had been of soldiers getting wounded and dying. I had not given any thought to what happens to civilians who must struggle to survive.

Going north

After about a month, as the days began to drag, we were given orders to pack up to leave to go north — to the fighting.

We boarded the old "40 or 8s" — freight cars that held 40 men or 8 horses — although we packed many fewer men in the cars. The journey was long and cold, and the fall rains that seeped through the old cars made the trip uncomfortable. After several days of wet travel, we arrived at a staging area outside of Livorno — Leghorn in English — and were housed in squad tents.

Nights were chilly and damp. The men kept warm and dry by filling the bottom of a five-gallon can with sand and pouring gasoline over it. The flame would last for hours. The men gathered around these cans, told lies, kept warm.

We were told that the town was off limits to GIs, but the officers could go. We refused to go where our men were not eligible to go. We saw white officers from other outfits going into town.

All the officers in the other units in the 92nd Division, "the Buffalo Soldiers," were white. Ours was the only one in which all the officers were black.

The white commander of the 370th Combat Engineer Regiment had been so brutal to his black soldiers that they had put a contract out on him — offering to pay $10,000 to the GI who got him.

One evening he went to town with his adjutant. When they returned late that night, very drunk, they both fell asleep in the commander's bunk. In the morning the medics took six slugs out of the adjutant's feet. On the outside of the tent was a chalk circle where the commander's head would have been, had the adjutant's feet not occupied his pillow.

That commander never went into the line with his regiment. He gave orders from behind the lines.

*

The second night after we arrived in Livorno, a very pregnant woman came running to our command post yelling: "Spee-ay; spee-ay (spy)." We followed her to a field where we found a man. She said he was shining a light toward the enemy, and they had sent a signal back. He denied it.

I told two of my men: "Get a rope and tie him to this tree. If nothing happens, release him in a couple of hours." When he saw what we were about to do, he got on his knees and begged not to be tied there. We took him prisoner and sent him to the rear. We cleared the area, and within 15 minutes the Nazis began a massive artillery barrage.

The woman had likely saved many lives. I asked her how I could reward her. She said she was expecting a baby any day, and she would need milk. I went to the mess sergeant and got a case of evaporated milk to give to her. She knelt and kissed my hand.

The barrage also targeted a British battery that was stationed to the right of us. After it subsided, Col. Ray ordered me to get trucks to evacuate the wounded. When we arrived, a British captain, smoking his pipe, informed us: "It really wasn't that bad. We had one chap who cut his hand falling over a gun emplacement, and some of our equipment was damaged, but we're in good shape. Thanks for coming. How about tea tomorrow afternoon?"

That experience taught me that when soldiers and materiel are properly dug in, the amount of damage shelling does can be minimal. I called my men together the following morning and related what I had seen. I sent them back to their equipment with instructions to dig in.

Ray called the battery commanders together on the following day and told them about the experience. Most reported that their men had been digging "like they are trying to reach China."

Artillery fire hit us the first week we were in place. We suffered no casualties. The experience caused the men to dig in deeper; some in the gun positions began to dig underground caves in which they slept. Another advantage of the caves was that they could have a candle in their dugouts to read or write letters without fear that the enemy would see the light.

As the months of the war crept by, we were involved mainly in artillery duels, and they were infrequent. It soon became apparent that we were in for a long session, especially when we received the order that artillery ammunition was to be rationed to one round per gun per day. The reason given was that we were to save enough ammunition for a big push.

But the enemy wasn't shooting often at us either. Our fire superiority kept their guns silent. We had their gun positions so well marked that when they did fire, we had a heavy counter-battery operation going within seconds.

Feeding the "families"

We had too much food. The daily ration was always adequate, but it was increased 20 percent for all units in combat.

I told the mess sergeant to give our men all the food they wanted and give the extra food to the dozens of hungry women and children who gathered outside the fence. They had done nothing to bring on this war, a war that had closed all stores and taken all the able-bodied men away, that had caused them to face starvation and disease each day.

Some of the soldiers who had made friends with women began asking the mess sergeant for additional rations — to feed their "families." There was plenty to give. As a result, these women disappeared from the group outside the fence.

Some of these relationships became so serious that when combat was over men stayed in Italy with their new wives and families. But, during the war, they would arrange to visit one another, to play bridge, or just to talk. There were a few pregnancies, too. No one talked of abortions — not in Italy.

Perhaps the greatest evidence of how well my men had integrated the neighboring community was seen on Easter morning. As the families headed to the local Catholic Church for morning services, 14 of my men accompanied their "families." Many of the "wives" and children were wearing new outfits purchased by GIs on shopping excursions into nearby Lucca. Most of the GIs were either Baptists or belonged to Sanctificationist churches back in the States.

It was a pleasure to see how the young children clung to their "darker fathers." Also, it was an exhibition of how humanly outgoing were these black soldiers from the States. Some of my GIs had not only learned the language, but acquired many of the gestures which characterize Italians when they speak. Also, their "children" had begun to pick up American slang — first, of course, was "O.K."

*

The war dragged on. Most of the time there was little activity. However, now and then at night the Nazis would pull their huge railway-mounted gun out of the mountains near LaSpezia and fire a few rounds that landed in or near Viarreggio. The shots were not very accurate; the whirring effect of incoming rounds might cause some terror, but the shells did little damage.

One day a flight of P47s, flying almost at wave-top, fired rockets at the target. After their sortie we never had any more shots from LaSpezia.

One day I was on the road to Pietrasanta when I heard a Nazi gun. The shell hit about six feet to my left, and behind a small tree. Fragments from the bursting shell went to my front and rear, deflected by the tree. Almost immediately, another round was fired and hit behind another tree. I had taken two steps backward after the first shell hit, thus most of the fragments were deflected by the second tree. Two fragments cut my jacket and one of them burned my arm. Before another round could be fired by the Nazis, our counter battery hit the gun with about 20 rounds. I was never that careless again.

Shortly after this encounter, we were alerted to a plan for a limited offensive to gain higher ground for better observation. The attack jumped off on Feb. 8, 1944 and continued through the 10th.

We were armed with 155mm Howitzers and ran short of ammunition. I jumped into my Jeep, armed with an automatic rifle, and led three 2-ton trucks to the 92nd Division ammo dump. There was not one round of 155mm ammo there. The warrant officer told me that he thought that there was some in the 5th Army dump.

As I drove over to that dump, I had visions of infantrymen, huddled on the hill, being blasted by enemy fire as our guns sat silent. A 2nd Lieutenant was in charge at the 5th Army dump. I told him what I wanted. He asked: "Where's your requisition?" I was so angry that I turned my automatic rifle on him, and declared: "We've got men dying up there on that hill. This is my requisition."

I told my men to load up on 155mm ammo, and I told the officer my name, organization and serial number. I never heard any more about it.

We delivered the ammo to each of three batteries. After I told Ray what I had done, he phoned 5th Army headquarters and we got more ammo.

However, a number of men died needlessly on that hill because of that supply snafu. I would find out how many later in September.

*

Standing in the entrance to my office one afternoon, I noticed a white GI walking along the road outside our CP. He was wearing the Buffalo arm patch worn by members of the 92nd Division. All the enlisted GIs in the 92nd were black. He was white, blond and blue-eyed.

I called to him. He came up to me and saluted. That made me more suspicious. No one was supposed to salute in a combat zone. I asked him what he was doing in our area, his name, his serial number, and outfit.

He told me he was on an errand for his CO, and gave me the correct name of the officer. I knew the officer well. We had socialized in Chicago. He told me he was from Chicago and said he had been a member of the Illinois National Guard. He even gave me his street address. That was a mistake. The address he gave was for an even number on Howard Street. There are no even numbers on Howard Street that near the lake.

I told the guard outside my door to keep him covered. I went to my phone, called the outfit, gave the name and asked if the had a GI by that name who was on a special mission here. The commanding officer said there was such a man, and that he was on guard at that very moment right outside his CP.

We took our "guest" back to Division, and they learned he was a Nazi spy. I couldn't understand why they would be so stupid as to send a white GI. If they had sent a white officer of the rank of captain or higher, I would not have thought anything unusual. All the senior officers in all but our battalion were white.

For arresting the spy, I received a congratulatory letter from the G-2 (intelligence) section.

*

One of the vexing situations that all black soldiers had to face was that we were fighting a war against the racist policies of Nazism, but we were in a seg-regated army. No one spoke about it openly, but the irony was infuriating to all of us.

For example, there was one white artillery battalion attached to the 92nd Division. There were 28 officers in that battalion — all white, of course. The division had hundreds of black officers of the junior grade. Our battalion, the 600th Field Artillery, was the only one with black officers above the rank of lieutenant. So, Division gave the white battalion the Principessa dei Piemonte — a large luxury hotel — for a rest hotel. The battalion, in turn, gave guest memberships to all the white officers in the division.

The black officers were given the Excelsior hotel, a nice hotel, but not nearly as posh as the other. Officially, the Excelsior hotel was the division's rest hotel for officers, but no white officers ever showed up there.

(More than 50 years later, in the summer of 1987, I returned to the Excelsior Hotel — on my honeymoon with Priscilla [my third wife]. The woman at the desk had sung in the local cabarets when I had been there as a young officer.)

*

The commanding officer of the headquarters battery was also the battal-ion's communications officer. As such, it was my responsibility to make recon-naissance of routes for future locations as we made plans for forward move-ments.

I was on such a recon walking down the streets in Forte del Marmi, north of our location in Tonfano. Suddenly, there was the scream of incoming artillery fire. I dived into a ditch and buried my head in my hands — as we had been taught to do. Almost immediately I was aware of someone else in the ditch. The shelling lasted for about five minutes. When it ceased, I raised my head to find my companion in the ditch was Warren Frank Spencer, a friend from Evanston whose sister, Margaret, I had dated in high school.

"Frank," I yelled, and we began hugging each other. He was in a medic unit and had just returned from delivering a GI back to his unit. We exchanged chatter briefly before continuing on our separate missions.

I had been gone from my unit longer than anticipated. Soon I was aware of a vehicle approaching the location I was surveying. The vehicle contained two of my sergeants. "We were concerned for your safety, especially after the shelling," Bailey explained. "I'm O.K.," I replied. "But thanks for coming to look for me." He said, "We don't want anything to happen to you."

A similar show of affection from three of my men came after they'd been sent on an errand south of Firenze. When they returned to our headquarters, they brought three potted plants. The sergeant in charge of the detail explained: "We knew how you liked flowers, Captain. So, we stopped in Firenze to get you these." I was touched that they thought that much of me to get some plants. Trying to keep these alive would take a great effort, but I would try.

Battle

Suddenly, we were given notice to prepare for a major battle. There was a flurry of activity as units began securing additional supplies.

During this interval, my friend Aurelius Miles came to visit. He joked: "Don't get too close, I haven't had a bath in 45 days, and I know how I smell. I can't stand to live with myself any more. I'm on my way to the bath unit in Viarreggio."

Two days later I learned that on his way back to his unit, his Jeep ran over a land mine. The mine killed his driver and cost "Reo" both legs. He had been champion tennis player before entering the service. Reo had a joyful disposition even after the injury.

I didn't know what a full-blown attack would be like. My only previous idea had been what Hollywood had portrayed.

When the kickoff came, one artillery battalion fired 1,228 rounds in the first five minutes. By the time all the artillery battalions had finished their preparation fires, the area into which the infantry was charging was one huge cloud of dust. There was no way for them to know which way they were going without looking at a compass.

As the attack went forward, we began digging in around Carrara. I found a place where someone had been digging out sand for construction. I ordered my men to begin using the sand to shore up the entrance. We had hardly begun when we came under enemy fire.

A 10-year-old kid who had been traveling with us was hit by a shell and it chopped off his legs at the knees. He bobbled about on the stubs for a minute

Capt. Brownlee on leave in Rome.

or two before he lay dead.

The next shell exploded near and fragments hit one of my sergeants in the hip. I tried applying pressure to a vein, and it slowed down the bleeding but I knew I would have to get medical help. The shells were coming in at regular intervals. I saw a Jeep near the entrance to our embankment. I told the sergeant to be ready to run to the Jeep after the next shell exploded. We both ran, and I got the Jeep started and out of range before the next shell came in.

As we got out on the road, we ran into a column that had been halted by the fire, and was lurking in the shelter of a hill. As fortune would have it, there was an ambulance near the head of the column, and I was able to turn the injured man over to the medics and get back to my command.

By the time I returned, our batteries were in operation, and their counter battery silenced the Nazi battery.

Our commander ordered me to go to the top of a nearby hill to see about establishing communications for our next push. I had to ride up the face of a hill in open sight of the enemy. I made the trip up without incident, but as I started down, a single enemy gun started firing at my Jeep. I realized the gunner was counting on my continuing at the same pace. I told my driver to stop. Then, when the next shell exploded ahead of us, I told the driver to speed ahead, then, stop. By alternating at irregular intervals, we made it safely to the bottom of the hill.

We made our next battalion headquarters under a road viaduct, which gave us overhead protection.

As I made another recon down a road, I came to a house and entered to find bowls of potato soup on the kitchen table. The soup was still warm. As I went out in front of the house, I was met by a young lieutenant colonel. He challenged: "What are you doing back here, Captain? The fighting is way ahead at LaSpezia." I pointed out to him that the shell fire we saw just ahead on the hill was brown. That was Nazi fire. Our explosions were black.

As we talked, a shell hit near us and we jumped into a hole. When the firing was over, he jumped into his Jeep and I didn't see him again until combat was over.

Less than an hour later, I ran into the division artillery commander, a gruff, red-faced man who parted his fiery red mustache in the middle and brushed it to either side. He said: "Brownlee, we need some forward observation. Do you see that church tower up the hill in Ortinova? Well, bring us wire line from that church into your switchboard. We can keep in touch through your board." I said "Yes, sir" and got in touch with my wire sergeant. We took a Jeep and two miles of wire and rode up the hill.

When we got to the crest, we were met with a good deal of rifle fire. We ducked, circled around the top of the hill, and came up at the end of a piazza where there seemed to be no fire.

Taking the end of the wire, we both raced across the piazza and entered the church door as rifle fire seemed to overtake us. There was a circular staircase up to the belfry, and while the sergeant reeled off the wire, I climbed up to the tower. I looked out and almost immediately there were rifle shots ringing the bell overhead. I ducked and tied the end of the wire to the stair rail. I told the sergeant to take the wire we had left in the Jeep and connect it to the line we had brought up the hill from our switchboard.

I placed a field telephone on the end of the wire in the belfry. In fewer than 15 minutes, the field phone rang. I answered. It was our switchboard. I asked him to connect me to Division Artillery switchboard. I asked to speak to the division artillery commander. When he answered, I told him that this was the team he had sent to Ortinova.

"What's it like up there?" he asked. "Hotter than the hinges of hell," I replied. "Well, don't get burned," he quipped.

I had one last obstacle. How do I get back to my unit without getting killed? Somehow, I summoned enough courage, or whatever, to race across the 20 yards from the church door to the crest of the hill. Actually, I had covered half the distance before the rifle fire started. It missed me! I dived over the crest of the hill and lay there, heart pounding from excitement, relieved that I was still alive. My sergeant came over to where I lay: "Are you O.K., sir?" I nodded.

"Let's go get some chow. I'm starved," he said. I had no interest in eating at that point. I was just enjoying being alive. I don't remember the return trip, or the rest of the day.

The following morning Ray came to me and said: "I know you got that line into Ortinova at 11:45. Well, what you don't know is our infantry units entered that town at noon — 15 minutes after you had finished. Some dope at division headquarters had reported that our men had already taken the town. That's why the Div Arty commander sent you in." I was frightened all over again to realize how close a brush I had had with death.

Mule pillow

We had been going for more than two days without rest, but we had to keep moving. Our next assignment was to repair a wire break some miles ahead. When we reached the point, we found that enemy artillery fire had cut the line. The same fire had killed a mule, which lay belly-up in the road. I had barely eaten over the past 48 hours, so decided to take a minute then to open a can of C-rations — lima beans and bacon. The next thing I remember was the sergeant's waking me where I had fallen asleep, my head on the dead mule's stomach. It had been a very comfortable pillow.

I slept in the truck for the next few miles. I remember the sergeant telling me that we were to make a connection with another unit on the other side of the mountain. We were given the coordinates to a road junction on top of the mountain.

When we got there with our wire line, it was past midnight and pitch black. We waited, and waited. When dawn came, we saw that the other unit had arrived before we had and had left a big loop of wire over a branch of a tree. We had waited five hours for the other team to arrive.

When we spliced into the line, the captain at the other end asked: "What the hell kept you?" Between swear words I told him that we had been there five hours waiting for them. Courtesy would have had them wait until our connection arrived. He apologized.

By this time, the Nazi retreat was so fast that we could not keep up with them. Our big guns could be towed at only 35 miles per day on a paved highway.

We stopped next at Hotel Elisabetta in Rapallo. The hotel owner was a partisan, and he welcomed us with open arms. I had been there less than a half hour when he came to me and asked:

"Will you do me a favor? Two men have come to ask me to accompany them to partisan headquarters. One of them owes me lots of money. Some people have been killed to liquidate a debt, if you understand what I mean." I told him that I would be glad to go with him.

When we got to the door, and the pair saw me, armed with a Tommy gun, they were suddenly in a hurry to leave. He turned to me and said "I'm sure you saved my life. I'll never forget you."

I had hardly returned to my room when the medical sergeant came. He said there was a young boy who wanted medicine for a baby. I said I would go with him, but I remembered the previous episode — I was not sure that this was not a ruse to kill a GI.

The boy led us to a small house about two streets away from the hotel. When we entered, there was a young woman in her early 20s holding a baby whom she said was her sister. The parents had been killed in air raid about a month previously. The baby was red with fever and I knew that I could not get our doctor to treat civilians.

I remembered that aspirin sometimes reduces fever. I took a tablet from the sergeant, ground it in the palm of my hand using the butt end of my gun, and pushed some of the granules into the crying baby's mouth. The baby coughed and spit, but swallowed some of it. I left some aspirin with the young lady with instructions to keep trying to get some into the baby, and we returned to the hotel.

About four hours later, I was told that the young boy was there to see me. He asked me to follow. I entered the house to see the baby asleep in a crib. The fever had gone out of its face and the young lady was smiling.

She disrobed and stood naked before me, smiling. Once again I realized that sex was a universal currency. Somehow I felt ashamed that a she felt that she had to pay for a humanitarian gesture. I smiled, said thanks, but no thanks, made an excuse that I had to go back to lead my troops into combat — so as not to hurt her feelings of having been refused. My gesture was not too far from the truth.

When I returned to the hotel, we were lining up to move again. I took my position in the column in the Jeep behind Ray, and we started down the winding road that led into Santa Margherita. As we entered, the streets seemed deserted. Then, we heard the shout: "Gli Americani! Gli Americani!"

Doors burst open, and people seemed to come from everywhere. Young ladies were all over Ray's Jeep, kissing him and his driver; two middle-aged women jumped on my Jeep and kissed me and my driver. Later, Ray teased me about attracting only old hags.

The streets were so crowded with happy people, mostly women and children, that our column could not move. We knew we were under orders to proceed, but it was impossible unless we ran over people. Finally, Ray began to inch his Jeep forward, and I followed in mine. It was the greatest ovation we had ever seen.

*

Later, on our trek to Genova, we came to a small village called Bogliasco. There the progress of the division was halted by the demands of a Nazi lieutenant in charge of six coastal artillery guns. He sent orders demanding that the division surrender to him or he would blow us off the map. This was about noon, and he gave the division until 2 p.m. to decide.

The division commander ordered all artillery to line up, hub to hub at the base of the hill. He gave the Nazi lieutenant until 1 p.m. to surrender or we were going to take the top off the hill with our firepower.

While I waited, an attractive lady approached me and asked if I were a Protestant. I said I was. She motioned me to follow her. My first thought was that she was leading me into a sexual liaison. We arrived in the basement of a building where there were about 20 men and women — mostly women. Next thing I knew we were in a Baptist service conducted in Italian. I could not follow the words very well, but I hummed the music.

I learned later that anyone professing Protestantism had to worship underground — same as the early Christians in Rome. I was surrounded by a group of very attractive women, but I felt a warmth and friendship which was based on a religious camaraderie. I returned to my command post strangely refreshed.

At about 12:50, the German lieutenant and his gun crew emerged from their position, hands in the air. They were taken prisoner and returned to the rear.

We moved forward on toward Genova. As we neared we were told that there would be a division review in Garibaldi Square (Piazza). As we approached the square, someone on the second floor of a building on the opposite side of the square opened fire with a machine gun. We hit the ground. A unit of our cavalry moved forward. One blast from one of the guns from the armored vehicle took out the entire second floor of the building. The military review continued.

"Peeka neeka"

About the first of May, we were still in combat, theoretically. We were ordered to move our battery to village about five miles north of Genova — a village named Campomorone. This was a sleepy little village. The men began to clean the howitzer. As they worked in the plazza, teenage girls peeked from curtains and made teasing remarks and giggled.

A young girl approached me, a 10-year-old named Maura. She spoke to me in elementary Italian, which I could understand: "Tell your men not to pay any attention to those stupid females. They were flirting that same way a week ago with the Nazis." I smiled, realizing that the men didn't care with whom the women had relations the previous week. They were interested in what they could get now.

"The men are just enjoying themselves. They are grown, and they know how to take care of themselves," I said.

"I know what men want," Maura replied. "I am shocked that your men would want to be involved with women who were being intimate last week with the enemy."

I was impressed with the worldly knowledge of a 10-year-old. I began a conversation with her and learned that her father had been a police officer who had been killed during a bombing raid by the British. She lived with her mother and a five-year-old sister, Renata. She described how much trouble they had staying alive during the conflict and that their mother went hungry sometimes just to be sure her children were fed. I reached into my kit and produced three cans of C-rations.

I asked her if she had ever been on a picnic. She said she did not know the meaning of the word. I tried to describe it. I asked if she would meet me on the following day and bring her sister. She agreed. About noon on the following day, Maura and Renata met me in the Piazza. Maura told me how much they had enjoyed the food I had given her and they had saved some so that they could eat later.

I asked them to get into the Jeep, and took them on a ride up through a little place called Tre Re. There was a grassy plot and we stopped and I spread out some Army goodies. We laughed and played games and had a delightful time. After several hours, I took them back to the piazza and arranged for them to meet me two days hence. Again we went to our picnic spot (Maura called it peeka neeka).

When we got there, we found a man sketching. He introduced himself as Rudolfo Bellati, an artist. All joined in the picnic, and he invited me to visit him, his wife and baby son.

Two days later, I went to visit him in his second story apartment. He apologized for the limited living space they occupied but said that they had been running from the Nazis and had felt lucky to have this spot. He showed me some of his paintings, and I was impressed with the quality of his work. I asked him what he had done before the war. He seemed embarrassed when he told me that he had managed the family's estate. His wife described the vastness of the family's holdings. She was very young, and had married him only a few years before.

I soon realized I was talking to someone who had never held a job before, who had grown up in a privileged state, but who had studied art and had become a very good artist.

The couple owned a radio and we tuned into some station that was playing dance music. She said she loved to dance. He didn't. We began to dance to "Jalousie," and were quite an adept pair. In fact, we danced most of the evening, and Rudolfo watched and applauded. I asked if I could come some day later and bring some food. I was told that I would be welcome, food or not.

There were several more peeka-neeka with Maura and Renata and a few more visits to the Bellatis before our organization was ordered to move down the road to Celle Ligure and into what appeared a luxury complex. There were apartment units surrounding a double tennis court. Each officer had a five-room apartment, fairly well furnished. In the evenings, we had movies on a large screen placed at one end of the tennis court complex. I could lie in bed and watch, and lie back and go to sleep after the film ended.

One afternoon in Celle Ligure I looked out my apartment window and saw two dirty, little girls talking to an MP on guard near the tennis courts. I recognized them. They were Maura and Renata. I raced down stairs and when they saw me, they ran into my arms, crying for joy. They had found their friend.

In halting voice, between sobs, Maura told me that a young boy in Campomorone had found a hand grenade, and had tossed it at their mother, killing her. They had no place to go, so, they came looking for me. They had been traveling three days, and had nothing to eat for the last day and a half.

I took them up to my apartment, got them fed, and put them to bed. They slept all that afternoon and night, and awakened the following morning, very hungry. I got them breakfast, and had them remain in bed while I had my orderly wash their clothes and hang them out to dry.

After several days in which the little girls had become darlings of the men in the battery, I began to wonder what I was going to do with them. After all, it had not been a problem to have little Italian boys who were orphans attach themselves to a unit, but I had not seen nor heard of having young girls in a unit.

Ray and I must have been thinking the same thing about the same time. He came to me and suggested that I start looking for some place to leave the girls. I told him that both their mother and father had been killed. He empathized, but he could not authorize my keeping them there.

I talked to Maura, and told her what Ray had said. At first she insisted that she knew of no relative. Then, two days later, she told me that she remembered that her father had had a younger sister, unmarried, who lived in Santa Margherita, but she didn't know where. She was not sure that her aunt was alive, or where she lived. I decided that we would go in search of her.

My driver and I loaded the Jeep with food and two blankets and headed for Santa Margherita. Once there, it took almost three hours before we got a lead on where she was staying. She was suspicious when an American officer came asking for her. When she saw the girls, she began to laugh and hug them, until Maura told her what had happened. Then, all of us cried.

Because the aunt was living in a single room, we had to help her find a bigger place. Also, we had to give her some money to pay the rent for the new place. At that time, the rent for the place was two cartons of cigarettes for a year. I left the food we had brought, and promised to return later to see how she was making out.

Several months later, when our organization had been ordered back to bivouac in the pinetta south of Viarreggio, I stopped to see her. She was not there. A neighbor said she had married and had moved south to Napoli.

I still remember the day we let them off, and how my driver, Ell Futrell, and I cried as we drove back to Celle Ligure.

*

VE Day came and went, with us paying little attention. Even though I was a captain, I was as unimpressed as my men were on that historic day. We had been out of the fighting a week before the announcement, and had been out of contact with the enemy for about two weeks prior to that.

After we had been ordered into Campomorone, I was given a seven-day leave at the officers' rest hotel in Rome. My executive officer, Lt. M.N. Smith, and I got into a Jeep and with my driver, Ell Futrell, headed for Rome.

What I experienced at Rome's hotel made me sick to my stomach. In the entrance to the lobby of the hotel, there were some 12 American officers and three prostitutes. An American officer would bid $25 and the women would run to him. Another officer across the lobby entrance would yell $30 and the women would run to him. As each bid increased, the prostitutes would run to that officer. I had passed through the entrance when the bidding had reached $45.

We reached the hotel in time for lunch, and we were ushered into a dining room. Suddenly, I had a stomachache. Maybe it was triggered by what I had just witnessed or maybe it was because I was hungry. Just as we sat down, the waiter automatically poured a glass of red wine for each of us. Smith said: "When I have a stomach ache, I drink a glass of red wine." I picked up the glass and drank. It was the first time I had tasted any alcohol in my life. So here I was, a 30-year-old artillery captain tasting his first alcoholic beverage. I hated the taste. However, my stomachache disappeared. (Priscilla and I always refer to red wine as "medicinal.")

Almost everywhere we looked, we saw prostitutes. We went to our room where we found an American officer about to go to bed with a naked prostitute. He said he had found the room vacant, and that he wouldn't be but a short time. Would we give him a break and wait for about a half hour? I looked at Smith and we seemed to agree. Rome was not for us.

I wondered how much trouble we would have getting my driver, who was at the enlisted men's hotel. To our surprise, when we waded through the flesh market in the lobby we found him sitting on the steps.

"We want to go back," I said to him. "Good. I'm sick of Rome," he replied. We got our baggage, and got into our Jeep and headed north.

Telegram: "Come home!"

Now that the war was over, we had to think of how to prepare our men for reentry into civilian life. The army solved some of that for us. Men were offered the opportunity to re-up, get $300 and a 45-day furlough in the states. About 85 of my 120 men took that option.

I was offered an immediate promotion to major, command of an artillery battalion, and a promotion to lieutenant colonel in six months.

I wrote to Vera asking her advice. I received a cablegram reply. It read: "Come home! Love, Vera."

We had been told that we could buy all the items we wanted for our personal use from the Officers Exchange. I knew that as a civilian I would be wearing underwear and knew that I could not beat the price I could get them for at the exchange. I bought several dozen pairs of socks and two dozen sets of underwear. I packaged them to ship home to Vera to keep for me.

Two days later, before I had chance to go to the post office to ship the box, two officers from the Criminal Investigation Detachment (CID) came looking for me. They told me that they suspected that I was involved in black market operations, and showed me a copy of the list of clothing I had purchased.

Luckily, I had not shipped the clothing. I opened the box, and they counted exactly what I had bought. They saw it was in a box addressed to my wife. They seemed disappointed. They said that someone had reported that I was involved in black market activities. They apologized. I was angry. I made them repack and reseal the box, and told them that I would bring charges against them if they showed up again.

Several years later, back in Evanston, I would learn who had triggered that search. I was waiting for a hamburger in a small shop on Church Street, when Wardell Sutton entered.

"I almost had your ass for black market activities back in Italy, but you were too smart for me," he said. "I sent those guys to search for the stuff you were selling in the black market. I knew you were in it. They told me you still had the stuff and reported that you were shipping it home. You hadn't had chance to sell it yet."

I was so angry at him that I wanted to wipe up the playground with him again the way I had done when he got me expelled in the fifth grade. I said: "Wardell, you know you are a liar, and if I hear that you have repeated that lie again, I'll whip you until you bleed from every pore before I sue you." I never heard that story again.

Six of my men had made arrangements to marry and remain in Italy; three had married and were planning to bring wives home to the States.

Some were extremely bitter as they thought about the discrimination they would face when they returned to the States. This subject was the topic of frequent conversations. There were a few men who had been drafted from southern states; they vowed to never return to Dixie.

One of them had written home to have his family move to Chicago. He would not even return to the South to help them move.

He showed me the P38 German pistol he had purchased as souvenir. "If I run into that same sonovabitch I watched raping my 15-year-old sister back home, I think I would shoot him. That's the same bastard that was in charge of the draft board. We had sent my little sister away, and he had the nerve to tell me that if I told him where she was, I wouldn't have to go into the Army. I told him that she had run off to marry a man in Nashville. So, I had to go into the Army."

I said nothing, but I knew that he was going to find discrimination in Chicago, New York, or any other northern city. The vestiges of slavery were a continuing epidemic in America — a poison that will pollute the nation's system for many a century, because it is a poison of the mind, nurtured by fear.

While we waited to go home, we also grieved. Early in September 1945, we received a request from the Army's graves registration unit for volunteers to help pick up bodies of soldiers who had been killed during that abortive February push. I volunteered and took about a dozen of my men to help.

We were not prepared for what we found. The bodies had been lying in

Les (first row, center) and National Guard colleagues at Ft. McCoy, Wisconsin after the war, in 1948.

the sun and rain all summer. Some bodies were missing heads. Some bodies were missing limbs. Some had maggots eating where deep wounds had been inflicted. There was the question as to which head belonged to which body, which leg should be placed with which body.

After the first day, I went to my tent and cried. This is what some parents lovingly raised sons to meet? I was glad, only, that I knew none of the cadavers personally, although one was a friend of one of the men who had volunteered. He broke into unrestrained crying. I sent him back to the area.

After three days of this detail, we had collected all the bodies and we went back to our duties.

Homecoming

The trip back to the States was almost uneventful, except for a winter storm that sent waves over the superstructure of the ship before we were given an elevator ride skyward. When we landed at Hampton Roads, where we had embarked, we were hurried aboard a train and whisked away to Camp Grant, Illinois for mustering out.

Vera had been living in a large one-room apartment on Chicago's near South Side. When I entered that apartment on the third floor, we embraced almost immediately. After a flurry of kisses, we began a most energetic embrace that lasted for hours. We couldn't get enough of each other. The dinner she had planned was ruined as we were too busy for her to turn off the oven where the food was being kept warm.

Perhaps four hours later we surfaced enough for her to turn off the oven. We didn't want food. We wanted a nap, then sex again. That continued all the night, and into the next day, when she said: "You didn't get a chance to look at the new dress I bought for your homecoming." I smiled, kissed her again, and turned to look at the dress thrown carelessly on the chair at bedside. "It's very pretty," I said, and we both laughed.

Chapter 5

Return to campus

In the months before I returned Stateside, I had heard that colleges were crowded with returning veterans using the GI Bill. I started making applications to schools immediately. I applied to the University of Wisconsin, Harvard Law School, University of Chicago and Northwestern University. Wisconsin wrote to welcome me back.

I galloped up to Madison to prepare to re-enroll. Everyone seemed glad to have me back, but cautioned me that I was going to have trouble finding a place to live. I was told the returning GIs were sleeping in pup tents in Camp Randall stadium, outside the football field. I didn't believe it. I went there and counted 19 pup tents pitched there. I knew I could not bring my wife to live under such conditions.

House

All during the time I was overseas, I had saved money so that I could pay my tuition when I returned. I had saved a little more than $3,000. Now it made more sense to use that to buy a home. We were not sure where we should look. That problem seemed to be solved when Vera's father, James Burr, claimed that he had connections with the Chicago Board of Education and could get her a job as a teacher. We felt certain that he knew what he was talking about.

Some new duplex homes were being erected at 69th Street and Evans Avenue in Chicago, and we paid $1,500 down on one of the homes.

Before Mr. Burr could make his connections, Vera applied to the Evanston Board of Education for District 75, and was hired. It was the first day on the job for Dr. Oscar Chute, and we were delighted. Her starting salary was $1,700 a year for the ten-month school year. Now we needed a house in Evanston.

We learned of new houses being built on Leland Avenue. We liked what we saw. We took our remaining money and made a down payment on a house at 1811 Leland Ave., and planned to sell the Chicago house. However, before we could sell it, we got an offer from a family to rent it for more than the monthly payment. We decided that we would collect the rent and pay off the mortgage. We carefully saved the money we received above the mortgage payments so that we would have that in case of emergency.

Medill

I went to try to enroll in the Medill School of Journalism at Northwestern University. The dean of the school, Kenneth Olson, was out of town. In his place was Charles Allen, head of the advertising sequence in the school, and assistant dean. He looked at me and said: "Sorry, we are filled up. Maybe there will be an opening next term."

I went home dejected, only to find a telegram from Harvard Law School stating that I had been accepted for the class starting Feb. 25, 1946. I flew to Cambridge, Massachusetts, only to find that the housing shortage was the same there as it was in Madison.

I returned to Evanston and decided to try Medill again. This time, Dean Kenneth Olson was there. He said: "Well if you're good enough for Harvard, I guess you're good enough for us."

He told me that it was true that the Evanston campus was full. However, if I enrolled at the Chicago campus, I would be one of their students and Evanston would have to make room for me the following term.

I enrolled in two classes on the Chicago campus: radio script writing and advanced fiction workshop. The Chicago campus was on a semester basis; the Evanston campus was on a quarter system. So, when the next quarter opened, I enrolled at the Evanston campus as a junior.

There were mostly males in the journalism school. All were veterans except one, who was handicapped. We had been through a war and we wanted to make the world a better place. As a result, we were very serious students. All of us were married, and we didn't have to waste the time that bachelors needed to chase skirts.

For that first quarter I received three A's and one B, and vowed to do better the following term — and I did.

Sigma Delta Chi

In 1947, my senior year, I was voted into Sigma Delta Chi, the journalism fraternity that was later re-named the Society of Professional Journalists.

I did not know at the time that I was the first African-American to join the fraternity. When news of my initiation spread to chapters in the South, some chapters threatened to withdraw. In an effort to show them who I was, Northwestern sent me as a delegate to the national convention in Washington, D.C. that year. I was told I was being sent with the hope that the southerners would recognize that I was a worthwhile candidate.

One gentleman at the convention, in a wheelchair, said that since he had met me he had changed his mind, and would fight to keep his chapter in SDX. I offered to shake his hand. He refused, saying: "Just because I believe that you are qualified to be a member does not mean that I want to fraternize with you."

I realized that Washington, D.C. was still "Dixie." Nevertheless, I took part in the sessions and voiced my opinions on some of the issues being discussed. My arguments were received with an appreciation of their validity.

I was sworn in with the now-late Michigan Sen. Arthur Hendricks Vandenberg, who had the greatest collection of filthy jokes that I had ever heard. He kept all of us laughing.

We were served meals at round tables seating a dozen. The white waiter who served my table always served me first, no matter where I sat at the table.

Then Floyd Arpan, our faculty adviser, came to me and said: "The organization's annual banquet is being held in the National Press Club. No Negroes have been allowed in as guests. The officers are prepared to waive this restriction in your case for the banquet only, just as long as you don't try to enter the club at other times. How do you feel about that?" I told him that I had been invited to visit an old Army friend, Brig. Gen. Steve Davis, and I would rather use that evening for that purpose. He smiled and said: "You were always the diplomat."

I did go to visit Steve in his large home. He was married to U.S. Rep. William Dawson's secretary and their combined incomes made possible a luxurious dwelling, even in Washington, D.C. Steve and I were friends from Fort Custer, and we had a lot of catching up to do. It was a much more pleasant evening than I could have had at the banquet.

The convention offered one more feature. Each of us would get a chance to shake hands with President Harry S Truman. On the day we queued up to walk past him, I was the only African-American member of that entourage of more than 100. He shook each hand perfunctorily as any candidate learns to do. When he came to me, he held my hand and asked questions about my background, my schooling, and if I were a veteran. I told him that I had been a captain of artillery in Italy. He smiled and said that he had been an artillery captain during World War I. Our conversation may have taken as much as five minutes while those behind me in line waited to shake his hand.

That interlude would have a surprising sequel. When Truman was running for reelection in 1948, he came through Chicago on a "whistlestop" and met the press from the back of a train.

I was there with a Speed Graphic camera, as part of my press photography course. He saw me, waved and yelled: "Hello, Les, how the hell are you? It's good to see you!" I waved back, of course. Heads everywhere turned toward me.

Members of the press entourage wanted to know how I knew Truman on such a personal basis. I told them that I had met him at the White House the year before. That didn't satisfy some. So, I had to tell them the entire story. They treated me with more respect.

After we had returned from Washington, Floyd Arpan told me that none of the southern chapters had withdrawn because of me. He added: "You saved the union." We both laughed.

*

I was Number Two in my undergraduate journalism class. Manny Steindler was Number One. I ended my senior year at the end of the 1947 summer school with a national award to my credit. A picture I took of little boys putting their underwear back on after swimming in a flooded street was printed in the Gary Post-Tribune and won me a prize from Sigma Delta Chi.

Without thinking about it, I enrolled in the graduate school that September.

I undertook several significant projects in my graduate studies.

Arpan, our photography instructor, asked me to take photos of a faculty dance to be held at the Woman's Club of Evanston — a bastion of racial segregation. When I arrived at the front door with my camera, I was told to go to the rear door. When I knocked at the rear door, one of the employees said, "Colored are not allowed in here." I told him that he had better talk to Arpan about denying my entrance. He left me at the door while he went to get Arpan. Arpan told him in no uncertain terms that I was the hired photographer, and that I had better be let in or the club could face suit. The man, scowling, stepped aside and I entered to take photos. These would later be sold for a dollar each. I made $88 on that gig.

The final project in Press Photography was a photo story, a sequence of photos that told a story. Most of the class selected subjects in Chicago. I had a table-waiting job in Scott Hall, and couldn't take time to go to Chicago for photos. I decided to do my sequence on the food preparation process in Scott Hall.

Not only did I get an "A" for my project, the university liked it so well that I got $150 for the project. I was the only student to get an A in Press Photography that quarter.

Another project was in Dean Olson's class in editorial management. Each student was to select a newspaper in some town and analyze its coverage, its advertising and circulation.

I was familiar with the Capital Times of Madison, Wisconsin because of my years as a student at UW. My report showed that the newspaper tended to cover primarily areas where people of the upper socio-economic status circulated — with the exception of crime. Almost invariably the only time people of lower economic status got in the news was when they were in trouble with the law.

Also, the newspaper tended to treat extremely wealthy people as if they were freaks. I pointed out areas of the city that seemed to be completely ignored, showing that the newspaper was doing a disservice to advertisers.

William Evjue, the newspaper's editor and publisher, got a copy of my report — some 672 typed pages, and on a visit to our campus praised the report highly. I was told by a fellow student that in a talk to one of the classes he said that the newspaper had already started implementing 11 of the 13 recommendations I had made, and would soon be starting on the other two.

My final project in the advertising sequence — which was my minor — was to show that African-Americans were brand conscious when it came to purchasing household products. To accomplish this, I interviewed 421 families in Evanston's black community, asking each to tell me the brand name when I mentioned a product. For example, if I said "oatmeal," most answered "Quaker." The results showed that brand recognition in the African-American community nearly matched that found in a similar study done by a research organization for the Chicago area.

I needed the three credits from the course for my Master's degree. About a week after I had turned in my report, with copies of the individual survey responses, I got a telephone call to report to the instructor's office. I was asked the whereabouts of some 100 pages of back-up surveys that I turned in with my project. I didn't have them. I suspect that someone in that office had, intentionally or not, destroyed them. Now, the only way to validate my study was to do the entire survey all over again. I was heartsick.

Curtis MacDougall

I decided to earn my needed credits in a course taught by Dr. Curtis MacDougall, whom I had heard lecture while an undergraduate. In that first memorable lecture, he pointed out a plot by people in authority to make sure certain minorities "were kept in their place." That way, there would be a constant source of cheap labor. At the same time, minorities were convinced they lacked the ability to achieve, a self-fulfilling prophecy.

As his student, I was further entranced by his knowledge, his insistence on excellence, his commitment to the highest of ideals. He was a severe taskmaster who elevated Northwestern's journalism courses to true college level and taught us how to work on a real newspaper.

He taught us to not take someone's word for anything, but to put our hearts into the search for truth and a solution to problems. He also was an ardent foe of racial discrimination.

His liberal views were unpopular with many Northwesterners and right-wing Evanstonians. But most of his students were veterans returning from a war that had a great deal of social significance, and we listened to him as if he were the oracle at Delphi.

He was the only one I knew at the time in faculty and administration at Northwestern University who dared conduct an overt campaign against bigotry. He fought to get black teachers in the Evanston schools, and he was in the forefront of the group that integrated Evanston Hospital.

As a student, I followed him to his home and met his family — including a 4-year-old daughter named Priscilla. Shortly after taking the course, I asked him if it was OK if I adopted him as my father. He smiled and said: "I suppose I could use an extra son."

After this discovery, I made any excuse I could find to visit and talk with my newly discovered idol. Very soon, Vera and I were frequent guests at the

MacDougall home. Every time I received an award or promotion, I received congratulations from him.

I learned well from my new "father." I was valedictorian of the Master's degree class, though I didn't attend the ceremony. I was busy working. Mother did not attend, either. By that time, she had moved to California, where my sister Agnes was a gospel pianist. She never returned to live in Evanston, but I knew her heart was with me that very special graduation day.

Ebony

While studying at Northwestern, I learned of a new magazine, Ebony, published by John Johnson, who had done well with the small sized magazine, Negro Digest. The small magazine was economically feasible because so many large magazines were writing about the conditions involving the nation's largest minority, and it was possible to pay an author or publication only a small price for reprint privileges of a digest of the original article. Also, very little office space was needed to edit that publication.

Ebony, on the other hand, imitated the very successful LIFE magazine, which counted largely on photos to give depth to stories.

My studies at Medill were confined to the morning, and it allowed me time to spend half the day writing at Ebony magazine — at half-salary, of course.

It soon became apparent that I was writing about as much as those who were working full time. This job lasted for two quarters, and ended when required subjects were offered in the morning and afternoon.

I asked Johnson for a leave of absence for a quarter so that I could finish my studies. His response was interesting: "I don't believe in giving leaves of absence. We can teach you more here than you can learn at that university. If there is an opening here when you finish, I'll consider rehiring you at the time."

In the meantime, my reputation as a photographer had spread. I was engaged to do two large weddings in the community. I made more than $3,000 on them.

I got into movie picture making of children's parties. For $25 I would give parents a 50-foot roll of film of their child's party. It was up to them to get it processed. I was so busy making money at photography that I didn't have time to look for a journalism job. I had already turned down an editorship job in Nashville, where I would have been the only African-American on the staff.

Chapter 6

Journalism

As I finished my graduate degree and September approached, I got a telephone call from the Chicago Defender, a prominent black newspaper founded by Robert S. Abbott in 1905.

I was interviewed by a short, rotund, young man named Charles Browning. He promised to pay me $75 a week and put me to work writing feature stories. I accepted.

At the end of the first week, I asked for my check, and he gave me one for $30. I asked what the check represented. Browning said that I was on trial that week, and would get my regular salary from then on. I gave him back the check and told him to keep it, and I walked out of his third floor office. When I reached the entrance, near the switchboard, the operator told me that Browning wanted to talk to me. When I returned, he told me that it was normal to give new employees a test, and to pay them less for that period. I told him that at no time had he told me that I was being tested. I told him that I didn't like working for people who made up the rules as they went along. He told me to return next week and I would get the rest of my money. I told him that he had my address, and when I got the rest of my money I would consider returning.

He said that I acted like someone who didn't want to work. I told him that I still opposed slavery, where the employer told the employee what he had earned after the work was done. I told him that I was giving up a lucrative photography business to work for the Defender, and I didn't need the job. He made a telephone call. Soon a secretary arrived with a check of $45, and I promised to return on Monday.

After the shaky start, the editors liked my writing, and my work was frequently featured. Of course, no one suggested increasing my pay.

*

When the New York Life Insurance Co. came into Chicago and proposed clearing an area that contained many run-down houses to erect a modern housing complex, I was asked to do a series of features extolling the benefits of modern housing.

The tenants who were being removed were promised priority consideration for admission to the new complex. There was just one catch: people who were being moved out could not afford the new housing.

Because New York Life had constructed a similar project in New York, Browning wanted me to spend a week there gathering material to report on the success of that project.

He scheduled the trip over Christmas weekend of 1948. I suggested postponing the trip until after the holidays so Vera and I could spend Christmas together. Browning wouldn't hear of it. I told him that I would go if my wife could go along with me — at the newspaper's expense, of course. Browning balked, of course, and I suggested that the newspaper send someone else. Apparently Browning had sold my writing ability to New York Life. The company, which was picking up the check for the trip, wanted no one else. That meant that Browning had to go back to get the additional funds for Vera.

Browning liked to play "skin of the teeth" games. After he got the money pledged by NY Life, he still tried to get me to go alone, right up to the day we were to leave. When I walked out and told him I was going home to my wife, he had me stopped once again at the switchboard, and had me return to his office. He produced the money. But all his games had wasted time, and now it was questionable whether I could make it to the train station in time. He had his special driver speed me to the station, where Vera was pacing the floor waiting for me. We literally had to run to the train, where the conductor had already called "All aboard."

My training as a reporter demanded that I gather material on all sides of a question. So, at the same time that I talked to people who were extolling the benefits of the new housing in New York, I also reported on those who had been moved from the area and who did not have adequate income to return to the better housing. I gathered and reported on the settlements given to those whose housing had been taken, and the problems they had in finding housing with the resultant funds.

The editor didn't like that. When I read the reworked copy, I demanded that my byline be removed. This also triggered a big fight. According to the reporters' unions, this was our right. But the Defender was not party to the unions and therefore felt it was not obliged to follow the rules. Because this was the first of a series of articles I was supposed to write, I told Browning that he could get someone else to write the remaining three articles. He relented. My byline was removed.

I tried to be cleverer in writing subsequent articles. For example, when I quoted someone who was pleased with the new housing, I included reports they made about the difficulty some of their friends had with the operation.

These also were cut from the final article.

I tried to explain to Browning that the newspaper's credibility was in jeopardy when we purposely gave one-sided reports. He rebutted that if the "greater good" was achieved by withholding some information, then we could justify our actions.

*

It seemed important to management that my feature writing talents be called upon to help boost circulation — especially on the national level.

Browning decided to have me travel through the larger cities in the South, writing a series of features that could help boost circulation in those localities. For example, one might be labeled "This is Memphis" and I would write several articles extolling the contributions of the black leadership in that city. The feeling was that those leaders would tell their friends — and enemies — about the series and people would rush to buy newspapers. Also, by sending copies of this series to black leaders in other southern cities, they would be looking forward to my visit to their locations.

The idea made me feel like a not-too-well-kept whore. I was being paid the same piddling salary as back in Chicago for a puff job on these cities. I wanted to, at least, report on some of the conflicts, the lynchings, the struggles that the people had in those cities. That was not the way Browning saw it. He wanted me to report only on the accomplishments of the leaders. I realized that I would do the job that I knew a reporter should. I realized also that it would be edited to fit Browning's ends. While I was struggling to fit this concept into my consciousness, a more basic problem arose.

I was to take my car, my camera and my typewriter on this safari and to be on the road nine months of the year. I balked. I told Browning that I was a married man and did not intend to stay away from my wife for that long. His response was pure Browning. He promised to supply me with the names of "interesting" women in every city I would visit. He said, "I'm sure you'll find the variety most rewarding."

This cavalier response made the situation worse. The idea of leaving Chicago with the names of the south's leading whores was revolting. And he made it clear that the office was not going to pick up the tab on my entertainment.

When I suggested that I go three months, and return for a month, then, go for another three months, he refused to listen. He said, "The plans are already made. Go start packing your bags."

Chicago Daily News

Jay McMullen, a Medill dropout, had stopped by the Defender office to get some information on a series he was writing. He asked me: "What the hell are you doing working for this crummy joint?" I had never questioned it. He was working for the Chicago Daily News, and I had done better in all the classes at Medill. Why shouldn't I be working for the Chicago Daily News?

True, no blacks had ever been hired by any of the downtown dailies. The thought of being a "pioneer" never crossed my mind. I was just looking for an exit from an unhappy situation.

I picked up my phone, called the Chicago Daily News and asked to speak to the managing editor — as protocol had taught me was the way to proceed. Everett Norlander, the managing editor, referred me to Clem Lane, the city editor. Norlander explained that he left the hiring of reporters to the man who would be working closest with them.

I told Lane I had a master's degree from Northwestern's Medill School of Journalism, that I had worked for Ebony magazine, and was currently a feature writer for the Chicago Defender. He told me to come in and bring my clippings.

That was early in December, 1949. When I arrived, I was not prepared for the greeting I received. At least six former classmates from Medill left their desks to shake my hand before I got to the city desk. Three others, who had been classmates at the University of Wisconsin, including Dan Sullivan and Bill Newman, came to shake my hand. When I arrived at the city desk, Clem Lane smiled and said: "Well, that reception answered one of our concerns."

He sat at the desk while I squirmed. He read every article I had written for Ebony. He didn't look at a single one from the Defender. He explained: "We know how the Defender slants its stories." After he had finished, he sent me in to talk to Norlander, who asked, bluntly: "What can you bring to the Daily News that we don't already have?" Without hesitation, I replied: "A much better understanding of the South Side community than you have exhibited so far."

He thought for a minute, and asked: "When can you start? I told him I could start the first week in January 1950. We agreed. My starting salary would be the one dictated by the Newspaper Guild — $75 a week. I can remember being happier only when I took Vera to the altar.

When I reported to Browning that I had been hired by the Chicago Daily News — the Midwest's most respected newspaper — he asked: "Why on earth would you do something like that? We have always been able to work things out."

*

I was extremely nervous on my first days at the Chicago Daily News. I felt that every eye in the city room was watching me. Even so, everyone was friendly.

I was ushered into the office of the publisher, John S. Knight. He seemed very pleased with my background and would demonstrate this on more than one occasion.

When I emerged and mentioned to Bill Newman that I had met the publisher, he said: "I've been here years and I've never met the publisher." Bill Newman and I had known each other since our years together at the University of Wisconsin, so I felt comfortable joking with him. I said: "Just as soon as you are a Negro he will invite you in to meet him." We both laughed.

The greatest source of comfort during those days was Margaret

Whitesides, secretary to the city editor, Clem Lane. She became my guardian angel the day I arrived. Her attention to me made others in the newsroom even friendlier and more considerate.

She seemed to run the city room as far as the managerial side was concerned. She came to me, smiling (I never saw her when she wasn't) to give me advice about perks the newspaper offered. Sometimes she told me about another reporter who had information that might be helpful to me for some story I was working on. I honestly believe that her friendly assistance helped me become a better reporter. It was she who pointed out to me that Time magazine had called about writing a story about my joining the Daily News.

6-heads

My first assignments were the ones given to all newcomers — writing "6-heads." These were stories that could be condensed to two paragraphs and were given a #6 headline. The practice made one seek ways to condense information so that only the most significant information was included.

The city editor had placed a note on the bulletin board stating that one of the best stories ever written was: "Ice skating was good in all city parks today." His note said it gave all essential information necessary for a significant number of the city's residents. I worked hard to emulate that practice.

In my opinion, the best person in the city room at condensing stories was John Justin Smith, a nephew of a former CDN editor, Henry Justin. John was a WW I veteran who had a combat injury, and was one of the friendliest persons I ever met.

I learned very early of the power of the Chicago Daily News — even to change a man's color.

I was sent to cover a meeting in the prestigious Drake Hotel. The bulletin board listing the meetings and rooms had no mention of the meeting I was sent to cover. I went to the desk to ask. I waited until the clerk had finished talking to a man ahead of me.

He looked up and asked: "What do you want, boy?" I began, "My name is Brownlee from the Chicago Daily News..." His demeanor changed immediately. "Yes, sir ... How may I help you, sir?" I asked my question. He seemed not to be able to stop "sirring" me as he gave me the directions and offered to escort me to the room.

In those days, I was a curiosity at some of the places I was sent. On more than one assignment, I was asked to show my press pass, and then queried about how long I had been working for the newspaper.

I found no hostility until one day John Justin Smith called me to the desk and asked: "You know about the racial disturbance at 72nd and St. Lawrence, don't you?" I assured him that I had been reading about it. "You don't have to go if you don't want to, but you would be more valuable to the newspaper if you didn't have to restrict yourself because of race." "I'll go," I said before he could continue. "You don't have to if you think it's too dangerous," he said. My pride as a combat veteran required me to go.

Les with other Chicago journalists.

He sent along Bud Daley, a veteran news photographer. As we walked down the block to where the police stood in front of the house where "Negroes" had moved in, whites who were gathered on their porches made insulting catcalls. I expected this. Some stones were hurled in our direction, one hitting me in the back. When we reached the police post, a white police sergeant grabbed me by the collar and yelled at me:

"Geez, ain't you got no sense? You could get lynched out here!"

Bud Daley snatched the sergeant's hand from my collar, yelling: "Get your hands off my reporter." The sergeant let go of my collar, but hustled me into a squad car and took me into the next block, away from the tension. I called the office and reported the story, and took a street car back to the newspaper. The first assistant city editor was giving Smith a rough time because he had sent me.

I came to Smith's defense. "I asked to go," I volunteered. The assistant turned to me and said: "I don't think you know how rare you are. We can't afford to lose you!" I was surprised at that appraisal of my worth to the newspaper.

*

My original seat partner was Peter Lisagor, who was to become a legend as a reporter for the newspaper and an icon for the Chicago Headline Club. He watched me laboring over stories during my early days and said: "Relax, kid! You're going to do great."

My first "real" story at the CDN came as Lisagor was transferred to the

Washington bureau. Clem Lane looked up from his desk and yelled: "Pete! What the hell ... are you still here? You're due in Washington. Get outta here!" Lisagor asked, "What shall I do with this story I've been working on?" Lane replied, "Dammit — give it to Brownlee."

Peter handed me a folder filled with handwritten notes. "This is all I've got," he said and patted me on the back, adding: "You'll do well. Don't worry!"

I read his notes and they made little sense to me. I gathered from them that there was a female clerk in the county clerk's office who was buying a great deal of tax foreclosed property. I tried to find out as much as I could about this clerk. She lived in a modest home. She was a widow whose children had left the nest. She seemed to have no expensive tastes and had a wonderful reputation in her community. Why had she bought more than a half million dollars worth of lots?

I learned that there were more than 250,000 vacant lots in Cook County that had been seized for non payment of taxes. Many of the lots were purchased before the Depression, and the former owners did not have the money to pay the taxes. Even those who had owned lots for years were unable to pay the taxes and lost their properties. I found out that if anyone else bought a lot that had been seized, the former owner could purchase the lot back within two years by paying the taxes and penalties. This meant that anyone who bought such a lot would have to wait two years before he could get clear title.

I learned also that the lots that this clerk had purchased were back on the tax rolls, and the taxes were being paid by the former owners. Suddenly — and in the middle of the night — the crazy quilt pattern began to come together.

The trouble for Cook County was that it could collect no taxes on the vacant lots, and the two-year waiting period discouraged most buyers. Getting them back on the tax rolls was a challenge. The answer was simple: The secretary would buy the lot, then execute a quit claim deed and sell the lot back to the original owner. In that way, the owner did not have to pay back taxes, but he would start paying the current taxes.

Although it was not the expose that we started out thinking we had, the story did a lot of good. Many people who had lost lots began to use the nominee system to regain their lots, and the county's taxes increased as a result.

*

Shortly after this story, I was placed on the "banquet beat" — the 4 p.m. to midnight shift, when many stories dealt with reports of speakers at banquets. I liked this shift because it gave me an opportunity to meet some of the more important people in government, business and industry, and it gave me the opportunity to do more writing, instead of just reporting. The number of bylines I collected increased.

Another feature was the number of invitations I received from schools — especially in the inner city, where teachers wanted to give their students a live role model to emulate.

As a result of these forays, I talked more than a dozen young people into

Les captivates a young audience (photo undated).

journalism. At least three went on to become stars in the field: Russ Ewing, a
TV reporter; Monroe Anderson, a reporter and TV executive; and John White,
a Pulitzer Prize winning photographer who was inducted into the Chicago
Journalism Hall of Fame at the same time I was in 1993.

Charles Cleveland was the political editor for the newspaper. His desk was
just behind mine. One day he said to me: "Congressman Dawson said that if
the newspaper wanted to interview him, then we should send you. Are you
willing to go?"

Of course I was willing to talk to the black congressman from the 1st
District of Illinois. This district included the downtown business section —
where few of the movers and shakers lived. But it also included a large section
of the South Side — largely inhabited by blacks.

Dawson was courteous when we met as he asked me: "Do you know why
I insisted on the newspaper's sending you? Because this increases your value
to the newspaper. Ever since I was able, I've been trying to upgrade the status
of Negroes. I try to get the few black Republicans to be sure and slate a Negro
in every contest where there is a black Democrat running. In that way, no matter who gets elected, there will be a Negro in office. But you can't talk to those
lunkheads."

He told me that the mayor and police superintendent were using the police to harass black policy wheel operators (a lottery type of gambling), but were letting the Mafia-run wheels go untouched. "The mayor wanted me to help him on certain projects. I told him that I wouldn't until he stopped harassing my people. He said to me that gambling was illegal and that the police were just doing their job. I asked him that if it were illegal for Negroes to operate gambling operations, but not for whites. He told me that police had a plan and he was sure that they would eventually get to them. That was a year and a half ago, and he hasn't got to them yet."

I asked Dawson what story he wanted me to write. "I don't want a story, Brownlee. I just wanted to meet you and put you on the right track." When I returned to the office, I reported our conversation. Clem Lane said there was no story there yet, but advised me to keep in touch.

When I got back to my desk, Dawson was on the telephone. He said: "The police are helping the Mafia kill off negro policy wheel owners who won't go along with them. If you report this, the police will get you, too."

I was reminded of an incident that had occurred when I was courting Vera. I had become friends with Howard Geter, Jr. His father was a lawyer who had two of the Mafia policy wheel operators as clients.

Howard, his father and I were playing rummy in the senior Geter's apartment when the telephone rang. He was told that the wheel had been raided by Police Sgt. Tim Allman, who headed the gambling squad. Geter was told that the raiders got "everything" — the wheel, all the money and the records. The operators were to appear in court the following day. Geter said he would have to stop playing and start preparing for the trial.

About an hour and a half later there was another telephone call. The wheel's operator told him to forget about the court date. The caller said that they had been able to reach "their man" who was on vacation in Florida. "Their man" had telephoned Allman and told him to give back everything his squad had taken and to forget about the raid. He was warned that if it ever happened again, the sergeant would be in "deep trouble."

Geter, noticing the startled look on my face, told me that Chicago had two police departments. One belonged to the city and the other belonged to the Mafia. The Mafia's department was the more powerful.

He told me that his brother, who was well known in New Orleans as a fine tailor of men's clothes, had received an order from the mayor's chauffeur at the time for 18 suits at $150 per suit. The driver who placed the order was a Sgt. Reynolds, who paid for the suits in cash in advance.

Reynolds' name would surface again when I was at the Chicago Daily News. The next time he would be Captain Reynolds of the 18th Police District, immediately adjoining the 5th District, where most blacks lived. But that's another story.

The next time I got to talk to Mayor Martin Kennelly alone, I asked him if he had heard anything about police harassing black policy wheel operators, but leaving the white owners alone.

He looked startled, but said: "I'm sure the police have their plan of operations." The next day, I received a call from the mayor's office. He wanted to see me. When I arrived, he and Police Commissioner Tim Prendergast greeted me in the mayor's office.

Prendergast spoke: "You seem to know a lot about what goes on in the Negro community." I replied, "I know people in the Negro community who tell me things. What's so unusual about that?" Prendergast spoke again: "If you could give me a report of what's being talked about, or what's happening in the community, it would be worth $50 a week to us."

"I'll report anything that's worthwhile in the newspaper, and that won't cost you a cent," I replied. "How long do you think I would stay alive if it was ever learned that I was on your payroll? In fact, I don't dare tell anyone about this conversation or I could be suspect." I never heard from them again.

*

Roy Fisher, who was to become city editor of the Daily News and later dean at the University of Missouri, joined me in an unusual experiment.

The near South Side of Chicago, which had some very elegant homes from earlier years, had become run down and occupied largely by poor blacks. The area seemed ripe for the kind of demolition and redevelopment that had become the pattern in many urban areas.

Editors of the Daily News posed the question: Is it possible to heal a slum by giving competent advice and not spending any money? In 1953, Fisher and I were given the task of finding the answer.

A block club already existed in the 3100 block of South Prairie Avenue. We attended meetings and offered advice and connected the residents with government officials willing to help fund an upgrade of the block without tearing it down.

During our project, and as the Daily News reported on it over the course of many months, we saw many of the houses spruced up and residents become proud of their community. To this day, the block is largely composed of lovely restored homes.

Ambulance chasers

One day I was sent to Provident Hospital on the South Side to report on an accident in which a number of "Negroes" had been injured. As we waited in the lobby, a policeman came downstairs waving a piece of paper. "I've got a broken leg. How much am I bid?" Several lawyers waiting in the lobby began to bid for the contract the policeman had convinced an accident victim to sign, leaving the space for the lawyer blank. I was two feet from the transaction that took place. I watched the lawyer count out $75 and give it to the cop. He turned the paper over to the lawyer and told him the room number of his new client.

I rushed back to the newspaper to tell the city editor what had occurred. He smiled and said: "Sit down, son. When we print this story, the cop will deny it, the lawyer will deny it, and both will sue us for libel. Just remember it as part of your education."

I became very seriously interested in ambulance chasing, and determined to learn as much as I could about it.

The city desk sent me to interview a young woman, a recent immigrant from Poland. She had been on the way to apply for a job when she turned her ankle in a street car track and was sent to Cook County Hospital for treatment.

There she was approached by a member of the ambulance-chasing firm that had developed the business to a science. The firm had a photographer who took pictures of torn-up sidewalks around the city. Another member of the law firm roamed the wards at County Hospital, signing up accident victims. That's where the Polish immigrant was recruited and signed with the promise that she would receive a lot of money from the city.

The city settled for $3,200. The law firm gave her $200. She came to the CDN and was sent to me. I told her to go back and ask for an explanation as to where the rest of the money had gone.

She returned with a piece of paper on which was written a list of charges, such as "rent of courtroom: $75, bailiff's charge: $100," etc. When I saw her penciled list, I could hardly believe that anyone would be stupid enough to put this in writing.

I told her to say nothing to the firm, and that I thought we could get the rest of the money she was due. She could not resist talking about it, and word got back to the law firm that she had been talking to me.

I received a phone call from the head of the firm. He was curious about what I knew. I went to his office. I told him that I understood that the woman was charged for rent of courtroom, bailiff's fee, etc.

Without saying another word, he reached into his top desk drawer, took out a wad of bills, and counted out ten $1,000 bills and put them on the desk in front of me. I recognized that this could be a trap. There could be someone near to photograph me taking the money. I picked up the money, tore the bills in half, left half on the desk and took the other half back to the city desk.

Later that day, I received a telephone call from the woman who said some-one had come to her home bringing $3,000 — the balance of the city's settle-ment. She wanted nothing more. We had no story.

But now the city desk was even more interested in exposing the ambu-lance chasing racket.

I was dispatched to an office where insurance records were kept. I went through a series of some 30,000 cards and logged the names of the lawyers and doctors who seemed to be working together. The chart that I was able to devel-op showed a coterie of some 150 to 200 lawyers who seemed to work with about 70 doctors.

Before we could come out with the story, a tragic collision between a streetcar and a gasoline truck at 63rd and State streets burned many passen-gers to death. We were prepared. We sent reporters to the homes of the rela-tives of victims and picked up the cards left there by ambulance-chasing lawyers, or their representatives.

We finally had our story. We printed the cards on a full page beside our story. The article nailed the law firms, and triggered an investigation by the bar association.

*

Whenever Clem Lane was about to give an important assignment, he called the reporter up to the city desk, smiled at him and asked him to take a seat near him. Then, he would discuss the assignment. Whatever he was going to ask, I HAD to do; I was ready even if it meant going to Hell to interview the devil.

Clem had cut his reportorial teeth during Chicago's notorious gangster era. He had reported on Al Capone, Bugs Moran, the St. Valentine's Day massacre. There was little that could startle him.

One day he smiled at me and said: "Sit down, son. They tell me that it is so easy to buy dope that one could walk up and down certain streets and buy it as easy as buying a newspaper. Do you think that's true?" I replied, "I believe that's true." He asked, "Do you think you could do that — walk on a street and buy some dope?" I answered, "I don't know, but I'm willing to try." He handed me a note as he said: "Draw $50 from the cashier and go see what you can do."

As I left his desk, I tingled with excitement. I knew I had to succeed, but I didn't know where to start. My mind raced through the neighborhoods where I had covered stories. I had seen evidence of dope activity along 47th, 43rd, 35th and 39th streets. But I was a stranger in those neighborhoods. I would have been suspect of being with the police, or an informant. If I had been suspected of being the latter, I was assigned a death warrant.

Then, it came to me. What about 35th street? Every Tuesday night before going to the weekly drill with the National Guard at 35th and Giles, I would stop at a restaurant around the corner on 35th Street to order lima or Great Northern beans, ham hocks and rice. It was a common sight to see someone who was "high," meandering down the street. Not infrequently, someone in the restaurant showed evidence of being high. People saw me there often. They must know that I was with the Guard. I would not be suspect.

The difference would be that I was there on Tuesday nights. This was a Wednesday about the middle of the day.

In an effort to try to lessen suspicion of anyone who might be watching me, I went straight to the National Guard armory. I shot the breeze for about 10 minutes with my supply sergeant. Then, I went to the restaurant. I spotted a teenager whom I had seen there before. He was not eating, just shooting the breeze with the well-fed waitress. I asked her, "How come you guys never have red beans and rice?" She replied, "Because I don't like red beans, and if there were leftovers, I would have to eat them damn red beans." Everyone giggled.

I had seated myself purposely next to the teenager. I turned to him and in a voice hardly above a whisper, I asked: "Y'know where I can get some stuff?" He looked at me for a long minute and said: "Don't go away." He left the restaurant.

As I ate my meal, I became aware of someone peeking at me from the edge of the restaurant's front window. After about 20 minutes, the teen returned and sat beside me, and asked: "Could you lend me five bucks?" I reached in my pocket and put the five dollar bill on the counter in front of him. He picked it up and shoved something in my coat pocket before he left the restaurant.

I tried to be nonchalant, slowly finishing my meal, making small talk with the waitress before I left. As soon as I stood outside, I reached into my coat pocket and pulled out a small package wrapped in tissue paper. I hurried back to the city desk and deposited the packet on the city editor's desk. He smiled and asked: "How long did it take you?" I replied, "Less than an hour." He winked at me and smiled: "Write it!"

Words poured out of the typewriter. Not only was I given a front page byline, but our radio ad featured my story.

*

I hardly had time to gloat over my success when I was called back to the city desk. Clem Lane smiled and said: "Great story, son! But maybe you could investigate another report I've received. I'm told there are women in the community who are using prostitution to support a dope habit. Have you heard anything like that?" I answered, "I have heard that, but I don't know it for fact. I'm not surprised, though, because people who are hooked on dope will do anything to get another hit." Lane said, "Why don't you draw $100 from the cashier and look into it?"

I was so flattered that I didn't have time to think about what the new assignment was asking of me. I was on the way back from the cashier's office when I asked myself, "Does he want me to have sex with a prostitute to get the story?"

I had heard dope flourished around 39th Street and Drexel Boulevard. If there was a place to start my study, that was it. It was early afternoon when I arrived in the community and saw a great deal of activity in and around a tavern. The blast of sound from a juke box almost deafened me as I entered. The place was packed. It seemed that there were equal numbers of men and women milling about, some with drinks in their hands.

As I neared the rear of the tavern, I saw a rather portly middle-aged woman seated on the last stool. I saw a man hand her some coins. She turned to face the rear of the tavern, and opened her legs. He opened his trouser zipper and stood in between her legs, pumping away. After a few minutes, he finished and closed the fly of his pants. The woman took a rag and stuffed it in between her legs. She then turned to the bar and yelled: "Hey, bartender! Give me another drink." She was a prostitute to feed her alcohol habit.

I crossed the street and entered the bar in a hotel. As I sat down on a stool and waited for the woman bartender, I noticed a printed sign on the wall behind the bar. It read: "FURNISHED ROOMS FOR RENT." The word furnished was underlined in red. When the bartender came to me to take my order, I asked:

"What do you mean 'Furnished'?" She answered, "What do you want — blonde, brunette, redhead?" I then asked, "What do you recommend?" She said, "There's a new blonde from New York who has developed a reputation for making johns happy." I nodded my approval and ordered a glass of wine.

The bartender went to a telephone at the back of the bar and spoke a few words into the instrument. She poured my wine and brought it to me. A few minutes later, the bartender nodded her head in my direction. I looked to my right where there was a door and saw a slight blonde coming toward me. She smiled as she neared me and asked: "Aren't you going to order me a drink?" I turned to the bartender, who brought her a drink. The woman, who called herself Blanche, and I made small talk for a few minutes until she said: "Let's go!"

I followed her out the door she had entered and climbed two flights of stairs to a room. She locked the door and smiled at me as she took off a wrap-around skirt. She was wearing nothing beneath the skirt. She was wearing a see-through blouse, which displayed small breasts with nipples which had been painted red. The blouse had opaque long sleeves, which I thought odd.

I felt the blood pounding in my head as I saw the woman lying on the bed. She asked, "Are you going to take off your pants?" I was certain that the woman was filled with venereal disease. I thought of my lovely wife and how stupid it would be for me to have sex with this woman, although I had given her the $20 she demanded as we entered the room.

I asked, "Can't we talk?" She replied, "Sure, we can talk, but in 15 minutes it's gonna cost you another $20." I had not made a move toward disrobing, but asked: "Aren't you going to take off your blouse?" She laughed and asked, "Do you want to fuck me under the armpits?" We made small talk and soon she said: "You owe me another $20."

No matter how I pleaded, I couldn't get her to take off her blouse. I began to believe that she did not want to disclose the puncture marks in her arms. I pretended to be angry: "Dammit. Keep your blouse on."

I stormed out of the room and returned to the office. When I reported the scenario to Clem Lane, he agreed that she didn't want to disclose needle marks in her arms. "Write, it, son!" he said.

Once again the story poured out of my typewriter. That story also received rave notices.

Everyone didn't rave, however. During my next National Guard drill, one of the officers, who was also a policeman, told me: "Watch yourself! You did not make friends in this community with your stories. If they think you are a threat, they will eliminate you." That made me uneasy — especially since I didn't know who "they" were, or how much of a threat "they" felt I was. For weeks after that, I entered and left that community with a great deal of caution.

*

One unforgettable story broke when I was fairly new at the CDN. I was sent to cover a fire that had broken out in a tenement on the South Side. The fire was in full flame when I arrived. I watched as firemen brought out the bodies of nine tots, some smelling of burnt flesh. The bodies were lined up on the sidewalk and covered with a tarp. I went back to the office and wrote the story — with tears streaming down my cheeks.

When Pete Lisagor left for the Washington bureau, Bob Herguth was given to me as a seat partner. From the very first few moments Bob seemed to always have a joke or a pun. He kept me laughing, sometimes upsetting the city room. We became fast friends down the years. I could seldom see him without breaking into a smile or laugh.

*

One especially happy episode occurred to me while I was returning from an assignment and was walking west on Madison Street near Wells Street. My foot kicked an envelope that skidded along the sidewalk. I picked it up, opened it, and found 25 $20 bills. No one else seemed to have noticed the envelope. No one paid attention to my picking it up.

I returned and reported it to the city desk. Clem Lane said that if he had found it, he would keep it. But if I felt worried about it, we could run an ad. The ad read: "Found money on a downtown street. Owner can have it if able to tell the amount and approximate location." Despite a flurry of responses, none came close to the amount and location.

After two weeks, Lane said, "The money is yours. Go spend it and have a good time."

I used it as a down payment on a 1947 Cadillac because Vera admired Cadillacs. She was to drive it more than I because it was easy for me to get to work by taking the Chicago and Northwestern train to the Madison Street station and walking across the concourse to the elevator and up to the sixth floor without leaving cover.

*

Not infrequently when I went to my mail box there would be a penciled note from Clem Lane, saying: "Damn good job on that story" and it would be signed with the curious "L" that was his trademark.

One such story was a report on an organization that delivered babies in the home. The assistants began by spreading newspapers over everything in the "delivery room." I was told that the ink used in newsprint killed any germs that might be around.

Of the three births I witnessed that night, I remember one in particular. While his assistant was spreading newspapers, the doctor was talking to the black woman in her late twenties. She was wearing a robe and was standing near a couch in the living room that was also the bedroom.

He had just asked her how long ago her last contraction had been when she gave a groan. The doctor pushed her down on the couch. Almost immediately her water sprayed the wall beneath her feet. Then, there was the baby boy's head. The entire birth process took less than five minutes.

The assistant cleaned up the baby, and before we left, mother was on her feet, holding her new son and smiling.

The editors gave the story a half page — with my byline. How well I remember the lead: "We rode in convoy with the stork, ushering new lives into the city."

George Lahey, who was known as a "newspaper man's newspaper man," who was always sent on challenging assignments around the globe, was talking to editors at the city desk. He saw me and yelled across the city room: "Hey, Les! That was a damn good story. I read it twice."

I couldn't have been prouder or happier if the archangel Michael had given me the keys to heaven.

Punch drunk

I had a chum who boxed at the Emerson Street YMCA when we were younger. He would ask me to swing at him so that he could spar his defenses. He was a heavyweight and I was a light heavyweight. I soon became aware that his punch had no sting. So, when he would punch, I would ride under it and clobber him. We used to laugh at him because we predicted that he would never make it as a boxer.

Imagine my surprise when I picked up the sport pages of the newspaper and saw his grinning face. He had just become the heavyweight champion for the Catholic Youth Organization. Somewhere along the way he had learned to hit. I learned another lesson — again. Never count somebody out before the game is over.

There is a sequel to that story. About two months after his championship, his sister brought him into the CDN sports department. On the way, he saw me and recognized me — almost. He called to me: "Ray! (my brother's name) How are you?" I could see by his manner that he was punchy. He was unstable on his feet. His speech was slurred. His sister was taking him to the sports department to do a story about youth who had their brains rattled by too many punches to the head. I never saw him after that.

Brother to brother

I met a lot of important people, though I didn't write about all of them. Though I reported on Dr. Martin Luther King Jr., I had long conversations with him that I did not write about. They were more "brother-to-brother."

Another VIP I met was Eleanor Roosevelt, wife of President Franklin Delano Roosevelt. We had two conversations while the Daily News was showing her that it was integrating. We compared recipes during two long lunches the CDN higher-ups invited me to, primarily because I was black. She had so much warmth, so much personality.

I also met band leader Duke Ellington. I knew Kay McDonald, a singer in his band, and she introduced us.

"Whatever Became Of...?"

I was assigned a column "Whatever Became Of...?" It sought out people who had been famous in the news in past years, and reported what they were currently doing. The column appeared daily at the bottom of page 3, and was extremely popular.

It wasn't as much writing as detective work. I prided myself on my writing skills, and this assignment did not give me the chance to do the kind of reporting of which I was fondest. So, I asked the desk for a reassignment. The desk refused, telling me that I was doing an excellent job and the column was so popular that they wouldn't take me off it.

*

Every reporter has them. They are the stories that never saw print.

A teenage girl came to the newspaper with a problem and was turned over to me: "The women in my parish are telling lies about me," the 15-year-old began. "They say I am having an affair with the parish priest, and that is a bald faced lie."

"What do you want to do about it?" I asked. "Well, everyone believes the Daily News. So, if you wrote a story saying that their stories were not true, then, the people in the parish would know the truth and those evil women would have to stop talking." "You realize, of course, that if we print your side of the story, we would have to print theirs, too."

"I didn't think about that," she replied. "Well, I guess I'll just have to talk to the Pope." I agreed.

Two weeks later I read an Associated Press report that the girl had gained an audience with the Pope. I marvel at the determination, the dedication, and the ingenuity the teen possessed.

*

While covering a fire in a two story building, I saw a woman stagger from the first floor coughing and gagging, trying to talk. A man, returning from work, exclaimed: "My daughter! Where is she?" The woman kept coughing and pointing to the building.

The man, brushing aside a firefighter's attempt to hold him, dashed to the front door of the building, got down on his knees and crawled in. Very soon, he returned on his knees, a blanket over his head, a very frightened six-year-old girl in his arms. Once outside the building, with tears streaming down his face, he kissed her face over and over.

The woman had stopped coughing and was crossing herself and muttering: "Thank God! Thank God!" I approached her: "A father's love for his child is very strong," I volunteered. Apparently, not thinking about her response, she muttered: "He doesn't know that it's not his child." That line never got into the story.

*

A secretary in the state's attorney's office and I became friends. We talked about our children. She had three; one had a birthday the day before mine. I sent a birthday card to the seven-year-old. She was very pleased. Later, at the appropriate times, I sent birthday cards to the other children.

One day, several moths later, I received a phone call from her: "I thought we had a lunch date," she said. I knew we didn't, but realized that she wanted to see me right away.

When I arrived at her office, I saw a large checkbook opened with a ball point pen pointing to a certain check. "I'll be with you as soon as I wash my hands," she said, giving me a knowing wink. The ball point pen was indicating the name of the prominent pastor of a large South Side church. The amount of check was $1,000. A hurried look through the check book revealed the names of other prominent South Side pastors, and the stubs showed varying amounts paid to them.

I copied as many as I could, and as rapidly as I could. About 20 minutes later, she returned with the remark: "My, my! Look at the time! I guess we'll have to lunch some other day." She hurriedly closed the checkbooks and put them away.

I scurried back to the office and to the city editor's desk to tell him about my scoop. Clem's words: "Sit down, son. When we print that story, will it stop many of those people from going to church?" I replied, "I suppose it will." He asked, "Do we want to discourage people from going to church?" I answered, "I don't think so." His last words: "Then, why not keep that story for your memoirs..."

Diversity

My being the first minority reporter hired acted as a stimulus to others, Hispanic as well as African-Americans. On more than one occasion, I was told by members of Hispanic groups that my success meant that they could be hired, too.

I doubt that my hiring did anything to upgrade the plight of women in newsrooms. At my hiring at the CDN, there were three women in the city room. Helen Johnson covered the Board of Education. Edan Wright did stunt work, such as parachuting into Lake Michigan or leaving purses — with a $5 bill and an address inside — inside telephone booths. (Of the five purses left in telephone booths, two were returned with the money; one returned without, and two not returned at all.) A third woman did similar feature type work.

The women's section was staffed almost completely by females; the features editor was a male, Tom Collins. He and I had a run-in after I was given an elaborate brochure showing about a dozen photos of attractive young women. It was the Polish community's offer of debutantes to their society. I was told that I should write a two-paragraph story about it.

I went to Clem Lane, noted that the largest collection of Poles outside Warsaw was in Chicago, said that this was an important event in the community and that we should do more than two paragraphs. He asked me to give him a memo to that effect. I did. He bucked it on to Tom Collins. Collins responded that I was just jealous because blacks were not in society.

I boiled. I cut out and pasted on a memo such items as "Mrs. Swift opened her apartment in Las Vegas," etc. I asked him to justify this as a contribution to journalism. He did not respond. Shortly after this, the Polish debutantes story appeared, but in the news section, not in the features section.

Several months later, I received a similar offering from the Snakes — an organization of black medics. Their daughters were being introduced to adult black society. I took this offering to Clem Lane on the city desk. To my surprise, about a week later these photos of debutantes appeared in the women's pages — a historical development to be followed by other Chicago newspapers.

Meantime, there was a report that CDN circulation was increasing sharply in the South Side black community.

And Northwestern rediscovered me. I was asked to speak to their "cherubs," a summer school in journalism for high school students from around the United States. During these sessions I was re-introduced to Dr. Curtis D. MacDougall, who was to have a profound effect on my future.

Defender, Again

I didn't enjoy writing the column I was assigned, so when I got a call from the Chicago Defender asking me to return as advertising manager, I seriously considered the offer. I was offered an increase in salary over what I was getting at the CDN. It took some soul-searching, but it represented a challenge that I wanted. I talked it over with Clem Lane and Ev Norlander. Both said they were in no position to advise me, but both thought it was an excellent opportunity. I decided to take the job. That was in June of 1952.

When I returned to the Chicago Defender, my first task as ad manager was to teach my salesmen how to sell. Their entire sales pitch was to ask potential advertisers: "Would you like to advertise in the Chicago Defender?"

I armed them with figures which showed the extent of the market, the need to inform this market of the advantages of getting their message across to the people in the market. Also, to develop the kind of message that would have the greatest appeal. As the messages were learned, the advertising revenue increased.

Then I had a battle with the management, which was Charles Browning. Every time a salesman got a new and large account, the management would take it over and call it a "house account," thus denying the salesman his commissions. I asked Browning, "Why should I ask them to go after larger accounts when they know they will not get paid for selling them?" When I finally was able to sell this idea, the sales increased.

I targeted certain markets for different seasons. We developed a summer campaign based on cold drinks and ice cream. I started a campaign for babies to coincide with National Baby Month.

I developed a food service campaign — including a food service show, for which we sold booths to various food distributors. I had a woman in the community who was an expert cook demonstrate how to prepare tasty dishes using products from companies that purchased booth space or advertising space in the newspaper. Our advertising revenue leapt as we successfully exploited this venture. Another feature that paid off was to have show visitors fill out a brand preference card. Each card turned in entitled the person to a bag of groceries. Food in the bags was donated by exhibitors.

After the very successful food show, we tallied the results of the surveys. Each company that came in first was approached with the suggestion that the company take out a "thank you" ad to the people in our community. Those who came in second and third were approached with the idea that they needed to increase their effort in the community to better their share of the market. All these campaigns succeeded.

Brownlee's way

The Defender had never had an ad from any of the merchants on State Street. When a new Robinson's Department Store moved in, I had our artists draw up an ad featuring their women's dresses. I met the owner and pointed out to him that this was virgin territory for a new arrival on State Street. He bought the first of a series of full-page ads. His customers from the South Side increased. I promised the account to the salesman who showed the greatest percentage increase in the next quarter.

Once again I ran afoul of Charles Browning. He argued that since I had brought in the ad, and since I was part of management, the account belonged to the house. I tried to tell him that his attitude was short-sighted. As men hustled to get this account, they would increase the overall revenue to the newspaper. He was adamant.

I went to John Sengstacke, the newspaper's publisher. I asked him who was to be in charge of my department. If I had a campaign to increase revenue, why should it be short-circuited by someone who was not in my department? Sengstacke listened and said nothing. Finally, I had had it. I told Sengstacke to look for another ad manager. I couldn't run a department if I were not in charge of it.

Browning backed down: "Why do you always want to quit when you are losing an argument?" he asked. "I try to avoid any situation where I am up against adamant stupidity," I responded. "There are hundreds of cases which show that the system I am advocating works," I added. "If you want this newspaper to continue increasing its advertising revenue, then we should take on some of these practices." Sengstacke spoke: "We'll do it Brownlee's way."

Pig roast

At the end of the quarter, ad revenue from all our agents had increased substantially. I took the results to Sengstacke to prove that I knew what I was talking about. He replied: "I know. I've been following each week's newspaper."

I scheduled a success banquet for all my salesmen at my house on Leland Avenue. We had a whole roast baby pig that was too large to fit into my oven, so I had one of the hotels roast it for me. It was quite a hit. That party raised morale among the salesmen, who said that nothing like this had been done for them before.

*

A woman working at the Defender as a secretary was also the mother of one of my salesmen. She kept asking to come to my department as secretary. She was a good-looking woman who had a lovely figure that she delighted in showing off. She let me know, in no uncertain terms, that she wanted me as a lover.

She was close to Browning, and was trying to work the transfer through him. When he approached me with the idea I asked: "Why should I transfer a secretary who is familiar with my operation for one whom I would have to teach from scratch?" His reply: "I'm sure you'll enjoy the fringe benefits." I turned and walked away from him.

One day when I was emerging from Sengstacke's office, she was waiting outside. She came to me and confronted me, grabbing my genitalia in one hand and holding my arm with the other. She asked: "When are you going to give me this?" Before I could answer, Sengstacke came out of his office and she let go of me.

For weeks afterward I had trouble dodging her. She would wait outside the building to waylay me as I emerged. I got in the habit of sneaking out the back of the building. After a while, she gave up on her campaign, which had become a source of embarrassment to both me and her son.

When I told Vera about it, she volunteered to come down to meet me after she finished teaching her class. She appeared once and met me. The secretary was outside in her car. When she saw me walking arm in arm with Vera she drove away. She seemed to have a hard time accepting that a man could be true to his wife. She also had a hard time accepting the idea that a man — any man — could resist her.

Laird

I had told Vera before we were married that the mumps had made me sterile when I was 15. She had accepted me with this incapability. But after eight years of marriage, she began to talk about having a child. We went to specialists who found her capable, but pointed out that my sperm moved too slowly to ever make a successful trip to fertilize an egg. We looked into adoption and were placed on an agency's waiting list.

Then Mother phoned to advise me that my baby sister, Maxine, was expecting a baby. Maxine was not able to keep the child or pay for the hospital delivery. Mother knew that Vera and I were trying to adopt. She asked if we were willing to pay the hospitalization and accept the child. We jumped at the opportunity.

Les with his son Laird, 1987

We turned a bedroom into a nursery and selected names: April Heather, if it were a girl; Laird Alan, if it came to be a boy. Early one morning on May 17, 1951, the telephone rang. I answered. The woman's voice on the other end asked if I were Lester Brownlee, I answered yes. She said: "You are the father of an 8-pound healthy boy." Vera, who was still in bed, asked who was calling. I turned from the phone and said: "Laird's here!"

She got up and we sat at the top steps of the second floor and talked all night. We picked up Laird at the hospital on the South Side. On the way home, Vera held Laird and I drove. I looked over at her and will never forget the look on her face as she worshipped the child she held in her arms.

Our lives changed drastically. We began to talk about Laird's future. Vera had an idea that would be revolutionary. She believed that a child's education was delayed too long before starting. She said the formal education should start when the child was about three months old, while the mind was still wide open. Also, it should be done at times of close touching — like when the child was being bathed, being fed, being caressed.

She sang children's songs to Laird while she bathed him, she pointed out pictures of animals in a picture book and pronounced their names. Later, when she asked him to point to a specific animal, he had remarkable accuracy. He would receive a kiss and a hug for each successful answer. This process kept on with the lessons getting more difficult. Finally, we read "The Night Before Christmas." He did so well on it that I made a tape recording of his reading the lengthy poem when he was two years, eleven months old.

He had composed several songs by the time he was five.

When we talked to Dr. Oscar Chute about Laird, he said that the school system was not prepared to accept a five-year-old who was reading at the level that Laird was promising. We turned to the National College of Education, which had a nursery school class for three-year-olds and pre-kindergarten for four-year-olds. The college had a number of students who were being trained as teachers. This permitted the luxury of having one teacher deal with an individual student if and when it became necessary. This allowed Laird to have a number of one-on-one instructors. He was extremely friendly, made friends easily, and he progressed rapidly.

People who met Laird marveled at his intelligence, his outgoing personality. We had promised Mother that no one would speak about his biological parentage. This was made easier to hide because it had been rather widely known among friends that we were trying to adopt. So, the presence of a new arrival in the home was merely a consummation of that effort.

My attempt to steer Laird into athletics was short-circuited by an accident very early. We were playing catch. His mother was watching. When he got ready to throw the ball back to me, he accidentally threw it up and hit himself in the mouth, cutting his lip. He cried. She brought him to her breast, and turned to me and said: "I don't want anything to hurt him. That includes all your athletics." So, he was never pushed into athletics.

Phoebe Ann McAllister often baby-sat for our son. She would become known as "Pam," her initials, by close friends and associates. She was a pupil in Vera's fifth grade class at Foster School. One day Vera said, as she handed me a piece of paper: "Do you want to see what our baby-sitter wrote?" I read the composition, and exclaimed: "My gosh, the girl can write!" That's when I took over. I was determined to make the kid into a journalist.

We took her with us on all our outings, and sometime to plays and operas. We continually told her that she could be anything that she wanted to be, but she had to believe and she had to keep trying. She sold her first magazine article when she was a senior, and I got her a scholarship to the University of Wisconsin.

She got her bachelor's, her master's, and her Ph. D. and became the first black woman to head an urban daily as publisher of the Ithaca (N.Y.) Journal. I was like a proud father when she was invited back to receive an award as a distinguished graduate of the University of Wisconsin.

Houston

That Christmas of 1953, Vera, Laird and I went to Houston to spend the holiday with her mother and Aunt Beulah. Her father joined us there later.

After we had returned from visiting Vera's mother, I received a telephone call from Carter Wesley, publisher of the Informer Group of Newspapers. He said that he had planned to get in touch with me while I was in Houston for the holiday, but that I had returned before he had the chance. He asked me to fly back to Houston to talk to him, at his expense. He said he had a proposition that he thought I would find interesting. I made plans to fly there over a weekend.

When we met, he praised my increase in the advertising in the Chicago Defender. He said that all owners of Negro newspapers checked weekly to see how others were doing. He said my name was circulating among owners as a person who might be able to bring new life to the Negro press.

He asked me if I would take charge of his newspapers as executive assistant to the publisher, with full authority and full responsibility. The salary would be twice what I was receiving at the Chicago Defender. I told him that I would consider it, but that I wanted to check first with my wife.

I telephoned Vera and she was pleased with the idea. She and her mother wanted very much to have all the family in Houston. I gave the Defender notice again, just when I was being promoted to vice-president in the Defender chain (with no increase in salary).

Staff upgrades

My first task was to evaluate the employees. I found that I had four writer-reporters, each receiving $30 a week. The sports editor was receiving $35 a week, and the person who was supposed to be the city editor was receiving $40 per week. All these employees showed that they were almost worth what they were receiving.

I needed better trained people in the newsroom. I needed an over-all editor, and I needed new editorial people who had some idea what news reporting was about. We had too many stories in which we were reporting unsubstantiated rumor, as well as some obvious inaccuracies.

I received an inquiry from Ernestine Cofield, a graduate of Lincoln University School of Journalism. I hired her at $50 per week. When Wesley heard of this he hit the ceiling, whereupon I took the stories that she turned out and made a cost per word comparison with other members of the editorial staff. I was able to show him that on that basis, she was more valuable than other members of the staff. He was not pleased with being shown he was wrong.

One day I read a story in a Dallas newspaper that impressed me. The story carried the byline of Lloyd General. My advertising manager said he knew him, so we got in my car and drove to Dallas.

He was not at home. We waited several hours on the front steps of his house until he arrived. He looked scared to find two men waiting to see him at 2 a.m. I told him who I was and told him that I would like to hire him to run the staffs of the newspapers in Houston at $55 per week. He said he would have to talk it over with his wife, and would get back to me. The following afternoon I received a phone call saying that he accepted the job. This time Wesley didn't raise his voice. I guess he had lost too badly in our past encounter.

General was soft-spoken and never given to vindictiveness, even when he had to entirely rewrite stories. The staff accepted his expertise in a good natured manner. They recognized that he knew what he was talking about.

*

There were two editions of the Houston Informer. The main issue came out on Friday, and a second smaller edition was published on Tuesday. The Friday edition sold for 15 cents, and the Tuesday edition sold for a dime.

I proposed to Wesley that we beef up the Tuesday edition by making it a "state" edition and increasing the price to 15 cents. He had doubts, but decided to go along with me because it promised to bring in more money. He predicted that we would lose circulation.

We made the announcement about a bigger, better Tuesday edition "for only 15 cents." The first Tuesday our circulation dropped by almost 300 copies, and Wesley was fit to be tied. However, that edition with its price increase brought in more actual cash than he had received before.

The next Tuesday the circulation was less than 200 copies lower than the normal run. The third Tuesday, with the headline "LANDLORD SLAYS TENANT," circulation jumped 350 more than any previous high. It never dropped back to where it had been when we started the increase.

*

I wanted to increase our state news, so every Tuesday when the paper came off the press, I would take 200 copies, get in my car and head out some route into a rural area. I would come to a town or village, and look up the pastor of the largest black church. I would introduce myself, tell him we wanted to print news about what was going on in his church community and leave him with five newspapers.

I would ask him to get someone in his community to sell the newspapers, send us 50 cents, and keep 25 cents. Also, someone was to send us news about what was going to happen in the church community. The person selling the papers should also ask for an increase in the number of newspapers to be certain to have enough for customers. We would accept up to five returns for credit. (The person merely had to tear off the dateline on the front page and mail it back).

I pointed out that a person who hustled could make some good money, as well as increase the flow of information about the community. This program went well and we began building circulation in rural communities.

Lily

On one excursion, I was in the pastor's living room talking to him when a young lady, a teenager, burst into the room, crying: "Preacher, don't let them take me!" she cried. He tried to calm her enough to learn what was bothering her. Finally, she said that her mother was sick and had sent her to work for the Taylors because the family needed the money. When she was working, "Ol' man Taylor got after me, pullin' at my dress. I run out. He said he was goin' to get the sheriff and put me in jail for stealin'. I ain't stole nothin!" And she started crying all over again.

The pastor explained to me that Taylor was known for his lechery. As he was talking, a battered Ford station wagon pulled up on the road in front of the house, which was set back about 100 feet. A voice from the station wagon cried out: "Preacher, send Lily out here!" I went to the door and saw two men in the front seat of the station wagon, one holding a shotgun.

I turned and asked the pastor what we should do. He shrugged his shoulders and said: "What can we do? If we don't send her out, they'll come in and kill us both and still drag her out." Lily began crying. He took her by the arm and half dragged her to the door and pushed her out on the porch. She stood there crying. Someone in the car said: "Lily, come on out. Don't let me have to come and get ya." Still crying, Lily walked slowly down the path and got into the back seat of the station wagon.

As it drove away, the pastor turned to me and said: "It's a downright sin. No better than under slavery, and we can't do nothin' about it. To make it even worse, Lily is his daughter."

I said that he may not be able to do anything about it, but I could report it in our newspaper. "Please don't! If Taylor found out that it had been published, he would try to lynch us all."

I realized the possible truth of what the pastor said. I left in such frustration that I forgot to talk to him about our newspapers. When I returned the following week, he would not let me in his house. To this day I've wondered what ever happened to Lily.

*

Another of our editions was in Galveston. The man who handled it brought news, picked up papers and sold them there. He put most on newsstands in the community. He also sold ads, and collected the money for the ads and brought that money in, too. His circulation was something more than 200 of the Friday's edition.

I tried to get him interested in the Tuesday edition. He said it would be too much work for him. When I offered to help him get started with the Tuesday edition, he got miffed. I didn't push it any further.

Two weeks later he became ill, bedridden. I took his newspapers to his house, asked him where I should leave them on newsstands, collected money from newsstands for the previous week's papers, and brought all of it back to him.

He was overcome with gratitude. He did not believe that one of the newspaper's executives would do all his work and still give him all the money.

The following week, when he was up and about, he came to me and asked: "Tell me more about the Tuesday newspaper." Within three weeks he had the Tuesday newspaper sales approaching 200. He was delighted. He hired a boy to help him with his work.

Jealousy

Carter Wesley suggested that I appear before various luncheon groups to try to win their support for the newspaper. My first talk was before a Negro businessmen's group. Wesley was upset when several of the men at the luncheon telephoned him to tell him that I was a much better speaker than he. He remarked: "I didn't tell you to go there to show me up." I asked, "What should I have done?" He replied, "You didn't have to show me up."

After that, I refused to accept future speaking engagements unless he ordered me to. I would tell people who inquired that they had to get his approval. He didn't like being put in that position, either.

Finally, I told him: "I refuse to go to speak in a mediocre manner just to please you. I will not speak anywhere until you order me to speak." He made few requests for me to speak after that.

*

I told him that I needed more people who could write news stories, and he suggested that I go to Texas Southern University and train them. I applied and was given four beginning English classes to teach.

I started to teach students to write for publication. At the end of the first semester, I was called on the carpet because I was not using the required textbook. I went before the committee and showed that of the 104 students I had, 17 had been published that semester. I challenged them to show any other instructor who had such a record.

I learned they were not interested in publication. They wanted someone to follow the text. We parted. I did get two of my students to come to work at the newspaper.

*

My next foray was to go to the Dallas Express to examine that operation. I found that the Dallas newspaper was in much better shape than the others. The editor told me: "We are far enough away from Carter Wesley that we can do a good job without his interference."

I was invited to spend the night with the women's editor and her husband. We had a delightful dinner and I went to bed.

In the morning when I was getting up, she came into the room and told me to remain in bed for a while. She hinted that she wanted to join me there after her husband had left for work. I thanked her, but told her that I would be afraid that her husband might return and catch us. She insisted that he never returned.

While we were talking, he did return. He said he had forgotten to take some tool that he needed at work. After he left that time, she breathed a sigh of relief and said: "You sure saved my neck. How did you know?" I said, "I had a premonition."

*

One day, as I was on my way home, I heard on the car radio that lightning had struck an oil storage tank in Kilgore, Texas. I was riding with my advertising manager, and asked him how far Kilgore was from Houston. He said it was about 200 miles north. The radio report said that the oil spilled by the strike had spewed into a black neighborhood, and had caused some fires.

Suddenly, I was a reporter. I forgot that I was an executive. We raced north. I went to the hospital, interviewed victims, and photographed the split oil tank and chickens that had been sprayed with oil. I had my film on a Greyhound bus at 2 a.m., and I raced back to write my story. It scooped all the dailies.

But I had not reckoned on Carter Wesley. He called me on the carpet and told me that I had reporters to do that kind of work, that I was an executive, and should act like one.

I countered by asking him which reporter we had that could have done that kind of job. He said that it was up to me to train them so that they could do that in the future. I agreed, but reminded him that it would take at least three years to develop someone to have that kind of expertise and news was not going to wait for us to be ready. He countered by saying that this was my problem, and he was sure that since I was such a brilliant person, I would figure out how to solve it.

I suddenly understood. He was jealous, and he was going to do whatever necessary to embarrass me.

He was always reminding the males to have nothing to do sexually with the females on the staff. One night when I finished work, I saw about five women waiting for a bus. I stopped my car and offered to give them a ride home. Apparently, he saw the gesture from his office window. The next day he called me in and told me: "If I catch you going to bed with any of the women on our staff, you just put your peter through your paycheck."

When I asked him what he was talking about, he told me that he had seen me pick up the women on the corner. I asked him: "Don't you believe in helping people, especially your own employees?" His reply: "If you want to be an effective executive, you have to control by fear, not favor."

I told him that I had commanded an artillery battery in combat by cooperation, and had brought all my men out alive. He said I was lucky. I had a reputation around the office for helping people, for never saying a harsh word. By contrast, when he came in, he was like an angry tornado. This attitude of his finally brought our relationship to a head.

Resignation

When I was hired, he told me that I was in charge of everything, except the training of drivers. "You young whippersnappers don't know how to train drivers. I'll take care of that."

I arrived one morning to find a memo from him on my desk asking me to explain how I had allowed three of our delivery truck drivers to be involved in accidents in one week. I took the memo and went directly into his office and pointed out that he had insisted on keeping the responsibility of training drivers. He replied that he had trained them properly, but it was my responsibility to see that they followed his training. He said that it was obvious that I had not lived up to my responsibility.

I said: "Mr. Carter, you'll have my resignation on your desk within 15 minutes."

I typed out my resignation, sent it to him by my secretary, gathered up my belongings and went home. He telephoned. He said that I was being too sensitive, that I should understand that this was the kind of give and take that made for strong leadership. I told him that his brand of leadership was one that led to insanity or murder.

I was not returning. When the word got around the plant that I had resigned, 16 employees handed in their resignations. They said they had learned that management could be friendly, and that they had functioned better under such leadership, and they were not going back to his tyranny.

An angry Carter Wesley got his lawyer to try to prove that I had talked them into resigning. Not only did they say that I had not talked to them, but if they were called to testify, they would recount the instances when Wesley had verbally abused them. They would tell how all this had changed when I took over, and they were not going back under his mean management.

Carter Wesley tried to get his lawyer to prove that what these people were saying was part of a conspiracy cooked up by me. His lawyer told him that there was no evidence that I had ever talked to his employees about anything but what they could do to improve their performance.

But now, I was out of work. I sat around the house for about a week, sulking, asking myself why I was so stupid to take this job without inquiring into the nature of Carter Wesley.

Several of the employees came to me and wanted me to start a new newspaper. They said that I could get all the employees at the Informer to come to work for me. I thanked them, but pointed out that I didn't have the capital to start a newspaper.

I decided that it was about time that the Houston newspapers had a black reporter. I gathered my clippings, my resume, my awards and applied. I was surprised at the response. The managing editor told me: "Your credentials are superior to anyone in the newsroom. If we hired you we would create a serious morale problem among our reporters. And we can't afford that."

"Home" to Daily News

I began mourning my happy days at the Chicago Daily News. Finally, I wrote a letter to Ev Norlander. "If you are planning a Houston edition of the Chicago Daily News, I am available." Two days later I received a telegram from Norlander: "Come talk to me. If you need carfare, wire collect."

I was overjoyed. We jumped into our 1951 Cadillac and headed for Chicago.

Here's what Norlander said to me: "I've always had a policy of not rehiring anyone who left the Daily News. However, you brought so much goodwill to the paper that I am willing to make an exemption in your case. When can you start?" My reply: "Immediately, Mr. Norlander. Immediately!"

That was 1953, less than one year after I had left the CDN. I don't know when I was happier on a job. The staff was glad to see me, and the contacts I had made before were glad to have me back. They began feeding me information for stories. I felt a surge of power, as if I were some sort of super-reporter.

I had the privilege of working with Bill Newman on several series. Several had to do with public aid — one series dealt with public housing and its problems, one dealt with health troubles of the poor. We won a special Stick-o-Type Award and $100 apiece from the Chicago Newspaper Guild for the series.

I worked with the team that exposed thievery by the Illinois treasurer — which won a Pulitzer Prize — and I developed expertise in urban affairs. My byline began appearing on just about everything I wrote. Also, some of the works were winning awards. It was pleasant also to see the paycheck getting larger.

Libel

There were occasional negatives. Few specters haunt a reporter's waking and sleeping hours as much as the fear of being successfully sued for libel. Imagine the ghosts that chased my sleep when I was informed that the newspaper was being sued because of a story I had written. I kept asking myself "How could I have made a mistake?"

The CDN had a policy of reporting very few divorce cases. I believe it was because the conflicting "'tis -t'ain't" charges that peppered most cases was difficult to report objectively. The only reason I was sent to cover one particular trial was because the family of the wife was so strongly on the husband's side. At the trial the wife testified "he snatched the baby from my arms and threw it against the wall." The woman charged in her lawsuit against me that she never said that.

Thus, it was a case of waiting for the transcript of the trial, which our lawyers ordered. I sweated until the transcript arrived. It proved that I had quoted her correctly. She still insisted that she had said that "he took the baby from my arms and tossed it on the bed and the baby rolled over and hit the wall." Nevertheless, we won the case and my sweet dreams returned.

The paper also had been threatened with lawsuits after the story I wrote about ambulance chasers soliciting business after the street car and gas truck accident. The city desk had sent reporters to the homes of the victims and collected the lawyers' cards. These cards were printed on one full page of the newspaper. The threats of lawsuits came whizzing in. It is probably true that none of the lawyers who were screaming had placed their cards in victims' homes — lawyers had made it a practice of hiring "runners" who went to the homes and even into accident wards at hospitals to solicit cases. Despite that technicality, none of the threats by these lawyers ever materialized.

*

After I returned to the Chicago Daily News, most of my beat dealt with urban affairs. I was to write many stories about the Chicago Housing

Authority, covering the board meetings of the CHA along with representatives of the other three daily newspapers.

I was always surprised to see Ruth Smith, a reporter from the Southtown Economist, then a weekly newspaper on the city's almost all-white Southwest Side. Because she never took notes, I asked her one day if she wrote her stories from memory. She told me that she never wrote stories about the CHA. She was there to inform her editors if the CHA planned to build any units in the newspaper's circulation area. The editors were prepared to do whatever was necessary to keep the low-class "Negroes" from moving into that neighborhood.

"Now if they were as educated and as well-mannered as you, I'm sure they would not mind," she said. I asked sarcastically, "You're telling me that all the people in your neighborhood have Master's degrees from a major university?" "Of course not. But they would not want all those who are not well behaved to move there," she continued.

"I'm surprised at you," I said. "You were trained as a journalist to check out the facts before you came to any conclusion. If you could just meet the officers in my National Guard unit, you'd realize how wrong you are."

I was back at my desk when I received a telephone call from Ruth. "I would like to meet the officers in your outfit," she said. I told her that we had our drills on Tuesday night at 8 p.m., and arranged to meet her at 6 p.m. in a restaurant in the Lake Meadows shopping area. Byron Minor, our battalion commander, agreed to meet me there.

She lit up when she met Lt. Col. Minor, who had a Master's degree in education from the University of Chicago. I think she was surprised to meet a light-skinned man with blue eyes and wavy hair who considered himself a "Negro."

After dinner, we three walked over to the Armory at 35th Street and Giles Avenue, and went into a room where the officers met before the drill started. As officers we had been instructed to call everyone to attention when a lady entered our midst. Ruth was surprised to see about two dozen officers standing at attention and staring at her. "I don't deserve this," she said, wearing a broad smile. "At ease," Minor said, and the officers resumed their seats.

Minor introduced her to each of the officers, and I thought I would play a joke on her. I pointed to one officer and asked her, "What's this officer's name?" She was the diplomat. She replied: "They are all so handsome that I couldn't be expected to remember anyone's name." All the officers laughed.

Minor gave Capt. Frank Marchant the job of squiring her around and telling her about the history of the organization, whose progenitors had fought in the Mexican war, and as the 8th Infantry, Illinois National Guard, in World War I, as part of the French army when no American commander would accept "Negro" soldiers. He chatted with her about the organization's combat record as the 600th Field Artillery Battalion in World War II.

After the drill was over, Minor and Marchant drove Ruth home. I received a telephone call at the office the following day. It was Ruth, thanking me for having invited her to meet the officers. Two weeks later Frank came to me before the drill started and shook my hand. "Les, I want to thank you for bringing Ruth to meet us. She and I are getting married." I doubt that I was ever more surprised about anything. They did marry, and Ruth was as "Negro" as anyone.

From time to time I would see her at a social function, laughing and joking with other "Negro" wives, as if they had been lifelong friends. She received nothing but rave notices from others in the community. As one officer's wife put it, jokingly: "Are you sure she doesn't have Negro blood?"

The Marchants had one son years later. I lost touch with them after the National Guard was ordered to integrate and I was transferred to a formerly all-white organization in the 33rd Infantry Division.

Real estate racket

African-Americans had difficulties getting bank loans, so they were prime targets for unscrupulous real estate dealers. These dealers would bid on a home in a changing neighborhood and offer the owner, for example, $12,000. Once the owner had accepted the offer, the dealer would seek out a "Negro" family and sell it for $18,000. He would take a down payment of $3,000 from the family. He would give the seller $2,000 as a down payment, and get a bank loan to cover the balance. The dealer would have the "Negro" family sign a contract to purchase the home over the same period as his bank loan. If the dealer's monthly payment to his bank was $125 per month, the dealer would charge $175 per month to the contract buyer.

In almost every contract the dealer had inserted a clause which stated that if the buyer was delinquent for 60 days, the contract was null and void and the buyer would forfeit all he had paid. Then, the dealer would start selling the same house all over again.

A lawyer who learned that I was interested in such cases gave me information that indicated the practice was widespread.

This lawyer, Mark Satter, discovered a case in Circuit Court in which one such dealer was suing a former partner for money he claimed the former partner had stolen from him. In making his claim, the dealer listed 19 buildings in a two block area in which the two had been partners. The listing showed the purchase prices and the sale prices to the "Negro" buyers. The court case claimed that one partner had defrauded the other of more than $750,000.

Because the practice was legal, there was little anyone could do about it. Satter told me of another case in which a young man had come to Chicago penniless, but had managed to accumulate properties worth more than $500,000 in less than two years. The practice was a serious indictment of the banks and insurance companies that made this practice possible.

My articles exposed this racket.

Speaking circuit

As a result of stories I wrote, I was invited to speak to many groups. The newspaper gave a $35 stipend to reporters who made speeches to groups on the reporter's own time. Reporters who had worked on some exciting stories were sought often to give more details on their experiences.

Some high schools in the inner city sought me as a role model, and the newspaper often allowed me to go speak on the company's time. I reasoned that the newspaper wanted to build readerships in those neighborhoods.

Sometimes it hurt to see the way students treated me — as if I were some kind of oddity one might find in a zoo. One young girl actually touched the back of my hand and seemed startled when I turned and smiled at her. I tried to assure them that they could achieve almost any goal they sought if they applied themselves to it. Their reply often was: "You know 'the man' ain't gonna let you go any place." I soon realized that "the man" had shackled their imaginations, their hopes. This kind of restriction was much more powerful than actual chains.

Some of their teachers were, knowingly or not, a part of the enslavement system, as was demonstrated by such remarks: "I don't think you should encourage youth to aspire to think beyond their abilities," or, as one principal told me: "We try to teach them to be good citizens and how to make an honest living at jobs they can understand."

I realized how much I had been blessed by having a mother who chased me away from the enslavement system of Evanston in the 1920s and '30s.

I was also discovered by some of the women's groups in Skokie and other white areas. I was asked to speak, not about stories I had worked on, but about how I had escaped the enslavement system. All were extremely courteous, but on occasion there would be some male who would ask: "Since you were able to achieve success, why aren't other Negroes achieving?" My frequent response: "How do you know that they are not achieving? How many do you know? How many of our doctors, lawyers, college professors do you know? Just because you have met only domestics does not mean that all in our communities are domestics. Many, if not most, are not concerned about what you think. They're too busy living."

One woman in Niles asked me: "Isn't it true that if there is sex between a white man and a Negro woman that there can be issue, but if there is sex between a Negro man and a white woman that there will be no issue?" I replied: "Don't count on that information." She told me that she had seen Negro women who had half-white children, but she had never seen a white woman with a half-white child.

I responded: "Negro women tend to keep their children, regardless of the father. White women give them up as soon as they can find a place to dump them." I told her about an agency in Evanston which called me and my wife often to ask we would be interested in adopting a half-white child. "That is probably why you don't see white women with half-white children."

I remembered this incident years later when residents of the Dewey

School community began adopting either black or Asian children to raise with their children so that their children would not be burdened with the culture's stereotypes.

On more than one occasion, attractive white women suggested that "we become better acquainted." I thanked them, but never took the offers. I would never have even considered cheating on Vera, but I also remembered a story that was reported to me as a teen growing up in Evanston.

The story was that this youth was invited into a woman's house. She disrobed. He disrobed. She yelled "rape!" Two men who had been waiting outside the bedroom came in with baseball bats and beat the youth into unconsciousness and left him in an alley, naked in sub-freezing weather. Another white woman who was walking her dog discovered him and called police. They took him to a black doctor who patched him up. My brother's response to that story was: "From now on, when I see a white woman coming toward me on the street, I'm gonna cross the street." And so he did for his entire life.

Maybe that story was apocryphal, but it was successful in deterring intimacy between races as far as black youth were concerned.

Chicago's American

One day I had lunch with Norman Glubok, a classmate from Medill. I complained that I wasn't writing as many feature stories as I would like. He asked: "Why don't you come to work for us?" He was a reporter for Chicago's American, a Hearst newspaper.

I was non-committal, and he asked if I would talk to their city editor, Wes Hartzell. I said I would. When I returned to my desk at the Daily News, my telephone was ringing. It was Hartzell. He asked if I could meet him late that afternoon. I could and did. In less than five minutes I was hired as a feature writer, choosing my own assignments, at $5 more per week.

My photo, along with those of Ernie Tucker and George Murray, was plastered on a large ad throughout the Chicago area. Vera brought me a poster when she visited me at a National Guard summer encampment. It seems that the newspaper thought I was important enough as a circulation builder to feature in a promotion.

My assignment at the American was to pick whatever I wanted to report and write about in the area of urban affairs. I chose primarily to write about the inequities minorities experienced in obtaining financing to buy homes. My ally, attorney Mark Satter, let me in on some of the discriminatory practices. I received several anonymous phone calls, threatening my life if I did not stop reporting on the issue. The calls made me more determined than ever to continue.

Not only did I write many stories about health and welfare, but I got involved in reporting on the Board of Education. I began to win awards for the newspaper.

Things went well for me until Hartzell left the paper, and John Madigan, assistant managing editor, took over. He came to me as I was writing a story and asked who had assigned the story. I told him no one — that Hartzell asked me to select my own stories. He told me that he would do that in the future. I folded my arms and waited.

I received the same treatment Fred Bird got at the Daily News after he wrote something which displeased a friend of Ev Norlander. He was told to wait for another assignment. He didn't get one for months. So, Fred Bird joined the American staff. Bird and I knew each other from New Trier High School, where he was editor of the newspaper, "New Trier Times," while I edited the literary magazine, "Inklings."

Seated close by were Tina Vicini and Hal Bruno. Hal was to be maligned later by John Madigan when he became engaged to a lady from India. Each of us was entitled to a three-week vacation a year. Hal asked for the three weeks at the end of one year and three weeks at the beginning of the next. After he had been gone four weeks, Madigan asked aloud: "When's Hal Bruno coming back? How long does it take to marry a nigger?"

Several seatmates looked at me and shook their heads. Many were aware of Madigan's foul mouth. Under Madigan's command, the assignments I received were those usually assigned to a beginner. He apparently wanted to be sure that I didn't get the kind of assignments that would bring me into stardom.

I was rescued when Ernie Tucker, an outstanding reporter, was promoted to city editor. He knew my potential, and the good assignments returned, and so did the honors.

Vote fraud

During my stint at Chicago's American, I noticed a discrepancy in the election returns from one of the West Side wards. The returns showed that some 400 people had voted, but there were only 22 applications for ballots.

I went to the ward to ask some questions. I found out that the alderman had run into trouble at a previous election, and was in disfavor with the organization. In order to regain favor, it was necessary from him to show that he could really turn out the vote. He had a mother of 10 busy writing out applications for ballots, to account for all the ghost voters. When I talked to her, she was afraid that she would have to go to jail.

I went to talk to my friend from the National Guard and later governor of Illinois, Otto Kerner, who was then a county judge. I explained that I could get her to come forward and tell, if she would not be sent to jail. Kerner agreed.

Since a congressional election was on the ballot in the precinct, I had to go to the District Attorney to get his OK. He agreed. I had to get her a lawyer. I called my Army buddy, Earl Strayhorn, who subpoenaed all the voters on the registered voters list and asked if they had voted. Only 21 admitted to voting. The alderman was sent to jail, but not before he had threatened to see that I was killed.

Mississippi

The managing editor, Luke Carroll, called me into his office one day and told me that he had learned that more than 51 percent of all "Negroes" migrating into Chicago came from Mississippi. The remainder came from 42 other states. My assignment was to go to Mississippi to find out why.

His caution: "I don't want one of those nigger-lovin' stories. I want facts." I don't know what he expected me to say or do. But I replied: "Mr. Luke, why don't you wait until I commit the crime before you indict me." His face turned red, as he replied: "Go draw money from the cashier for your trip."

I was not prepared for Mississippi any more than the state was prepared for me. I found "colored" signs over the waiting room, and over the drinking fountain, and I found a "colored" cab driver to take me to a "colored" hotel in Jackson.

The following morning I set out afoot to search the back roads of the Delta country. I found a new school building that had 23 books in the library. The principal explained that the federal government had provided funds for the building, but none for books.

I was looked on with suspicion by blacks because I talked like a "nawthunah" and wore well-pressed slacks and a sports jacket. They eased up when I showed them my press pass and told them that I was a newspaper reporter.

I soon learned that things hadn't changed much, if at all, since the abolition of slavery. The economy was still based on share-cropping, just had been when my mother was a child. This meant the white man still owned the land, and the blacks who farmed it got a portion of the crop. The farmers had no money for seed, but had to get it from the "company store" — on credit. All of the basic foodstuffs, such as flour and molasses, had to come from the company store — on credit. The white man kept the books, and most blacks were not educated enough to know if they had been cheated. The smart landowner saw to it that his tenants got enough to keep them on the land, but not enough to be free from the land. The "good" landowners would include candy treats for the children, as a gesture of goodwill.

The landowner — and his sons — also had the "right" to take any of the tenants' wives or daughters who appealed to them, and nothing could be done about it. A black man was helpless to retaliate after he found out that his wife and/or daughters had been raped by the landowner and/or his sons. Years later, a police sergeant in Augusta, Georgia, told a black couple whose wife had been raped: "She should feel proud that a white man wanted her."

After wandering through the Mississippi delta country talking to blacks, I was overwhelmed with the realization that there was a dearth of hope. The most I could find had to do with getting to Heaven after death. Despite the huge migration north, stories about blacks having a better life in Chicago were considered fictitious, more like fairy stories. The more positive the story, the less likely it was to be believed.

I went back to my room in Jackson, sat on the edge of the bed and cried like a baby.

The four-part series that I wrote won several awards, and Luke sent me a congratulatory note. The series was such a success that people asked for copies of it. The newspaper had it reprinted in booklet form and distributed thousands. The Chicago school superintendent ordered 1,200 reprints that he mailed to other school chiefs around the country.

I was at the American and its successor, Chicago Today, from 1958 to 1964.

Chapter 7

Broadcast

In January 1960, I was approached by radio station WBEE to introduce a news program starting at 8 a.m. daily.

I went to Ernie Tucker and told him about the offer. I requested to be transferred to the midnight to 8 a.m. shift. He helped me get the transfer without a hitch.

It was an ideal arrangement because the radio station was about five minutes away. Because I was at a newspaper, I had access to the latest breaking news. My first morning show was five minutes long. I could write it during the breaks I had in the evening. My shows were each hour on the hour until 4 p.m. Then, I would dash home and try to get some sleep before I had to report at midnight at the newspaper.

Many stories appealed to our audience of mostly African-Americans. There was a great deal of civil rights unrest all over the nation, including in Chicago. During that summer, Pam McAllister, Laird's babysitter and Vera's and my long-ago pupil who had gone to the University of Wisconsin with our help, came to work with me as an intern. She witnessed news stories that caused her to go home nights wide-eyed. One of them was Dr. Martin Luther King, Jr. speaking at Soldier Field.

(Pam McAllister Johnson, who calls herself my daughter, is currently the director of the School of Journalism and Broadcasting at Western Kentucky University following a successful career including several years as the editor and publisher of a Gannett paper.)

"Channel 7 Eyewitness News"

During my radio sojourn, I was asked to participate on a panel of news people who would be interviewed by a group of high school newspaper editors.

Also on the panel was Sterling "Red" Quinlan, vice president and general manager of then WBKB, Channel 7 in Chicago.

The high school newspaper editors were particularly critical of television, and Red Quinlan did not seem to be able to come up with plausible answers to their complaints — especially when it came to explaining public service shows. I kept taking him off the hook.

After the panel interview had concluded, Red Quinlan came over to thank me for coming to his aid. I countered by saying: "You know, of course, they are right." He asked, "What do you mean?"

I gave him some ideas I had about public service programming that would answer some of their criticisms. He reached into his pocket and gave me his card and said: "Come talk to me soon."

I met him at ABC Chicago's building at 190 N. State St. and further outlined thoughts I had on public service programming. I pointed out that there was no reason why such programming must run without a sponsor. The first example I gave him was of a junior Olympics — which would feature high school athletes in track and field events.

He interrupted my pitch: "When can you come to work?"

I was not expecting to be offered a full-time position. What I wanted was an opportunity to develop some programs, present them to him and have him buy them. In the meantime, I would continue with my other two jobs. He would not hear of it. He wanted me full-time. This meant a cut in income. Although the television job would pay more than either of my other two jobs, it did not pay more than I was getting from both jobs.

It was a big decision. I wanted the challenge of developing shows for television. I took the pay cut.

*

I went to work for Channel 7 in September 1964, and became disenchanted quickly. In order to get paid, an employee had to be placed in a departmental budget. I was placed in the local news department's budget. I met Dick Goldberg, who was the news director, and he said to me: "If you are going to be using up my budget, you are going out on the street to do some reporting. There's your crew. Here's your assignment."

I hadn't bargained for this. I had never done any TV reporting. However, I had a very friendly crew. The cameraman was Tony Caputo, a veteran from the newsreel days. My sound engineer was Ollie Oakes, and the lighting engineer was Phil Risser.

On that first assignment, Caputo had to tell me where to stand and how to hold the microphone; Oakes had to tell me to speak louder. Also, my questions were too long. I had to learn to shorten them to something a little more than an elongated grunt.

A newspaper reporter's practice of developing a story had to be jettisoned. All TV news wanted was an emotional expression dealing with a news event. The end may or may not increase a viewer's knowledge of the subject. As a result, I had the same kind of feeling on some of the stories as "coitus inter-ruptus."

As a print journalist, I had taken pride in my ability to ask questions in a mild manner, rather than in the style exemplified in Hollywood movies. I learned that my soft tones were not appreciated in TV news. So, I was sent to Columbia College at night to learn how to project.

I did one-up them all. I was reporting live from the scene of a bank rob-bery when I signed off my report, "Les Brownlee, Channel 7 Eyewitness News." How many times have you heard the phrase "eyewitness news" since then?

On the public service front, my initial project drew a major sponsor even before it had chance to be developed.

When the word got around that Channel 7 was going to conduct a statewide junior Olympics, we quickly heard from high school coaches, play-ground directors, and individual athletes themselves.

The junior Olympics attracted quite a crowd. In the 13 boys' events, the meet set 11 new state records, and in the 11 girls' events, the meet set 10 new records.

Before I could get my next project under way, Red Quinlan was gone. Dr. Tom Miller was my next top boss, and he was not interested in any of my proj-ects. I became a full-time TV reporter.

My knowledge of urban affairs gave me a jump-start on others in the field. Soon, we were getting the best of these stories — especially those that dealt with the problem-plagued school system.

My appearance on the tube was somewhat of an anomaly. Very few peo-ple, white or African-American, were prepared for a dark face on the tube. It resulted in my being asked to speak at a number of places — especially in inner city high schools, where students stared at me as if I were a three-legged drom-edary. Few instructors were prepared for the knowledge I exhibited on a num-ber of subjects. I imagine I surprised many because I displayed a lack of ego-tism.

One thing occurred that my bosses were not prepared for. Channel 7 had a huge increase in viewers in African-American — and Hispanic — communi-ties.

These were days with a great deal of tension over the integration of schools, and there was some stone throwing and fist fights. My presence at the scene of these disturbances had a peculiarly quieting effect, especially after our cameras caught photos of those involved in the violence. In some instances, the police subpoenaed film from TV stations and used the film to identify and prosecute those who were principal perpetrators.

Most of the stone throwers' objections were based on the belief that some "stupid niggers" were coming in to lower the standards of their schools. My presence was not welcome because I gave evidence of being anything but stu-pid. I was always courteous and well-mannered.

One protester told me: "We'd welcome some like you in our schools." My reply: "How do you know that you're not getting some even more intelligent than I?" There was no reply.

No picture, no story

Having been "raised" as a print journalist, I was not sensitive to the demands of television journalism. So when a group of the leading merchants along the city's "Magnificent Mile" stated that the city's taxing policies were doing more to create slums than all the slumlords combined, I rushed to the news director with the information that I had the inside track to the story. He looked at me and asked: "And what do we use as a picture, Brownlee? Do we show a series of slum buildings?" No picture, no story.

Another slap at my news judgment came when an informant told me of a meeting being held at the Metropolitan Sanitary District offices. The subject being discussed was the threat to Lake Michigan as a result of industrial poisons being discharged into the lake. I was reminded of the serious health trouble that resulted when the Chicago River carried human excrement into Lake Michigan, and bacteria entered the city's drinking water. Once again, without thinking, I dashed into the news director's office telling him about the story. "But what do we use for pictures, Brownlee? Waves?"

This was too big a story to let go just because we had no dramatic picture. I told friends on a newspaper and on another TV station. Both came out with top stories on the subject.

When the news director said: "Brownlee, I thought you said that we had an exclusive on that story," I replied, "We did. But how do we get a source to keep quiet about a subject after I tell him we are not going to use it?" He was not pleased — especially since another TV station made a great story out of it.

Informant

These stupidities made me only slightly annoyed. However, there was one which still causes my blood to rise each time I think about it.

During the civil rights revolution, several celebrities began to underwrite activities by inner city organizations to help them help themselves. Sammy Davis Jr. sent money to the infamous Chicago street gang known as the Blackstone Rangers (the name came from a South Side street) to open a restaurant. I'm certain I was assigned to do the story about that because many were afraid to have anything to do with the gang. The story showed how the gang had obtained a closed store, scrubbed it clean, painted it, and started with a menu consisting of a variety of beans — for 25 cents a bowl. The story was complimentary, and gave the gang a public relations lift.

Two years later, after the restaurant had closed (the gang had no business sense and the enterprise went belly-up for lack of profit), I got a telephone call from one of the gang leaders — the one I had interviewed on camera — asking to meet with me about a big story. I met with him on the South Side and he said he would give us the exclusive story in exchange for $5,000. He needed that amount as a down payment on a small farm in Michigan, and he needed it right away. He said the Chicago Police Department had a contract out on him and he wanted to take his wife and four kids out of the city.

Here's the story he was offering: A Chicago cop had a brilliant record for narcotics arrests in the Kenwood District. The reason was simple. He knew a prostitute in the neighborhood who would tell him who was pushing dope and how he could catch him or her. In exchange, the cop would allow the prostitute to operate without fear of arrest.

When he made a narcotics arrest, he would confiscate some of the dope and turn the remainder in with his report. The cop operated a "wet towel hotel," where couples could rent a room for two-hour stretches. A person who wanted to buy some dope would go to the desk and say he or she wanted to rent a room, and would put on the counter the amount to pay for the dope. The clerk would say: "Let me see if a room is cleaned up yet." He would go to a phone on the desk and talk to someone. Then, the clerk would return and give the room number to the person seeking to buy dope. When the purchaser arrived in the room, the heroin or whatever would be in a dresser drawer. In that way, no one would be caught exchanging money for narcotics.

The plan was this: I would do an off-camera interview with my informant. He would explain the operation to me. Then, with the arrangements I had made with a deputy police superintendent, we would go on the raid — cameras rolling — and have a fabulous story.

I was certain that this was a good story. First, we would have the actuality of the arrest. Second, we would have a first-rate story of how we broke up a narcotics operation. We would certainly win a national award for this story.

When I told the news director what I had, he snarled at me: "We don't do business with gangsters!" I asked, "Even if it means breaking up a narcotics ring and saving a man's life?" His retort: "No, we don't want it."

I couldn't give this story away. My informant did not trust anyone else.

Two weeks later, when I read in the paper that my informant had been shot by the police — six times — a half block away from where I had interviewed him for the restaurant story, I took the item to the news director and showed it to him. My voice trembled and there were tears in my eyes as I said: "Thanks a helluva lot. I hope no one ever sells you out like this." His face was flushed as I stalked out of his office. I went back to tell him: "Don't ever send me into that community again on a story — unless you want me killed, too."

I was bitter when he came to me about an hour later to apologize. I growled at him: "I know. You can't believe that a black man has enough intelligence to get a story like that." He answered, "That's not it. Les, I just don't believe that those people tell the truth. He could have been using us."

I shot back — "I want you to remember that when one of 'them' tells you that a theater you're in is on fire." As he turned away, he said, "I'll wait 'til you have calmed down before we talk again." We did not talk again for weeks.

Days of terror

There were specific advantages of having an African-American on staff, especially when there were racial flare-ups.

Once gang members were having a shoot-out at the all-black Cabrini-Green public housing project. I was not afraid to go into the Near North Side area and report what was going on. I never did find out who was shooting at whom. All I could report was the number and direction of the shots. No one was killed or injured.

But the advantage of being a black reporter was most evident in the days of terror after Dr. Martin Luther King Jr. was assassinated. I sat and cried openly as I watched the television report of the killing, not realizing that before the day was over I would be involved in two ways.

First, I did a "standup" in Soldier Field recounting King's famous visit there. There were tears in my eyes and my voice cracked as I tried to report my lines. I had to stop to regain my composure. The cameraman was set up in the stands. As I walked slowly off the field, he pulled back to show a solitary figure slowly walking off the field. We received rave notices about that presentation.

That night, all hell broke loose on the West Side, where Dr. King had lived when he conducted his walks in Chicago. Buildings were set afire, shots rang out everywhere. The sounds of women crying in their homes sent shivers down my spine as I tried to record the deep, deep sorrow of a people who had just lost their only living saint.

As I walked the streets and made notes of the total loss of direction a people could take, I was reminded of combat and the need to try to stay alive as I did my job. Thank goodness for combat experience.

There were very few people on the streets. Now and then, I would witness some youngsters looting a store and torching it. It seemed that they were angry at everyone and everything that was not owned by blacks.

I was scheduled to give a live report on the 10 o'clock news and I was having difficulty finding a telephone that had not been vandalized. I saw a police squad car, and they recognized me. I told them my dilemma. They told me to get into the squad car and they would drive me to a police station where I could make my report.

As we got out of the squad car, bullets hit the telephone pole just over our heads. We ducked and ran into the station. The shots continued, intermittently. I was ushered into a room upstairs where I could make my call to the TV station. The policeman turned the light on in the room. Shots immediately shattered the windows and knocked out the light.

I got Joel Daly on the phone and was making my report when more shots ricocheted off the walls. I got down on the floor and continued my report. Daly interrupted: "Les, what's that noise I hear?" I replied, "Those are bullets hitting the wall over my head, Joel." He came back with, "Be careful, Les, Don't get killed." I am supposed to have said, "Being careful was what got me through combat, Joel." Frankly, I was too frightened to remember what I said.

However, all who heard it said that my report was extremely coherent — even cool — under fire.

Two days later, a neighbor from across the street in Skokie came over to congratulate me. He told me how angry he was at several people in his temple who reported looting their own stores and making application to insurance companies. He said he almost wanted to punch one man in the mouth who is supposed to have said: "Hey, let the niggers take the blame for it."

No bullet holes

I was on the street following the killing of Fred Hampton, who headed the Chicago branch of the Black Panthers organization. The organization seemed a threat to the white power structure of the city, and especially an affront to the Cook County State's Attorney, Edward Hanrahan.

He had led a coterie of armed policemen to the house on the West Side where Hampton and some of his top lieutenants were asleep and ordered the occupants to vacate. Before they could obey, the police entered shooting. Hampton was killed during the firing. Hanrahan said that the police had fired in retaliation to shots by the Panthers. He pointed to what he called bullet holes in the door jamb as evidence.

I tried to find the bullet holes. All I found were heads of nails that were sunken into the wood frames. I found no bullet holes.

I learned another lesson: If you are black and seem a threat to the establishment, your life is in jeopardy. The realization angered me, but made me know that I was powerless to change it. Methods used these days are less brutal, much more subtle, but no less effective.

'68 convention

No one could have predicted the uproar that occurred during the 1968 Democratic National Convention in Chicago.

On the first day of the convention, there were a number of policemen in Lincoln Park. One was a former copyboy from Chicago's American newspaper who had been a friend of mine. He sidled up to me and said: "Watch yourself, Les, the word has been passed to get newsmen." When I tried to get more out of him, he shook his head and walked away. When I returned to the office, I reported what I had heard. Everyone laughed at me. However, before the evening had ended, three newsmen had been hit on the head by policemen. The office wanted me to tell them who had given me that information. I told them that if I told, the kid would be in trouble with his peers. I would not wreck our friendship by exposing him to harm.

The next night, a huge crowd gathered in front of the Conrad Hilton Hotel on South Michigan Avenue. From somewhere back in the crowd, someone threw a rock and hit one of the policemen standing in front of the hotel. A group of about a dozen policemen charged the crowd in front of them, swinging their billy clubs, and injuring some who were closest. This caused more rocks to fly, and the sergeant in charge of the detail called for tear gas. The canisters were fired into the crowd. That was the first of three nights that I got tear-gassed.

On the second night, National Guard troops had been mobilized and a group from my old outfit was deployed at 18th Street and Michigan Avenue as an unruly crowd marched south. The officer in charge gave the command: "Fix bayonets!" The troops obeyed. The crowd stopped. No one was prepared to be impaled on a bayonet. Then, from some place back in the crowd, the police fired more canisters of tear gas. The crowd began to run in all directions, screaming and coughing. I got a whiff of tear gas from that attack.

The next night, a group of policemen decided to clear the street in front of the Congress Hotel on South Michigan in the 500 block. About 20 policemen locked arms and began a sweep from Harrison Street north. An aged couple had just emerged from the hotel, and the woman asked her partner: "What's going on?" Both were bowled over by the marching police and left lying there, crying in pain. Once again, some police decided to use tear gas to clear the area. I was tear-gassed again.

After that, I was unable to keep food on my stomach for several days. I learned that once you have the police as an enemy, there is no hiding place or sanctuary. The police have the guns and the permission to shoot. What excuses they use later don't help pay your funeral expenses.

The '68 convention was later made into a Hollywood movie. Early in 1968, Haskell Wechsler, the noted filmmaker, started a movie which became "Medium Cool." The opening scene shows a TV cameraman taking a picture of a woman who has apparently been thrown from her car in what is supposed to be an accident. After he has filmed a series of shots, he turns to a crew member and said: "Now, you can call the paramedics!" The idea was to show that TV newsmen are so callous that they want to get their dramatic shots, even at the expense of someone's life.

The film showed a cocktail party given to help a female French journalist get some insights into the way presidential conventions are run in the United States. I was lucky enough to have a few lines in that scene. The film included a number of news people, and was set up to use their influence by way of promoting the film. Instead of actual cocktails, we were given weak tea to sip.

Rent strike

I did a story on a woman who was put out of her apartment on the West Side on the day before Thanksgiving. Her crime: she organized a rent strike in her slum building.

The tenants had been after the landlord to make repairs, which he refused to do. So, she went to the tenants, collected their rents, and deposited them in a bank account in her and the landlord's name. She sent him copies of the deposits and a letter, listing the repairs that were needed and stating that he could have his rents as soon as he made the repairs.

Les and his Channel 7 crew, 1972.

He went to the sheriff's office and got a notice of eviction. The sheriff's men put her furniture in the alley next to the building. Neighbors gathered, covered her furniture, built a fire for her in a 55-gallon drum, and sat and talked with her. After I made my report, I called the Salvation Army. Their workers picked up her furniture and other possessions, stored them safely, and gave her a place to sleep.

I learned a valuable lesson in law. A renter has no security unless that security is in the law. The renter has an obligation to pay the rent, regardless of the conditions of the building — unless the court says otherwise. She should have taken her complaint to the courts, and obtained a court order directing him to make the repairs. There was nothing in her rental-agreement that permitted her to withhold rents.

About two weeks later I received a phone call from a magazine editor in New York, asking me to write a story about the success of black business in Chicago. He would pay $500. I wrote it. I got my check.

The following week I got a phone call from the woman whose story I had reported. She thanked me for all my kindness, stating that she knew I didn't have to do that. Then, she asked if I had heard from the editor of the magazine in New York. I told her I had done the story. She told me that her "baby sister" was secretary to that editor. Suddenly, everything began to come together. It taught me a valuable lesson. Be kind to all people. You never know who knows whom.

Pay up or else

That was the same year that I got a call from the Nixon White House, offering me a job doing public relations for the chief executive. I refused. The next week I got a bill from the Internal Revenue Service demanding an additional $1,000. When I tried to find out what I owed the money for, I got nothing but a stern warning, "pay up or else." I realized that this was part of the Nixon vindictiveness that I had heard about. I paid. Years later, after he had resigned, the IRS sent me a $1,000 refund.

Gov. Richard Ogilvie also tried to hire me as his press secretary. I was not into politics.

*

Channel 7 was in third place among Chicago TV stations as far as the 10 p.m. news was concerned. Then, the station had a stroke of good luck. A new manager at Channel 2 demanded that Fahey Flynn, the station's top anchor, take off his bow tie. He was given an ultimatum, take off the tie, or leave the station. We rushed in and got Flynn. The very first week he was with Channel 7 our viewership increased by 15,000. It continued to grow after that.

Bill Fyffe, a news director who had done wonders at ABC's Detroit station, was brought in as the news director. He began to turn things around, including getting new outfits for all news personnel and crews. He seemed to appreciate my knowledge and promoted me to Education and Public Affairs Editor. Things were going well for me.

*

The FCC announced it was unhappy that we had no minority in any managerial position. The station had been searching for someone to take the job as Director of Community Affairs. I was summoned into General Manager John Sevarino's office and told I was going to take the job — or else. It meant taking a cut in salary, but since I had a mortgage and a family, I had no alternative. I became the first African-American to be a TV executive in Chicago.

My challenge was to improve the station's image vis a vis the community. One thrust I made was to convince Sevarino that there was nothing in our newscasts to give black youth any hope of a better future. I pointed out that we talked only about the bad in education. We were doing nothing to encourage high school dropouts to return and finish their schooling.

I got his go-ahead to develop one-minute spots called "Chicago Images." These were a series of interviews with former dropouts who had returned to school, received their diplomas and had gone on to some degree of success. These spots increased my popularity with youth in a way that I had not imagined. When walking down a street, I was frequently hailed by young people, who had hardly noticed me before. The response we got from the community was encouraging to the management.

*

I learned that the Schulze Baking Co., sponsor of the Peanuts comic strip, had arranged to give away packages of vegetable seeds as a promotion, in sets of six packages each. I arranged to get 80,000 of the sets and advertised that they were available to community groups.

We hired a horse and plow to dig up a field in the Woodlawn Gardens area so that residents could begin a garden. We gave a lot of the seed packets to a group on Chicago's West Side for the same thing. A group of nuns took some to plant in the depressed area where they lived and worked.

The community outreach program brought a great deal of good will to the station. My greatest success came when Sy Friedman and I decided to conduct a Scholarship Fair. I had asked our new general manager, Lew Erlicht, for permission. He said I could do it just as long as I did not expect the station to come up with any money to underwrite the effort. We tallied more than 24,000 attendees.

Emmy

I also helped win the station an Emmy for editorial writing. The editorial director had throat cancer and I took over writing the editorials while he was out. He died.

Lew Erlicht, at the 1975 Emmy Awards ceremony, accepted an Emmy for the editorials I had written "in memory of Con O'Dea, our former editorial director." I protested that I had written the prize-winning editorials and was told that I should understand the boss's motives in honoring a dead man. O'Leary later apologized to me and said that he knew that I had written the prizewinning editorials. He wrote me a letter confirming that — a letter that I had framed.

O'Leary's letter stated: "Congratulations on the Emmy for Outstanding Achievement in Editorials. I am aware that Lew Erlicht accepted the award in the memory of Con O'Dea. But please know that all of us at ABC are aware of your involvement in this area and that you were the writer/producer of the editorials that won the award. A tough call for Lew to have to make. I hope you can understand his charitable motives. With the outstanding success of the Scholarship Fair and now this wonderful award from your professional peers, it's certainly been a banner year for you."

Chapter 8

Discrimination

How is one supposed to handle racial discrimination? Should one tuck tail and run? Should one fight back with every legal weapon at one's disposal? If it's a merchant, should one organize a boycott to put him out of business? Should one laugh in the person's face and deride him for his stupidity? My Christian mother would smile at the offender and say, — as she left — "I'm going to pray for your soul." Most of the time when it happens to me, I smile and walk away. When the discriminator hurts someone I love, I'm tempted to draw his blood.

After a Sunday morning service at the First Congregational Church in Evanston, Vera and I decided we would have lunch at a new restaurant in the downtown.

We ordered bacon, eggs and French fries. When the waiter brought the orders, we saw that the bacon was raw, the French fries had not been cooked but smeared with grease, and the eggs were also raw. Vera shook her head. I picked up the check and headed for the cashier. The manager was standing at the cashier's station. I told him what had occurred.

He looked up and saw the waiter hurrying away with our plates. He told the waiter to halt and bring the plates to him. His face turned beet red. "I will not tolerate this in my restaurant. Get your things and get out. You're fired!" He turned to us, his face still flush with anger but his voice full of apologetic tone and said, "I'm so sorry that you had to experience this. I will not tolerate this in my place. Of course you can not pay for this. But please promise me that you will come again and please ask for me when you come."

He shook my hand and kept holding it as he repeated his apology as he walked us to the door. I promised him that I would return and we went home to eat. Somehow, the incident did not leave me feeling upset. I felt that the manager had handled it properly.

Several weeks later we did return. We did not have to ask for him. He saw us and came to us rapidly saying: "I'm so glad to see you again." He personally supervised our orders, and again, would not let me pay the bill. I thanked him, but felt so embarrassed by not having to pay the bill that I never returned.

I never felt too bad about his incident. I believe that was because I saw "justice done" immediately.

I didn't feel so magnanimous when Edgar Leach and Francis Bacone made tears come to mother's eyes at Evanston High School in 1932. Although, in retrospect, it was that act that triggered my move to New Trier High School and started my upward climb.

*

As a reporter with the Chicago Daily News, I covered a story in which a black woman had been discriminated against by a Woolworth dime store employee. The woman had answered an ad and went to the employment office and was given an interview. After she left, she remembered that she had left her gloves on the chair in the office. When she returned, she saw the employee tearing up her application. She sued, the employee was fired, and the woman got money in a lawsuit — and was given the job for which she had applied. That was another case in which I felt good that the culprit had gotten her comeuppance.

Movie

However, there is one instance of discrimination that hurts me even today. It happened when I was a reporter with the Chicago Daily News. I can't remember the name of the movie, but there was such a demand to see it that the theater was selling tickets for advance performances. I overheard Vera telling a friend that she wanted to see the movie. I thought it would be quite a romantic thing to take her to dinner at a restaurant near the theater and then to the movie.

I asked the Daily News film critic if he could get tickets. He picked up the phone, identified himself, and within a half hour a messenger had arrived with the tickets.

I telephoned Vera, and asked her for a date to dinner and the movie that she wanted so much to see. She was overjoyed. When we met, it seemed like a courtship starting anew, and both of us seemed elated and planning a happy evening.

We entered the restaurant and seated ourselves at a table. A busboy served us water and we waited and waited. Finally, the manager came to the table, and in a low voice said: "We don't serve colored here, would you please leave?"

Tears came from Vera's eyes, and I felt anger welling up inside. I stood up and said in a loud voice, "I didn't see a sign in the window saying that you do not serve Negroes in here. How in the hell was I supposed to know? You made my wife cry and I can't forgive you for that. I think you owe her an apology."

His face turned crimson and he asked: "Will you kindly leave quietly?" I retorted: "Why should I? Don't you want the rest of your customers to know that you don't serve Negroes in here?"

At that point, two couples who had entered at the same time as us got up and left. The manager was angry and started for me as if he was going to swing at me. I exclaimed: "Please do. It will give me reason to break your damn neck."

I said to Vera, "Come sweetheart, let's go before I break him into little pieces." We started out and then I turned and said: "How much do I owe you for the water we drank?" He said nothing, but hung his head.

That episode poisoned our evening. We didn't go to the movie, but drove silently home. There was no love-making that evening, nor for several others that followed. I kept trying to tell myself that I should forget it. In retrospect I realize that the incident was not too bad in that I didn't get hit — but it hurt the woman I loved.

I had a similar experience just a few years ago. Priscilla and I were out with friends and artists, Tom Seagard and Brigitte Kozma. The waiter pouring water into my glass deliberately spilled it all over the table and served everyone but me. Tom got more upset than I did. We left without getting my meal and I simply stated, "It was your pony tail, Tom!" The four of us enjoyed another restaurant.

"We"

The first day that Dr. Oscar Chute was superintendent of schools in Evanston's then District 75 was the day he hired Vera Lucile Brownlee. She signed a contract for $1,700 to teach the fifth grade at Foster School for a year.

Over the years as other vacancies occurred in the district's various schools, Chute appointed blacks to the positions. Such a practice had never occurred before, and the black community saw Chute as a champion of equal rights.

We had visions of his battling a defiant school board to hold to his position of integrating the school teaching staffs. Chute said there was no such opposition. In fact, on more than one occasion when he had made such an appointment, one or two board members said, "it's about time."

He and Charles Bouyer, the one black teacher at all-black Foster School, had become friends as a result of their discussion of the mistreatment of black soldiers during World War II. Bouyer was also athletic director for the all-black Emerson Street YMCA.

When Chute was asked to speak to the PTA at Foster School, he was apprehensive about appearing before an all-black group. After his talk, he asked Bouyer how he had been received. Bouyer said he was a great success — primarily because he used the term "we," unlike other previous speakers who had always said "you."

I speculate that Chute's upbringing in New England and his education at Colby College and Harvard University had failed to indoctrinate him with the gospel of segregation. So, his practice of appointing black teachers — and later black principals — was nothing more than trying to find good teachers to fill vacancies.

He and I had lunch together a couple of years before he died. He claimed he didn't deserve the laurels of a champion. We believe he does because he had the courage of his convictions not to go along with the racist practices that had been so long entrenched in the Evanston school system.

He sat in our kitchen in Skokie in the '50s, discussing with Vera and me how to get a black teacher into Lincolnwood School on Evanston's northwest side. Vera had been sent there once as a substitute teacher. The principal, Ms. Bassett, was shocked to see a black teacher sent to her school. She told the pupils, "Mrs. Brownlee will sit with you this morning until we can get a teacher for you." By afternoon, a white teacher was at the school and Vera had to sit in the principal's office for the rest of the day.

We told Chute that we knew a black teacher who looked white, and who was an excellent teacher. Her name was Barbara Lee. She even had blue eyes. He sent Miss Lee to Lincolnwood School. She was not only accepted, but the parents in the community came to revere her. She had been there about three years when the principal learned that her prize teacher was black.

The next year, the principal resigned. We always believed that she quit because she could not accept the idea of having a black teacher in her school. However, Chute said at the time she had resigned because she had cancer. She died in the year after her retirement.

In later years, we helped search for outstanding black teachers and had them placed in what had been all-white schools. Eventually, Evanston schools would have many principals who were black, and a black school superintendent, Joseph Hill, whose father was a pastor in the Church of God where my father had been pastor.

Another advantage of the desegregation of Evanston schools was that the real estate effort to keep areas segregated began to weaken. After all, if a family could not be sure to keep its schools all white, there was little reason to keep the housing community segregated.

Urban League

The Chicago Urban League had been limping along for years with an executive secretary and his secretary — and little else. Its budget was pitifully small — about $32,000 per year — and much of the executive secretary's time was spent trying to raise money in the black community.

When the board of directors of the league went to the annual convention in 1952 in Minneapolis, the Chicago Daily News sent me to cover it.

I knew that Edwin C. "Bill" Berry, executive secretary of the Portland, Oregon Urban League, had done a spectacular job of involving much of the Portland business community in that community. I sought out Bill and asked if he would consider moving to Chicago. He said yes. I recommended that he insist that the fundraising job be the responsibility of the board of directors, and that he be free to carry out programs. He was interviewed. He followed my recommendation; he got the job.

The CUL had never had an office before. This time an office was rented on the second floor of the Chicago Defender building at 26th and Michigan. Bill and I stood in the bare office and he said to me: "All right, you got me the job, now get me a secretary."

About a week before, an attractive friend from Evanston, Pat Walden, had asked me to find her a job. She had been secretary for the head of a savings and loan association. However, her boss was becoming more and more insistent upon her going to bed with her. He was indicating that unless she capitulated soon, she would have no job.

I sent her to see Berry. He liked her. She was hired. He said he had to get a letter from her previous employer. He showed me the letter he received. It stated that she was incompetent, inaccurate in her work, unreliable in attendance and just about every other derogatory thing he could say.

As Berry pointed out, with all these poor qualifications, her employer would have trouble explaining why she had received several pay raises, and been promoted to the top secretarial job in the company, and had kept her job for more than five years. "This letter is so transparent as to its vindictiveness that it is almost comical."

Bill and Pat developed into a wonderful working team. Pat's former boss did not give up. He kept calling her. I told her that I would get rid of his attentions. I telephoned him, told him that Pat and I were engaged and that if he didn't stop pestering her, I would go to his wife. If that didn't work, I said, I would personally beat him to a pulp. The phone messages stopped.

I was hired by the CUL to develop a newsletter to be used as a fund-raiser and enlist the involvement of businessmen to help in the cause. As a result of the success of the CUL newsletter, I was solicited by others to do newsletters. I eventually had four monthly newsletters.

Evanston Urban League

The more Bill Berry's effort showed white businessmen what their organizations were losing because of racism, the more those leaders wanted to see change. In fact, Berry had been very successful in getting some of these leaders on the CUL's board of directors.

We would follow the same pattern in Evanston, where we found that the vast majority of decent Evanstonians were against the kind of entrenched racism that had existed there for years.

Perhaps because of the obstacles Vera and I had experienced in trying to buy a better house, or perhaps because of the admiration I have for Bill Berry and his technique of friendly confrontation, I began to believe that Evanston needed an Urban League. I talked over the idea with Bill, and he agreed that we could establish a satellite chapter in Evanston. He would speak at our opening ceremony.

We rented space in the Fleetwood-Jourdain Fieldhouse in Foster Park and scheduled the meeting for late in November of 1960. I collected the names of

300 Evanstonians — about half black and half white. The late Mildred Robinson addressed the envelopes and mimeographed the invitations. A blizzard blew up on the night of the meeting. A tally of the attendees showed that 298 of those invited had shown up. Some brought relatives or friends. We had asked those who attended to sign up to work on committees. Almost all did.

Erwin "Bud" Salk became chairman of the program committee and began to arrange for programs that would expose some of the bigotry that had existed in Evanston for so many years.

He got a series of speakers to present their points of view, some of which angered the Evanston police department, especially when they told about police bigotry and brutality. Some of the speakers were leaders in the civil rights struggle. These especially angered the police, who actually roughed up some as they tried to enter. Many of Evanston's citizenry began to see what blacks had been talking about for years. They had not wanted to believe that their law enforcement officials had such a built-in bias.

*

One program pointed out the existence of an all-white caucus that nominated candidates for the Board of Education. The caucus had a rule that an organization had to be in existence for three years before it could become a member of the caucus.

As our organization approached the three-year mark, the rule was changed to read that the organization had to have existed for five years. It became apparent that the caucus was going to do its best to keep our organization out.

However, the caucus had not reckoned on being undermined by one of its own organizations. Each of the public schools was a member of the caucus. Orrington School — all white — had a black librarian. Her husband, who was greatly admired by the faculty at Orrington, was a candidate for a graduate degree at Garrett Biblical Institute on Northwestern University's campus. Orrington nominated him as a candidate to the Board of Education, and he was elected.

*

The Evanston Review reported on our activities. Suddenly, there was a groundswell of anger among white citizens, especially when they found that their finances were being used to support a segregated YMCA. The threat of withholding money from the Y caused the doors to swing wide open. Management began to beg some blacks to join, so that they could show that the organization was not segregated. Actually, not that many blacks wanted to venture into the bastions of white supremacy. They had already established their social and athletic milieu. But gradually, the more venturesome began to ease into some of the "white Y's" activities.

As reports of the threat to the Y spread, and as some of Evanston's leaders began to look at their other public organizations, more and more doors began to open.

As one leader explained it to me: "We have been so accustomed to being color-blind that we didn't notice that Negroes were being excluded. Some of us actually believed that they were not interested in belonging to these organizations."

Black alderman

One of the earliest efforts at change in Evanston came about with the election of Edwin B. Jourdain, a black Harvard-educated lawyer. When he announced his candidacy for alderman, about half the Fifth Ward was white, and half black. For years Peter Jans, a white man, had been alderman and no one had tried to oppose him.

But when Jourdain announced his candidacy, almost everyone in the black community was energized to see him elected. Many who had never voted registered to vote. Teenagers got busy campaigning for his election. He was sure of just about all the black vote, and his intelligence and charisma won a substantial number of white voters. He won handily.

His first foray was to stop Evanston theaters from forcing blacks to sit in the balconies. Also, he was instrumental in getting the police to stop some of their roundups of black youth. When the police made these arrests, he would appear and demand that they show him what evidence the police had to keep 15 or 20 youths in jail until the police decided to let them go. Needless to say, this did not please the constabulary, which had been telling the citizenry that it was protecting the city by putting all the bad guys in jail.

One of the community's allies was my dear professor Dr. Curtis D. MacDougall, who was also the editor of the Evanston News Index, a local paper. He was not infrequently approached by the city's racists to buttress their position. Once the police asked him to write an editorial advocating that the American Legion be deputized to be armed with clubs and stand on corners in the black community to "keep the niggers in their place." He refused. He said it was up to some of the leaders to make that recommendation, and he would comment on it editorially. When one of the leaders made that suggestion, MacDougall compared the idea to an army of occupation. The idea died a-borning.

In another instance of MacDougall's fairness, one of the white aldermen wanted the appropriation cut for funding the venereal disease clinic, pointing out that 90 percent of those using it were blacks. MacDougall's comment was that whites went to their private doctors for treatment, but poor blacks didn't have that kind of money.

He asked: "Where do these people work? Don't they work in our kitchens, take care of our children?" The appropriation for the clinic was doubled.

His willingness to champion human rights made enemies for him, enemies who would lie in wait to attack him from more protected bulwarks.

Expanded visions

Even Evanston schools began to change. Some members of the Evanston Urban League were teachers and volunteered to donate one evening a week to tutor students. Several churches offered their facilities for this program. The program started at three black churches, and served mostly black students. Eventually, the program expanded to eight churches — four white and four black — and helped both black and white students.

The league conducted a career fair, in which we had many people representing various careers and occupations to talk to young people about their futures.

Almost without exception, the applicants had limited visions about their futures. One teen girl, who was getting straight A's in chemistry, had no idea how she could make a career out of the study she loved. Fortunately, a representative of a chemical company was present, and found a college scholarship for the girl. Later his firm hired her.

I met a high school student who wanted to become an architect. His father said that since he knew of no black architects, he was not in favor of financing the boy's college education. I found and showed the father a number of blacks who were successful architects. He was surprised, and he changed his mind.

Many of the black girls spoke of getting jobs as secretaries, or file clerks. They had little vision of careers other than those. The career fair opened their eyes, increased their hopes that they could qualify to do more than those jobs.

Another feature of the career fair that we had not planned was the increase in friendships that occurred between the races. Interracial social events followed meetings to discuss and attack problems. Several interracial marriages resulted as a result of these friendships. Also, the friendships among high school teens increased, and the racial tensions seemed to diminish.

*

One day while we were living on Leland, Vera and I were visited by a representative of the First Congregational Church, asking us to attend and to consider joining their church. We visited, were warmly welcomed, and began attending. I became a member of the choir, and later was named a member of the board of Christian education of the church. Later, I was elected president of the Christian education board.

We were concerned about the curriculum, staff and facilities of our Sunday School. The church had a large building which had classrooms used only Sundays. The rooms were vacant the rest of the week.

I received a telephone call from a woman who was chair of the board of a local day care that served black children. She said the day care needed more space. I asked her to send me a letter asking to rent our church's classrooms Monday to Friday.

When I got the letter, I read it to the board. It hit like a bombshell. Some board members were sympathetic to the plight of the mothers who needed the service to keep working. But the idea of opening up the facility to several dozen black pre-schoolers in an all-white neighborhood frightened others.

After intense discussion, the board decided to ask the church membership to vote on it. One woman who lived across from the church school wrote that the presence of all those black children would be so unsettling that she would not be able to do her work of helping some 30,000 blind people nationwide.

The church community was asked to vote. Out of the hundreds of ballots, the vote in favor of renting the church school to the day care service won by two votes.

The church community came to witness the "invasion" and was impressed with the behavior of the children, and by the professional presence of those in charge of instruction. The church received a great deal of favorable publicity as a result of the gesture. As a result the day care people were able to raise enough funds to purchase their own building on the corner of Asbury and Emerson streets.

Second Black Family

Because Vera and I had been making more money, in 1959 we decided we wanted a better house. To aid in our search, we contacted John Bryant, Jr. We expected to locate a lot in our neighborhood and build on that. But we didn't find one. As we were looking in Evanston, a black family moved into neighboring Skokie, causing protests and police vigilance around the clock. They bathed the house in spotlights at night in an effort to prevent the threatened reprisals by white supremacist militants, none of whom lived in the community. The white family that sold the house fled the community because of the flak they took.

This squabble had barely died when Bryant asked us if we wanted to buy a house in Skokie. We were interested. A major reason was that our money would go further than it did in Evanston. And we found a house we liked on the same block as the other black family, the Jones'. But as we were preparing to move, we were contacted by an official in the Skokie administration, asking us to hold up on our move. The official said they feared that we were creating a ghetto.

We agreed to meet with the officials and talk. The meetings were scheduled at midnight in the village hall. At the first meeting, the police chief said that he didn't believe that he could provide protection for us if we moved in. I told him that I commanded a battery in the Illinois National Guard, and I could provide my own armed protection of my house. The idea seemed to frighten the police chief, who said hurriedly: "No, no. I'm sure we can get the protection."

The village manager offered a solution. If we did not move into that particular house, the village would help us find another house of comparable or better value. We agreed. There was one obstacle. We had put all our money into

Les and Vera hold a fundraiser for Gov. Otto Kerner in 1964. At right is friend Lily Venson, a Lerner Newspapers reporter.

the house the village didn't want us to occupy. We had sold our Evanston house, and had to vacate. The final arrangement was that we would move into an apartment in south Evanston, and the village of Skokie would pay our rent, pay for the storage of our furniture and pay an Evanston minister to help us search.

The minister showed us houses in Glencoe and in other areas of Evanston, but not a single house in Skokie. I told him that I was going to move into Skokie, and he had best get busy finding us housing there. We didn't hear from him again. It became apparent that his assignment had been to show us houses anywhere but Skokie.

We attempted to look at houses that appeared for sale, but each time we tried to look at a Skokie house it was withdrawn from the market.

I got some expert help from an unexpected quarter. One of the white members of the Evanston Urban League, Joseph Hackman, a professor of economics at Roosevelt University and head of a home building firm, came to us with a suggestion. He would shop for us and meet with us and tell us what he had found.

He met with us on several evenings to report what he had found. We rejected a number. But, finally, he found one that he felt had all the right features. The house had a large living room, a dining room, a large kitchen, four bedrooms — one off the kitchen for the hired help, a huge basement fully paneled and tiled all over, with a wet bar. We loved it.

So Joe Hackman bought it in his own name. He immediately turned it over to us with a quit-claim deed. He got financing from Oak Park Federal Savings & Loan Association. As soon as the loan firm learned what had happened, someone called from the firm to blast him for his move. He told the caller that this was the kind of thing that President John F. Kennedy had said he was going to take action against.

In the next mail, and without our having made any application, we received a payment booklet. Now, we had to go back to deal with Skokie officials.

We planned to move in the first week in January 1960. The village planned that move as if it were a military operation. An aerial photo was made of the entire area around our home. The names of every family in every house were printed on the photo. Each rabbi and each minister was contacted and asked to talk to their respective members to tell them of the proposed move, and to ask each family for its cooperation.

On midnight of the day before we planned to move in, Vera and I went to the house to make plans as to where we would place furniture. We were met by a detective from the Skokie police department who demanded identification before we could be admitted to our house. On every evening after our move in, one unmarked police car was parked down the block from our house on Keeler and one in a similar location on Grove.

The day of our move, we received visits from some neighbors who brought the traditional Jewish welcome — salt and bread. For the next six months, we were overwhelmed with invitations from neighbors who asked us to dinner, and who wanted us to know that we were welcome. Our biggest threat became one of obesity, as well as fatigue from too many nights out as guests of neighbors. Our next-door neighbors, the Fishmans, became very close friends. Lorraine has remained a particularly close friend.

We felt as if we were royalty in Skokie. At the same time, Vera was becoming a celebrity in the Evanston school system. During the summer of 1964, Vera attended summer school at the University of Wisconsin, where she worked on a master's degree in education. As a result of her work with teachers, Vera was appointed associate professor of Education at Northwestern, and placed in charge of screening all teachers from NU to the Evanston schools. Everywhere I went, I heard her praises. When I walked gown the street, I was known as "Mrs. Brownlee's husband." I was flattered to be considered that important.

Losing Vera

Each year, Evanston public school teachers were required to take a physical examination that included a chest X-ray. Each year for ten years, a small rise appeared on one of Vera's ribs.

In April of 1965, Vera underwent an operation to remove a cancerous spot on her lung. She had never smoked, and there was no history of cancer in either side of her family. We believe her cancer resulted from the radiation she was exposed to when she worked on the atomic bomb at the University of Chicago.

She seemed to recover well, attended summer school at U of W and completed her requirements for her MA in education. She started school in September and almost immediately began feeling ill. She was unable to keep food in her stomach. An extensive examination at Michael Reese revealed that she had cancer of the liver, and it was growing rapidly. She died Oct. 31. I was holding her hand when she breathed her last.

I was able to go through the motions of work each day, and would come home to a teenage boy who was overwhelmed by his mother's death. Laird would lock himself in his room and refuse to come out, refuse to eat, refuse to communicate with anyone. In addition to bereavement, I was haunted by the fear that I was going to lose a son.

"We're going to marry you!"

About two years later, George Collins, who had been alderman in the 24th Ward on Chicago's West Side, was elected congressman from that district. He developed the concept of a cotillion among the high school students in his district. He was able to get businesses to donate money for scholarships. He got Sears Roebuck Co., which had its headquarters in his district, to pay to film the entire process.

Collins got in touch with me to do the filming. I got one of my cameramen, Harry, and we produced a beautiful film. Sears had one of their PR people, Nikki Smith, work with me on the film.

After the film was finished, I got a fee of $2,000. I wanted to give some to Nikki, but she refused. I persuaded her to go to dinner with me at the Chicago Press Club. At dinner, she told me that she was delighted with her career, her life was going very well, and she had her son in a private school where he was doing well.

After dinner, I drove her to her apartment and met her 8-year-old son, Ray. It was instant love. We hardly knew each other before he was into my lap, hugging me, kissing me. Nikki said she was surprised. She had dated other men and he had never become close to them. Before I left, I invited them to visit me at my house in Skokie. They agreed. As I left, Ray yelled at me from the top of the stairs: "We're going to marry you!"

Laird was still deeply depressed, and rarely left his room. When Ray arrived, Laird came out laughing, joking. Laird and Ray acted like they had been lifelong buddies. We listened to the boys enjoying each other's company, and quickly decided then to take them to other places where they could enjoy being together. Soon, we were dating — just to watch the boys enjoy being together.

This went on for several months, and we were acting like good friends, with just a goodnight kiss at the end of each date.

In February Nikki got a notice from her landlord that her rent would be increased $15 per month starting April 1, 1968. She said she thought the increase was too much, and I agreed with her. That's when it happened. She asked: "Do you think anything will come of us, or should I sign the lease?"

Without thinking, I said: "Don't sign it."

For our wedding, we selected March 17 — two days after her 31st birthday. We arranged to be married in the small chapel of the Congregational Church where I had been a member for many years.

Nikki's parents had been Unitarian, and she said she felt uneasy attending the Congregational Church. So we switched and started attending the Unitarian Church in Evanston, which had a long-standing reputation of liberalism.

*

One Sunday early in 1970, we drove past 1308 Asbury Ave. in Evanston, a shabby 22-room house with a stucco exterior and a Swiss Chalet motif. The sign on the lawn stated that there was an open house. Nikki suggested that we go inside. I told her that there was no way that I could afford to buy the house. "All the more reason we should look," she said. I worked like a madman to figure out how to afford the house, then worked just as hard to restore it.

I learned that the house had been owned by Frank Lloyd Wright's dentist. Wright is supposed to have remarked that he did not like the way the house was designed. His dentist told him to change it. My challenge was to try to restore it in the Frank Lloyd Wright image.

When Abner Mikva decided to run for Congress from our district, we held a fund-raiser in the house, and were able to accommodate 503 people who paid $5 a head. I suspect that some of them were just curious as to what improvements had been made in the house.

The twins

I had legally adopted Ray. But Nikki insisted that she wanted a baby — and that because of my infertility we should try to adopt. We went to the Illinois Children's Home and Aid Society and were approved for adoption. We were told a baby girl would be coming to us.

The day we went to pick up the child, we were told that the baby had a mental defect, and since we were college graduates the agency thought it would be better to get us one that had a chance of going to college.

We were on the way out the door when the social worker said: "There are, however, twin boys, if you would be interested." I turned on my heel and returned to her desk. She told us that the twins had been adopted at birth. The adoptive mother was too young. She left the twins in a laundromat, and telephoned her husband to come to get them. He brought them back to the agency. The boys were 16 months old.

The day we went to get them, Ray carried one to the car and I carried the other. The Hispanic couple who had adopted the twins named them Jesus and Jose. We re-named them Curtis MacDougall in honor of my "adopted" father and journalistic idol, and Gerick Thomas. There was a family we had met at Circle Pines Center whose last name was Gerick, and Nikki had lost a brother named Thomas.

Les with sons Ray (left), Curtis MacDougall and Gerick Thomas.

Though we had a full family life, it was not enough to maintain our marriage. One day Nikki confronted me: "Do you know it has been six months since we had sex?" I had no idea how to check. I was not interested in sex, only sleeping and improving the house.

Nikki also accused me of not having any ambition because I was not interested in becoming an anchor person — like Warner Saunders. I tried to explain to her that I was a reporter, and that I considered that the highest achievement in journalism — the nation needed people who could dig out facts and get them to people so that they would be able to make more intelligent decisions about issues concerning their lives. These discussions began to drive a wedge into our relationship.

Next, she accused me of having an affair. But that made no sense because there was no time it could have occurred unless I was doing it at the office or on my assignments. Then, when that didn't hold together, she told neighbors I was impotent.

*

This was about the time that I did a story on the Cancer Prevention Center of Chicago. This was an agency that gave clients two full days of intensive testing.

I thought this was a good idea, so I went through the two-day test. My physician was Frank Spencer, my high school chum with whom I had shared a foxhole in Italy. When he got the results, he telephoned me and said: "They found evidence of blood in your stool. Why not go to Evanston Hospital and have them check it?" I did.

A surgeon said he found incipient cancer about the size of the head of a pin. He took out 13 inches of my colon just to be sure he had gotten it all. To this day I have doubts as to whether any cancer at all had been found. In 1994, Dr. David Winchester had to spend over two hours removing scar tissue caused by the operation, which had obstructed my bowel and brought me close to death.

While I was recuperating in the hospital from the original surgery, Mother died in California March 17, 1974. That knowledge hurt worse than the operation. I couldn't be with her those last precious minutes. I could not even attend her funeral.

Board of Education

I left Channel 7 in 1975 and went to the Chicago Board of Education as director of media relations at a salary that was $10,000 greater than I was earning at Channel 7. I did a couple of things I remember with pride. I started a crusade to improve reading and to recruit tutors. I also conducted an editorial writing contest for high school students. And I started a city-wide spelling bee, which still exists under the sponsorship of the Chicago Tribune.

Finalists in the spelling bee and editorial writing contest appeared on television, resulting in the Board of Education sending me a letter of commendation. As a result, I was asked to become a member of the Chicago Board of Education, and became its first African-American member.

Chapter 9

FAIR and Fiasco

About this time, I got a phone call from a New Trier High School chum. Lowell B. Snorf, Jr., whom we called "Snorky" with the irreverence of teenagers. He said he was on the board of the Illinois Fair Insurance Commission, which the Legislature set up because minorities were having difficulty getting fire insurance at reasonable rates.

The legislation created an insurance pool in which insurance companies doing business in the state had to participate. The plan was known as the FAIR plan, an acronym for Fair Access to Insurance Requirements. Snorf asked me to handle publicity for FAIR, and I agreed.

I got in touch with Charles Rice, an artist I had worked with on a project for the South Side Merchants Association. He had wanted to set up his own ad agency. This would give him the nest egg to start his own business, I thought. He designed a very attractive ad. His design showing an African-American gentleman was striking, and got the approval of the board immediately. We got a list of all the minority owned newspapers in the state, and began placing the ads.

Fire prevention

It became apparent that placing ads alone in newspapers was not enough. What was needed was a program that worked to reduce the number of fires in inner city communities. I approached the FAIR board with an idea that it approved. I ordered several hundred T-shirts with the inscription: "Outlaw Fires in Lawndale!" These T-shirts were handed out to youngsters through Ald. George Collins's 24th Ward precinct captains.

I hired women to go into the schools, showing films about how to prevent fires, and getting youngsters to look for sources of fire hazards in their homes.

The result was that fires were significantly reduced in Lawndale. We were unable to document the percentage because the fire department's districts overlapped, but anecdotal evidence showed a significant drop.

In Woodlawn we conducted the same campaign. I had learned that the Blackstone Rangers were setting fires in the community so that landowners could collect insurance for the burned buildings. I had no direct contact with the leaders of the Rangers, but I met a community leader who did have connections. He reported to me that the gang leaders would accept $800 per month to set no new fires in Woodlawn. I took the offer to the board. The board agreed. So, each month I made a check payable to my contact, who cashed it and delivered cash to the gang leader.

We also distributed T-shirts with the insignia "Outlaw Fires in Woodlawn."

The result: fires were reduced more than 90 percent. The alderman, Bill Campbell, made a report to the City Council, which gave the FAIR plan board a plaque honoring the success of its fire prevention effort. Board members were ecstatic, and all took turns in giving me a pat on the back. No one offered to give me a raise.

Trouble

When I first started placing ads for the FAIR plan, I took copies of the ads to the manager, Lloyd Shook, to show that the ads had been placed and to support my billing. After a while, he told me that he had no place to keep them, and suggested that I find a place to keep them. I trusted Charles Rice. He said he could store them in the basement of his office. I made the mistake of never checking back with him.

I made another mistake that was to bedevil me later. He was divorced, and his wife was trying to get money from him. So, when I made the checks out to him to pay for the ads, I would go with him to my bank so that he could cash them without his wife knowing how much he was making.

About that time, the FAIR plan changed managers. The new manager, checking results of fire prevention in East St. Louis, found out that ads had not been placed in the local newspapers for about a year or more. He called me in and asked me about it. I checked with Rice and asked him to get me copies of the tear sheets for ads in those newspapers. He couldn't find them.

When I reported this to the new manager, he had already checked with other newspapers and found that they had not received orders for ad placements in a long time. In fact, no one seemed to have received ad placement orders for some time shortly after Rice had hired a man with apparently no advertising experience, Joe Coste.*

Rice and I were ordered to turn our records over to the U.S. district attorney's office. Rice said he had no records. I turned over all my records, including check stubs and bank deposit slips.

Rice and I were indicted on a charge of using the mails to defraud. The checks that I cashed for Rice so his wife would not find out about his earnings were used as evidence of a conspiracy. The money paid to the intermediary to give to Woodlawn gang leaders also backfired. Federal investigators wanted

* Not his real name

him to name the gang leaders or face a charge of income tax evasion. If he named them, he would be dead, and I knew it. To keep him alive, I had to act as if he had never received any money.

When the indictment came down, I called attorney Don Johnson for help. His law firm took my case. He received copies of statements made by Rice, and I was shocked to learn what Rice had said. He denied receiving money for ads. He also denied placing the orders for another project we did, comic books about fire prevention.

I remembered the man who handled the printing for the comic books. Don went to see him. The man said that he had printed at least 80,000 of the books. He said that he would be willing to make a deposition to that effect.

Don reported to the prosecutor's office that we had a witness. A day later the printer said he had a visitor who threatened to cripple him if he testified. His description of the man fit that of Joe Coste.

We located Coste's estranged wife, and she said he kept two sets of books. She would testify. We reported this to the DA's office. She was beat up so badly that she was hospitalized.

It was at that point that we realized that Coste had a pipeline into the DA's office, and that we could no longer share information with that office.

Rice and I were named as co-conspirators. Don's plan was to ask that the two of us be separated so that we could bring evidence that Rice was guilty and I was not.

A threat

On Sept. 10, 1979, a week before I was to go on trial, I came out of my office in the Chicago Board of Education office and was confronted by a small teenager. He asked me for a cigarette. I gave it to him. As he lit it, he said: "I was on a bus and two men in the seat in front of me were talking. The tall guy said if Les Brownlee testifies against me, his twin sons are going to get hurt bad." I grabbed the teen by the collar and demanded that he tell me who said that. He said he didn't know. He said he knew me from television and came to give me the warning.

Instead of going to lunch, I went to Don's office and reported it. He said: "It's clear that that message was sent by Joe Coste."

I went to talk to a friend from the National Guard who was a deputy superintendent of police. He said: "Les, we can give your sons protection, but if they want to get you, they'll eventually get you. The police would have to move in with you, go to school with your boys. The boys couldn't play outside any place where they could be within rifle shot. And this would have to go on for years." I realized the impossibility of this kind of arrangement.

*

Nikki had asked me for a divorce, and would be taking the twins with her. Both Laird and Ray were old enough that they were out of the house.

She said she didn't believe me when I told her that I was not guilty. She said I had taken the money and put it into the house. She said that the house would have to be sold and that she would take the boys away from Evanston. About this time, she moved her lover into the house on the ruse that he would make improvements to increase the house's value.

The idea of her lover being in the house didn't bother me. I was far more concerned about the welfare of the twins. However, I was upset when she threw all of my newspaper clippings in the alley. They were rained on and irreparably damaged.

Confession

When the date of the trial came, the DA's office told my lawyer that if I pleaded guilty to one of the 15 charges, the office would ask for clemency. I didn't want to do this, but I could see that if I testified about what I knew the boys would be exposed to violence.

I confessed to a crime that I had not committed. I cannot remember a more painful experience than making that confession.

(I later wrote a letter to the judge explaining why I had taken a plea. The judge had been puzzled at the sentencing hearing and said, "Something is wrong here.")

*

I was sentenced to one year in the Metropolitan Correctional Center, which meant I went to work in the daytime and returned to spend the nights in a locked dormitory. There were a few chores, like polishing the marble floors when it was my turn, but the inmates who were there were convicted of "white collar" crimes, and were considered no threat to anyone in the community.

My first night in the MCC, I smiled while lying on my cot. I was free from Nikki.

*

Curtis MacDougall had attended my trial and wrote a letter of reference to the court, as had dozens of my friends and colleagues. After I was released from the MCC in 1980, I had no place to go. Dr. Mac invited me to join his household.

I was eager, and to pay for my lodging I cooked for the family. Dr. Mac's wife, Genevieve, a brilliant junior high school teacher in Winnetka and organizer of archaeological digs in Kampsville, Illinois, liked my cooking but complained that I put weight on her small frame.

Life in the MacDougall home was good. I moved into the very bedroom that Priscilla MacDougall and I now share. At that time, Priscilla was married and living in Madison, Wisconsin, where she was employed by the Wisconsin Education Council. I was already in love with her, and my love has only grown stronger. More about that later.

Another vote of confidence from the journalism community came soon afterward. I was asked to become a member of the Board of Directors of the Chicago Headline Club, an organization of 400 or more Chicago journalists.

Chapter 10

Radio and Teaching

I had not been in the MCC a week when I was offered the post of manager of a 10-watt community radio station on the South Side. The pay was $800 per month.

Around the same time, I received a telephone call from Lya Dym Rosenblum at Columbia College, asking me to teach one course. I considered her a friend and liked the idea of sharing some of my experience with students.

So, I was able to run a radio station and teach while serving my sentence.

The South Shore Community Organization had received FCC approval to operate the station. I was asked by the president of the board to develop a program that could address their concerns, needs and wishes. The main problem I had was that there was no one on the board who had any experience in the media, and no one who had any experience in business. Some had conducted successful bake sales or rummage sales for their churches, but there was no one there who had any experience raising the thousands of dollars that would be needed to properly run such an operation.

Programming consisted heavily of music because it was cheapest and easiest to obtain. However, we had some significant interviews with people who were leaders in the community, and in state and national government. I was able to schedule these because I was known in the media.

A weekly half hour devoted to local poets was quite popular.

There were news shows, featuring information of and about the community as well as state, local and national news.

Also, I conducted a class at the radio station to train students in news writing and broadcasting. Some of these trainees went on to successful careers in broadcast news.

Because the South Shore community was proud of its racial integration, a great deal of our radio programming reflected activities and concerns of these groups. The station became an important unifying agent in the community, and gathered an important audience.

Money was short because we did not accept advertising. And the problem of raising enough funds to meet weekly payrolls was like a soap opera in itself.

In an effort to get beyond the meager fund-raising efforts of bake sales and car washes, I presented to the radio station's nine-member board of directors a plan based on one of the strengths in the South Shore community: the churches. I proposed having a coalition of the churches and the radio station rent Soldier Field and produce a gigantic choir festival. Each church would sell tickets to its members, friends and others. Each church would have a section of the audience and would place its choir in the center. Soldier Field could seat 100,000 persons, but I had no doubt that with proper promotion we could fill the place. Each church would receive 70 percent of the profit from its sales, and the radio station would receive 30 percent.

Most thought the plan was too ambitious; most were afraid that our group could not get the support from the churches. One member of the board was a pastor of the church around the corner from the station. He thought it was a brilliant idea and argued loud and long in favor of it. A few others on the board felt that it could succeed.

Not only did that majority vote down the plan, I was ordered not to mention it to the churches in the community.

The pastor of our neighboring church was so angry that he decided to conduct his own choir festival in his church and turn the proceeds over the station. His effort resulted in a standing room only crowd in his church, and he gave me a check for more than $5,000 he had raised in his lone effort.

Other members of the board were impressed both with his success and his generosity. The board gave him its official thanks, and started to argue about how to spend the money. I was never more disgusted.

Harold Washington newspaper

During this period Harold Washington, at the time 1st District congressman, and I planned a newspaper that would be circulated primarily in his district. It would be issued once a month, and would feature activities being conducted by the Black Congressional Caucus. Most of the activities of this important group of legislators never got into the mainstream press. Only when there was some conflict did the mainstream press consider reporting the activities of those embroiled.

Our plan was to hire top flight editors and reporters to handle the principal stories, and to use advanced journalism students — mostly black and Hispanic — to write the lesser stories and to act as interns for the top journalists.

Because Washington was representing the 1st District, which included all of downtown, we did not feel that we would have trouble getting adequate advertising.

Les speaking at a journalism event (undated). Seated beside him is his mentor, Curtis MacDougall.

As far as distribution was concerned, we believed that this would best be done by the precinct captains in their respective wards. This would allow them a monthly opportunity to contact their voters and would give the voters information not readily available in the mainstream press. Also, we thought that many members of the Black Caucus would want copies to circulate among their constituents. This could develop into a national medium.

Then our plan suddenly ended: Washington was drafted and ran for mayor. So, we tabled our plan. It is still a good idea.

Chapter 11

Priscilla

Priscilla Ruth MacDougall first came into my life during my years of marriage to Vera. At that time, there could not have been any other woman — let alone a cute schoolgirl I thought of as my "little sister."

My first awareness of Priscilla as a possible candidate for my heart came in the late 1960s or early 1970s. She was a lovely woman who smiled at whatever I said.

I can't remember how many times I proposed. I did almost every time the two of us were alone. Her refusals were always gracious. She treated my questions as if they were jokes.

One of my boldest approaches occurred in the Circle Pines Center near Kalamazoo, Michigan. The center was established in the late 1930s by a group of liberals who believed in the cooperative movement. Priscilla was there in 1971 on her honeymoon with her first husband. I caught her alone and said, "You know, we should be married." She shook her head and smiled as if I were joking. I never gave up dreaming and trying. I guess I finally wore her down.

I was considered a member of the family. Once, at one of Dr. Mac's parties, one of his former students asked Bonnie, Priscilla's younger sister, who I was. Without hesitating, she replied: "He's my brother." I did indeed feel that close to the family. And during Dr. Mac's final illness in November 1985, I sat with him in his room and the intensive care unit as a member of the family. I held his hand when he was in a near-coma. I felt that this was my father, and I was watching him breathing his last. I felt as if my own life and soul were draining away. When he died, once again I felt a huge void in my life.

After Dr. Mac's death, Priscilla — by then divorced — and I were thrown together arranging the memorial service, disposing of some of his books and papers, and arranging for scholarships in his name at Columbia College,

Eastern Illinois University and Roosevelt University. We also developed the Curtis D. MacDougall Freedom of the Press Foundation at his alma mater, Ripon College in Wisconsin, which honored him a few months before he died with Ripon's highest medal of honor.

One Sunday night early in 1986, as she got out of the car to enter a small restaurant, called the Main Café, where we often ate while we discussed disposing of the estate, she said something about how she saw me as her brother. I retorted, "I see you as my wife." After dinner, as I climbed out of the car at my apartment, I said again that she should think about marrying me. She didn't respond with a "yes" or a "no." However, she telephoned me from her home in Madison and asked, "Are you serious about this marriage business?" I replied, "Absolutely."

She wrote me a long note about the difference in our ages and our careers in different states, Illinois and Wisconsin. But she was talking! She began planning the wedding.

I had not even kissed her.

Because she could not put up with my junk-filled, cat-fumed apartment, we searched quickly for the perfect house. We found it on Dobson Street in Evanston, and moved in during October 1986, almost a year before we were married.

Before we announced our engagement, Priscilla conferred with her nieces, Jennifer and Stephanie, if they approved our union. Priscilla would not even think of marrying anyone whom her nieces did not like. I had been doing everything I could think of to endear myself to them. They approved.

Their mother, Bonnie, was already on my side. She had told Priscilla, "Dad respected him and Dad could smell a phony a mile away." For months after that, every time I saw Bonnie I'd say, "Thanks, Bonnie."

When we told Priscilla's mother, Genevieve MacDougall, on Mother's Day in 1986, Priscilla's mother exclaimed with an air of understanding unique to her, "Well, I guess you've got my daughter."

I had loving relationships with them all. The girls stayed with me when Priscilla took her sister to Mayo Clinic in 1988, and Priscilla and I took care of her mother during her last two years.

My sister, LeJeune, said after she met Priscilla, "You've got a really, really good one this time." My brother, Raymond, thought no one was as good as Priscilla.

Up to that time, I had been expecting someone to veto our marriage. I felt I was floating on a warm, pink cloud in a fairyland. All marveled at my luck. I still do.

The wedding Sunday, July 5, 1987 was at the Woman's Club of Evanston — the same one which did not want me to enter, even as a photographer, when I was at Medill decades earlier. We came up with a list of 570 people to invite. The club could accommodate only 350. We cut the list judiciously, and 315 attended.

Lester Mondale, a Humanist writer, Evanston Unitarian Church minister

Photo by Bob Black

The wedding of Les Brownlee and Priscilla MacDougall, July 5, 1987.
From left: Monroe Hutt, Carole Brewer, Laird Brownlee, Marletta (Marty) Martenia,
Ray Brownlee, June Hutt, Les Brownlee, Priscilla MacDougall, Genevieve MacDougall,
Bonnie Cottrell (Beck), Stephanie Cottrell (Bryant), Jennifer Cottrell (Miller).

in the 1930s, younger brother of Vice President Fritz Mondale and dear friend of Priscilla's father, asked: "Do you, Lester, take Priscilla to be your wife, to love and to cherish, to honor and to comfort, in sickness or in health, in sorrow or in joy, in hardship or in ease, to have and to hold from this day forth?" I eagerly exclaimed, "Oh, but I do!"

I had waited a long time to say that to her. I was 72. She was 43.

All the men in the wedding procession wore tartan ties — the MacDougall Clan uniform. Priscilla, Jennifer and Stephanie had purchased them when traveling in Scotland that April. Bagpiper Will Norman led us into the reception at the Orrington Hotel. Dr. Mac's ashes were in a box at the reception.

I promised to never call her Mrs. Brownlee. She promised to stay out of the kitchen.

What was my fascination with Priscilla based on? Of course she was — and still is — a good-looking, sexy chick. But she has the high intelligence and integrity that I had not encountered in any other woman since Vera.

I marveled that in her profession as a champion of school employees, she makes school district administrators and other attorneys cringe.

Tom Seagard, who with his wife Brigitte Kozma are both outstanding artists and owners of the Mill Road Gallery in Sister Bay, Wis., says of Priscilla: "She saved my life!" That's only one piece of evidence of her legal wizardry. As a surprise for my 85th birthday, Brigitte did a fine portrait of my mother Rosa and me at about the same age, using my 1993 Hall of Fame picture.

Many of the Wisconsin education personnel Priscilla has represented over the years have become close friends, especially Della Tesch of the Appleton

Public Schools and Jim Wittlieff (and his wife Barbara) of the Greendale School District, Vicki Marg of the Marathon schools, Helen Hurdis of the Clinton School District, and Jeanne Griffith, former head of the University of Wisconsin-Whitewater.

A poem I often recite to Priscilla, from Shakespeare:

Let me not to the marriage of true minds
Admit impediments. Love is not love
Which alters when it alteration finds.

Les and Priscilla

Chapter 12

Columbia College

By 1982 Columbia College wanted me to teach full time, so I handed in my resignation at the radio station and took the full-time college post. I had been teaching journalism one night a week. That income — (that weakly income) — helped pay my bills, which included child support for my sons.

Lya Dym Rosenblum, who was in charge of the journalism program, had hired me to teach the one course. The course I designed was titled "The News Reporter," and outlined the qualities needed to become a good one.

After the first semester, I noticed that the curriculum lacked two courses which I considered essential: Media Law and History of Journalism. When I pointed this out, Lya asked me if I would teach them. I agreed, and suddenly I was teaching three courses part-time.

Columbia students brought a wide variety of abilities to their studies. Some had been out of school for many years and their verbal skills showed a lack of proper use. Some evidently never learned the proper use of the language, but wanted to learn journalism.

Some of these students expected instructors to teach them all they needed to know in a three-hour course, once a week for 15 weeks. At the other end of the ability spectrum were recent graduates of better high schools whose verbal skills had been better honed. But all needed the assurance that the instructors would perform an educational miracle and turn them out as competent journeymen in four years of college.

At first I thought it was wrong to take students' money and promise to make them journalists when they exhibited little ability. I soon learned that I was wrong. It was almost impossible to predict who would do the extra study to develop the necessary skills.

Of course, some felt that just being in journalism classes would somehow qualify them as reporters. Several of these ended up as bus drivers for the Chicago Transit Authority.

However, others surprised me. This was true of some women who had had a child, were working and raising that child alone, but who wanted to prepare for a career in journalism.

Sometimes when a baby sitter was sick, a mother would show up in class, child in tow. Some would study long hours at night to get their lessons, after working a long day.

One who enrolled in my class, Rachel Morrow, was six months pregnant. When the baby arrived, she sent me a telegram at the college to announce it was a boy. A few at Columbia wondered if I was the father. She returned to Columbia Oct. 16, 2004 to praise me at my professor emeritus ceremony.

Not all students finished in four years. Some had to drop out and work for a year and save money for tuition. Some had money enough to go only part time. However, they continued to return.

One such woman took seven years to finish. Her writing had not been very good when she started. However, she practiced all the time. She had no trouble getting a job when she graduated.

One came to me in her senior year to say she was pregnant and would have to drop out. She said that sometimes during pregnancy a woman get sick, and she might have to miss classes. I told her that if she had to miss classes, I would permit her to make up the work. I refused to let her drop out. She had a big smile on her face as she faced me at commencement.

One man had been a policeman but wanted to be a reporter. He said to me, "My writing skills ain't too good, but I'll work hard to learn, if you'll help me." We worked hard together. He graduated on schedule, and got a job in a small city near Chicago. Several years later, he received an award for outstanding reporting. I felt as if I had won the award.

Lessons in teaching

To my students I applied certain lessons I had learned, some inadvertently. Once as a young man I had followed a lovely young woman home with pure lechery in mind. I'm sure she was not unaware of my interests.

At her home she told me that her 12-year-old bother was a member of a Scout troop that was losing its scoutmaster. She lowered her eyelids seductively and asked, "Would you help out temporarily until a new scoutmaster can be found?" My lechery had goaded me into agreeing.

I met with the nine 12- and 13-year-olds and found that all were having trouble with math. I reasoned that it was because math meant little to the areas in which they lived.

I asked: "Which of you is the fastest sprinter?" The bully in the crowd insisted he was. "How would we find out?" I asked. All agreed we could hold a race. We did. The smallest kid turned out to be the sprint champion.

"If you are a manager of a baseball team, why is that important to know?" I asked. No one seemed to know. I pointed out that if a manager was lining up his batting order, he would want to have the man who was fastest in the position where the team might need someone to bunt. They could follow that reasoning. I went forward from there: "Can he get to first base before the third baseman can field the bunt and throw it to first base?"

They began to see what I was getting at. So, we went to a baseball diamond to get the answer. My girlfriend's brother (who was the fastest sprinter) beat out all the attempts to throw him out. But most important, they could see that math mattered a great deal in sports.

We did the same thing with football and basketball. Soon, using the stop watch I left with them, they were timing and computing everything they could think of. Suddenly, math became very important to them. As their interest in math grew, my lechery seemed to diminish.

I realized that I used a basic principle in salesmanship: Let the customer handle the merchandise. By the time the new scoutmaster came, the boys were into all sorts of math games.

Another three lessons I brought to my teaching I learned in the Army.

While we were still in basic training, we were told that we were going to have to hike 25 miles in eight hours. I went to my sergeant to plead: "I don't think I can hike 25 miles in eight hours." He replied: "Maybe I can't either. But tomorrow when we start out, you walk with me, and I'm going to try to keep putting one foot in front of the other. Let's see where we are at the end of eight hours." At the end of seven hours and forty-one minutes, we had traversed the 25 miles.

Another lesson: Never underestimate the ability of anyone who is motivated. The blue-eyed general who commanded the 80th Division Artillery when we were transferred from Fort Custer, Michigan to Camp Forrest, Tennessee in 1943 told our commander, Lt. Col. Marcus Ray: "Frankly, Colonel, I don't believe that Negroes will ever make good artillerymen." Col. Ray's response: "General, we hope to prove you wrong." The general retorted, "Your men don't look healthy, Colonel. Tomorrow morning I want to see if they can march the four miles in 50 minutes that the army requires of healthy troops."

Col. Ray assembled the entire battalion and told the men what the general had said. Fire kindled in the men's eyes. They would show him. We hiked two miles out and turned around and hiked back, singing at the top of our lungs "This is the Army, Mr. Jones," the lyrics of a contemporary popular song. We did it in 37 minutes.

The general's face was florid. He would show us. He ordered the soldiers who seemed most tired to do push-ups. All performed gallantly. The general knew he had lost that round. Col. Ray gave all men the day off.

Another lesson started when I was first commissioned as a second lieutenant in Fort Sill, Oklahoma. The black soldiers who fought to get in line to salute the first black officer they had seen told me that my commission was not for me alone. I was part of many men's dreams — we were part of the same team.

Les teaching at Columbia.

In return, I gave each a voice in the command. If the unit was given a problem, I would assemble all my officers and non commissioned officers and outline the problem. And I would ask: "Has anyone any idea how we might best go about tackling this problem?" At first, men were reticent to make a suggestion. But when they saw that I was serious and would take their suggestions seriously, more and more men would volunteer suggestions. Also, when a corporal — the lowest non-commissioned officer rank — made a suggestion and I took it, the men began to respect me all the more.

*

I tried to make this arrangement with the students I taught. I told them — and I meant it — that once they were my students, they would always be my students. I tried to establish a personal bond with each student, so each knew that I was there to help them succeed. In this manner, many came to me with personal troubles. I tried to help each find solutions.

One student with a problem was a promising young lady who came to me at the end of the first semester of her senior year. She was in tears. Her father had just told her that because he had lost his job, he would be unable to pay for her last semester in college.

Priscilla's mother had started a $500 a year scholarship to outstanding editors or reporters on the college newspaper. I saw to it that she got that scholarship. I arranged for her to get a loan for the balance of tuition. One week after graduation, she had a full-time job. Susan Jancowski, now married and living in Washington State, has had a successful career.

The shortfall I found most prevalent among students — the good and the not-so-good — was lack of confidence in their ability to succeed. Thus, my job was the same as the coach of a junior high school team. Not only does one have to teach how to do whatever is the job, one has also to assure the kid that he can do it.

Not infrequently I discovered a student — most often female — who demonstrated exceptional ability. I asked this student: "May I take you and your mother to lunch some day?"

At the luncheon I explained to the parent that the student had shown exceptional ability in journalism, and I wanted to enlist the parent's cooperation in making the student's career a success. In each and every instance — and there have been at least three dozen — the student has gone on to become a success.

Perhaps I have been fortunate enough to enlist all the power in the family to help the students succeed. One told me that the talk with the parent was instrumental in preventing her parents from divorcing. "When my mother told my father what you had said," she told me, "they stopped arguing and started planning what each could do to help me. In less than two weeks, all of us were united in seeing that I got a good education. They even started dating again."

"I am great!"

My challenge as an instructor at Columbia was to be more of a coach than one who merely showed how to do it. So, I developed some tactics.

In my advanced news reporting class, which came after lunch, I made the class stand, stretch and repeat individually, as I pointed to each: "I am GREAT!" One student wrote in the college newspaper later that she at first had thought the practice was silly. However, before the semester ended, she felt that she was great, and tried hard to live up to that belief.

*

My syllabus for Advanced News Reporting required each student to submit a minimum of ten stories to media for publication. The first required each to write a letter to the editor and turn it in in an envelope addressed to the selected publication, and with the correct postage. I graded the letters and put them into the mail. Class members were surprised to see how many were published. This exercise made them read the newspaper, in search of their letters.

In my most advanced news reporting class, Covering Urban Affairs (which I based on a course Curtis MacDougall taught at Northwestern, Reporting Public Affairs), the final project required each student to write a feature story to be submitted to a publication. Each student had to turn in the feature to me in an envelope addressed to the editor of the publication with the correct postage. In almost each class one or two were sold. In one class, four were published.

*

Priscilla and I, in an effort to narrow the gap between student and professional, gave two parties a year until the turn of the century when we brought it down to one a year. It's something Dr. Mac did from 1948 until his death in 1985.

The Curtis D. MacDougall Party is held the last Saturday in November. Priscilla teaches one course on Saturday afternoons — "Law and Society" — and we invite all our students to attend. We invite also members of the media and others so that students rub elbows with editors and reporters. Some make important contacts that lead to jobs. The idea is to reduce the apparent barrier that many see between student and professional.

*

My students made it clear that efforts by the "ruling class" have been effective in creating a feeling of inferiority in females and minorities. Many believe that they cannot, or will not be permitted, to succeed because "the man" will try to stop them. Therefore, why try? My challenge is to get students to believe that they can succeed despite "the man."

This is especially difficult to convey to some women. The first exercise I gave all students in my beginning classes was to write their obituaries. I told them I wanted them to dream, and dream big. In their obituaries, many women identified their crowning achievement as being the wife of someone of importance — such as "wife of anchorman Joe Smith." Not a single male student identified himself as the husband of an outstanding woman. Both women and many of the minorities seemed to be unable to escape these psychological shackles.

These kinds of psychological barriers made me believe early that I must do whatever I could at Columbia College to prepare students for careers in journalism. I received offers over the years from other institutions (including the University of Kansas) to take positions at as much as twice the salary. I resisted.

TV writing

Most students we received wanted to major in broadcast journalism — specifically they wanted to be in television. The majority of these were females who somehow had visions of being on air, and having an exciting life with a big salary.

They felt that we were making a mistake to tell them that they must learn how to write — even for broadcast. I tried to coax my students into communicating with someone who has made it, to ask them what is needed and how best to prepare. A few followed my suggestions and were amazed to find that what we had been telling them is true.

One example is Chicago's outstanding Anita Padilla, who rose steadily to her present position by working in small stations in Moline, Ill. (a job I got her through Priscilla's mother's cousin Al Uzzell, the station manager there) and

Orlando, Fla.

I emphasized the importance of their getting stories published. Many people who do the hiring ask applicants to submit clips and references. But many students feel doors will open if they just get a diploma.

I have used the true example of an attractive female who squeezed through the broadcast journalism sequence in the 1980s. She applied to a number of stations, but was unable to convince any that she had enough skills to warrant hiring her. Starting in 1994 she began to pester me with demands to use my connections with television stations to get her a job. My response was always the same: "What can I tell them that you can do?" I suggested that she take a few more courses to develop the necessary entry skills.

A full load

By the early '80s, I had been teaching three 3-credit courses during the evenings as a part-time instructor when the staff of the college's newspaper, "The Columbia Chronicle" went on strike because of their adviser. The newspaper staff asked Dr. Lya Dym Rosenblum to assign me as adviser. She asked me if I would take over. I agreed. That meant I was teaching five courses as a part-time instructor. A full load for an instructor is considered to be three or four courses.

The syllabus for the newspaper sequence required that students who wanted to work on the newspaper have a B average and take certain beginning reporting courses. Entrants then took a 2-credit course on principles of the newspaper along with a 4-credit practicum on producing the newspaper.

Daryle Feldmeir, a retired top editor of the Chicago Daily News, was named the new department chair. He made a few changes to the curriculum, but agreed with the syllabus for the newspaper sequence.

At the time, all full-time instructors in our department were former newsmen from the Chicago Daily News. They included Eric Lund, a former assistant managing editor, and Nick Shuman, a former foreign news editor.

The part-time faculty consisted of many outstanding practitioners who taught courses in the areas where they were working. Most part-time instructors were selected because of their eminence in their specialty. For example, Bill Gaines, Pulitzer Prize winner for the Chicago Tribune in investigative reporting, was teaching investigative reporting.

Undoubtedly, one of the outstanding features of Columbia's journalism program was — and probably still is — the availability of internships for students in their junior and senior years. Because there are so many news outlets in the Chicago area, and because the college has so many connections among its full and part-time faculties, internships come easily. Many of these lead to full-time jobs, either directly, or through referrals.

It was our experience that the graduates who averaged a B or better had little trouble finding employment and advancement. Those whose grades averaged C or lower had more trouble.

Productive days

Those were halcyon days for the department, and I wanted high school journalism students to know about the quality of our offerings with our faculty of distinguished journalists. In addition to teaching classes, journalism educators have an obligation to develop a strong "farm team" in journalism among high school journalists — and especially among minorities.

I discussed with Feldmeir a high school newspaper contest to encourage the student journalists. He agreed, and I developed the program in conjunction with the Chicago Headline Club, the local chapter of the Society of Professional Journalists.

The J Department handled the administrative part, and the Headline Club did the judging. Award certificates would be signed by the heads of both units. The contest showed that the best endowed high schools tended to take home the most prizes. There were exceptions. Kenwood Academy, in the shadows of the University of Chicago, often had winners. On one occasion, DuSable High School had a winning newspaper. In most instances, inner city schools didn't even submit entries because their advisers didn't believe they had a chance.

Awards were given for the best three in each category: news reporting, feature writing, sports writing, editorial writing, in-depth reporting, photography, art-work, and overall excellence. The first year of the contest drew about 30 entries, not much of a turnout. I lobbied for an outreach program that permitted me to go to an inner city high school once a week to help that school improve its journalism program. I couldn't get other members of the Headline Club to volunteer to do likewise. Some expressed fear of the "dangers of the inner city" — specters that their reporting had created. Nevertheless, the number of entries grew each year.

My experience teaching high school students at Columbia College's summer institutes drew more favorable results. More than a dozen enrolled in journalism courses, most at Columbia, and have gone on to successful careers in journalism.

Gangs

We held high school seminars on the college campus between semesters. The Headline Club provided the speakers. We began to get more applicants from all around the area. However, we were still receiving too few minority candidates.

Some of the teachers in the schools from which the minority candidates might come suggested that major deterrents for male candidates were street gangs, which were always recruiting. Those who refused to join a gang were subject to punishment, including death. Also, once in the gang, the youth's activities were dictated by the gang. So, if the gang leader had not given permission for the youth to attend these "out-of-turf" functions, he would be subject to severe punishment for attending.

One high school journalism teacher told me that gangs determined such basic things as attendance, as well as any other activity a leader might wish.

This control would explain why so many schools had such poor attendance records, and why test scores were so low.

"There are many youths in our communities who don't want to belong to a gang," she said, "but death could await them if they don't. People who criticize our youth for their shortcomings should be aware of the ominous threat gangs are in our communities."

This made me recollect an encounter I had with a teen gang when I was reporting on a student riot at Crane High School on Chicago's West Side for Channel 7. I was confronted by three gang members as I prepared to do a standup next to a brick garden wall. The gang leader demanded: "Who in hell gave you permission to be in this 'hood?" One member of the gang was standing with his back to the brick wall and to my left. The leader was to my right and slightly in front of me. The third was behind me and slightly to my left. I handed the microphone to my sound man as I said to the leader: "I did not know where I should go to get permission."

As I spoke, I turned to my left and grabbed the youth behind me and slammed him into the youth whose back was to the wall. Both sank to the ground with a groan. The leader, to my right, saw what had happened and ran.

My white crew was amazed, and relieved. The cameraman asked, "How did you know what to do?" I told them, "These punks operate on a power theory. If we had given in to their power play, they would have done whatever they wanted with us." We left the two on the ground groaning. I received word later at the office that I had better not return to that 'hood.

The episode reminded me how uninformed were so many who castigated black youths for not attending classes. When I would point out the kind of problems these youths faced, those afflicted with an overdose of naiveté would state: "Why don't they call the police?" My response: "Call the police? The gang members would be gone when the police arrived, but within the next few days something severe would happen to the youth who called the police."

In one instance, a mother said she was going to call the police. For days after that, her house was vandalized. Her windows were broken, glue was poured into her front door lock, feces were strewn across the door mat, two dead cats were hung on her front door.

The police began a systematic drive-by watch on her house. They caught a culprit. It was her son. At the police station he said the gang leader ordered him to vandalize his own home. If not, the gang would see that his mother had a serious accident. The mother sent her son to live with a relative in another section of the city.

Successful campaigns to get rid of the gangs in any neighborhood involve the total community and the police. In one case, each time a teen did something that was anti-social, the police were called and the offender was arrested and jailed. Some people in the community swore out warrants and appeared at trials at which the accused was tried. The aggressive behavior by an angry community caused the gangs to run for cover — to seek more passive communities.

Some believe that a law should make all members of a gang guilty of conspiring in any crime proved against any one member. In each such instance, any gang member would have to prove that he had no way of knowing that an antisocial act was being planned.

Others have suggested the creation of a "hotline," which a youth who is being coerced could call to alert authorities. It seems inconceivable that a society could be brought to its knees by a group of youthful terrorists.

$1,000

When things seemed to be going well in the J Department at Columbia College, Daryle Feldmeir was attacked by a rare disease that caused physical and mental deterioration. His death had to be a release.

I did not know how to accept Nat Lehrman, the new department chair. He had been president of Playboy magazine.

I don't want to believe that his actions against me were based in racism, but I have searched for reasons to explain them. He took me out to lunch right after he arrived and immediately asked me, "When are you going to retire?" He thus set forth his attitude toward me. (He retired almost ten years before I did.)

When a new office for the college newspaper was being designed, Nat never spoke once to me about it. Instead, he held frequent conferences with the editor — who was visibly embarrassed by his not talking to me.

Lya Rosenblum told me she was trying to get more of the better full-time teachers to teach classes in summer school. She said that she was planning to offer an additional $1,000 to each. She asked me if I would agree to teach under such a condition. I agreed.

The following week, Nat announced that he was removing me as adviser to the newspaper and was going to give me $1,000 to teach our introductory course, Introduction to Mass Media, because I had a reputation of being a strong teacher. This would keep more students in the journalism sequence. To this date I am waiting for the $1,000.

Headline Club

In 1989, I became the first African-American president of the Chicago Headline Club. I won a national award for the chapter.

When I was Headline Club president, I was approached by a woman reporter for a community newspaper who wanted to know where she could see copies of the winners in the Peter Lisagor Contest, sponsored annually by the club and named in memory of the brilliant former Washington correspondent for the Chicago Daily News.

Our practice had been to farm out entries to the various chapters of the Society of Professional Journalists to judge. The Chicago chapter reciprocated by judging their contests. These chapters sent us the results, but did not return the entries. As a result, we didn't have the entries.

Les, late in his career, hard at work at Columbia.

I wrote a column for our newsletter suggesting we needed to change that policy and acquire a place to display these winners so that others could see them. Nat sent a memo accusing me of conflict of interest because the college had planned a residuum where communications could be exhibited. If he had checked, he would have known that I had offered to give material to our school, but was told it was not in a position to accept it.

On no occasion did he ever apologize, or admit he was in error. I had long before labeled him as an enemy and was cautious in all my dealings with him.

Earlier, when I was involved in working with high schools, I had been given additional student help. He took away my student help. I think he expected me to come crawling to him to beg. I did not. Instead, I worked late at the office, or went in on Saturdays to get the work done. He came in one Saturday and found me hard at work collating some mailing material. He asked, "What are you doing here?" I replied, "Some grunt work that has to be done." He seemed disappointed. I went further: "Someone has to do the dirty work. I'm glad I'm qualified to do it." He left without saying another word.

I suspect he was bothered by the fact that there were students who went to him singing my praises, or that high school teachers told him what a great help I had been to them on my own time.

Replacements

As the Daily News alumni retired, Lehrman brought in some excellent replacements. He hired Don Gold to head the magazine sequence and Rose

Economou to head the television sequence. Don's magazine students consistently won national awards. Jeff Lyon, a Pulitzer Prize winner from the Chicago Tribune, took charge of the science writing sequence. I was given the title of "Outreach Coordinator," whatever that means.

The three years after Lehrman retired were also difficult. Three staff members, one not even tenured, traded off acting as acting chairs until 2002 when Nancy Day, of Boston, was recruited by my esteemed colleague Rose Economou and hired to restore order and move the department into new quarters, quarters which will be housing a convergence journalism center named in part for yours truly.

The college had earlier lost the chance to hire another Boston woman as chair in 1994. Some on the faculty, who supported her candidacy, felt the administration had not hired her because she was female. I spoke out against the college's not hiring her and the paucity of women in department chair positions at the college.

One of my students, Bob Chiarito, wrote an article for the Columbia Chronicle about my concerns about the college's not hiring the first Boston woman and the lack of female administrators at the college. The college president denied the charge. However, my mentor and then Dean of the Graduate School, Lya Dym Rosenblum, immediately hired three new female administrators.

I sent her a thank you, meant not just for hiring the women, but for everything she had done, and indeed continues to do, for me personally. Dr. Rosenblum is one of the truly great people I have had the privilege of knowing.

Hall of Fame

Priscilla and I were at our time-share resort, "The Rushes" in Door County, Wisconsin in early 1993 when I returned a phone call from Dr. Jerry Field, who said: "Congratulations, Les! You have been elected to Chicago Journalism Hall of Fame — without a single dissenting vote." I stood speechless, and handed the telephone to Priscilla. I had never in my wildest dreams imagined that I would receive such an honor.

For days afterward I wondered if it were true. I went over my career and tried to evaluate each achievement to determine if I deserved the honor. I did not convince myself, but was not going to refuse it.

Maybe it was because I was the first African-American to be hired by any of the major Chicago daily newspapers? Or, maybe it was because I was the first African-American to be an on-the-street reporter? Or the first black local TV reporter and then executive? My Emmy in 1975 for TV editorial writing? Also, I was the first and only African-American to be president of Chicago Headline Club. Or what about the Scholarship Fair, the Minority Job Fair? Even as I totaled all my apparent achievements, I was still unconvinced.

If I was excited about the honor, Priscilla was ecstatic. First, her father was named to the Hall of Fame; now, her husband. She decided that I needed a new suit for the occasion — and she needed a new outfit. When we returned to our

Evanston home, our close friend Christine Shuyke Linnell and her husband Charlie had had a huge banner printed with the inscription: "STOP THE PRESS! CONGRATULATIONS!" The banner had been fastened to the molding just below the ceiling in our living room. Then came telephone calls and letters of congratulations from friends, former students, acquaintances. I was overwhelmed.

Priscilla gave the nomination speech — as she had done for her father. I gave my acceptance speech. I told of some of my experience with racism in Evanston and at Evanston High School and much of my history. Here is the conclusion of my remarks:

"America, in her magnanimous generosity, rewards those of us who are black with a cornucopia of obstacles. Perhaps it is to determine which of us are strong enough to survive. Those who do survive are much stronger than all who have not withstood the heat in a similar crucible — or who have no understanding of the same. Like a male who wonders what childbirth is like.

"I only know that when such obstacles arise, I see Rosa's pretty face, tears streaming down her cheeks, and I have the determination to continue the struggle.

"Each time I won an honor, she would smile at me and say, 'Oh, I'm so proud of my big boy'!

"Tonight, I wish she were here to put her arms around me and say, 'Oh, I'm so proud of my big boy'."

Chapter 13

A Fairy Tale Life

This book came about because people kept telling me I should put on paper the stories of my life.

Priscilla says the exact date of origin of my efforts was an evening in 1990 with the late NU professor Jean Hagstrum and his wife Ruth in their Evanston home. "You must do it, Les," Hagstrum had said as we sat over dessert and coffee.

From that evening on, Priscilla became insistent. She suggested I take a sabbatical. It had never even occurred to me, although I had been at Columbia College since 1979, that I could take a semester off just to write. Teaching and Columbia College had become my life, and the thought of writing full time again had simply not occurred to me.

But, the first day of the spring semester of 1995, the year I turned 80, I put paper in my typewriter at 9 a.m. sharp and started writing. Priscilla was impressed.

When I started writing about my fairy tale life during that sabbatical in 1995, I expected to end my story with my induction into the Chicago Journalism Hall of Fame in March 1993.

However, other responsibilities kept interrupting my writing, and seven years rolled by. Priscilla urged me to take a second sabbatical to finish this book. I planned to spend several weeks at our timeshare, The Rushes, to write.

The weekend of March 9, 2002, we were in Madison where Priscilla was working on a major case.

On that Sunday, I found myself unable to breathe. Just as Priscilla was preparing to leave for her office, I staggered into the living room. Not more than 15 minutes later I was in the emergency room at Meritor Hospital and immediately admitted with congestive heart failure.

Not long after we returned from Italy the next month, I was admitted to Evanston Hospital and, on May 6, 2002, a defibrillator was inserted. When the doctors called Priscilla into the recovery room, I was still half-enjoying a nice sleep in the hospital bed. To get me to move, Priscilla asked the doctors standing beside my bed how long I should abstain from sex. A doctor responded, "six weeks." My eyes flew open and I exclaimed, "Six weeks? That wasn't part of the deal, take the thing out."

As all the recovery room attendees roared with laughter, Priscilla gloated, "got ya."

I call the bump in my chest "Suzie," the nickname we gave the big cannons in WWII. It did not give me a blast until just after midnight on Sept. 30, 2005.

*

The Chicago Headline Club has always been my "pet" professional organization and I sensed toward the end of the 20th Century that it again needed some rejuvenation. I had not been able to get to as many board meetings and events as during my presidency because of my bad back and knee injury (from the 1939 Wisconsin/Purdue football game which we won in the last two minutes, 14-13 from a score of 13-0). I saw that an enthusiastic technology reporter from the Chicago Tribune, Christine Tatum, was to become the next president. I seized the moment and took her to lunch.

In 2005, Christine, by then working at the Denver Post, was elected next president of the Society of Professional Journalists, the organization to which I was the first African-American member when a student at Northwestern in 1949. I will tell the tale of how the annual Les Brownlee Journalism Series was initiated, by this remarkable go-getter, in her own words:

> I forgot all about the bland cafeteria food before us when Les started talking about ways to launch dynamic programming that would excite working pros and inspire student journalists. We brainstormed and devised all sorts of clever ideas. And then reality hit, and I was left staring into my soggy broccoli again.
>
> "They're all great ideas, but how do we pay for this, Les?" I asked. He smiled that mischievous smile of his, and passed me the slip of paper he had stuffed into a pocket. It included the name and number of Les' longtime friend, Art Nielsen Jr.
>
> "Is this the Art Nielsen of A.C. Nielsen? The guy behind the Nielsen Family Ratings? Nielsen Net Ratings?" I asked. "You know him?"
>
> "Just give him a call," Les said.
>
> I did, and Mr. Nielsen didn't hesitate to give the Chicago Headline Club $15,000, one of the most generous gifts it had ever received. The primary stipulation, Mr. Nielsen said, was that money had to be used to honor his friend.
>
> "From there, the Les Brownlee Journalism Series was born."

As of this writing, the Headline Club is preparing for the 2006 Les Brownlee Series as well as preparing to host the 2006 national convention of

Les, late in his life, with young friend Elihu Haque, son of friends Elizabeth Conant and Fareed Haque.

the Society of Professional Journalists. Each year, a part of the series has been the Lifetime Achievement Awards banquet to honor many of the great Chicago journalists.

Billy O'Keefe, of the Chicago Tribune, designed the logo for the Les Brownlee Journalism Series after he wrote in the Columbia Chronicle that I, at 85, was the greatest teacher he ever had.

As if the Brownlee Series were not enough, my dear friend Tom Ward, a fellow student of Dr. Mac's at Northwestern, endowed an annual contribution to the Columbia Journalism Department in my name around the same time.

The National Association of Black Journalists decided to give me a life time achievement award in 2002 and in 2003 Eastern Illinois University made me its journalist of the year. The Chicago Journalists Association, formerly the Press Veterans and headed by Allen Rafalson, honored me with its Lifetime Achievement Award in the fall of 2005.

I let Priscilla convince me to have knee surgery and to retire at the end of the 2003-2004 academic year. I retired July 1, 2004, earlier than I had expected, from the institution Priscilla and I both love and believe in. On July 3, Priscilla had me on an Alaskan cruise ship.

Professor Emeritus

How much can a poor boy take? But lo, as if so many happy professional endings were not more than enough, Columbia College made me its first

Les' emeritus ceremony at Columbia.

Professor Emeritus.

The ceremony was emceed by Nancy Day and a former student, NBC's Anita Padilla, Oct. 16, 2004. Rose Economou, former students John Kass, Jim Sulski, Lee Bey, Danielle Haas and many others helped make the evening a epitomic event in my life. Columbia College president Warick Carter bestowed the emeritus status.

Retirement and emeritus status came only after I knew the journalism department was in good hands with the selection of Nancy Day as a department chair.

As I have written, after I was inducted into the Chicago Journalism Hall of Fame in 1993, I thought I had reached the pinnacle of my career and had planned to end my autobiography with that event.

After my emeritus ceremony in 2004, my reaction was the same. When I made a few brief comments at the event, I stated that all the accolades were like a "pre-obituary." I meant that I got to hear all the nice things about me long before I died, which I planned to be when I was in the triple digits age bracket.

In mid-2005, difficulty breathing led to a diagnosis of lung cancer. I started on a drug called Tarceva, which diminished the tumor in a lung. However, other physical problems occurred, such as embolli in a lung.

While I shall probably not live, as did George Seldes, to write as a centenarian plus five or six, and while I frequently quote my brother Ray's statement "You can't get out of life alive," I tell Priscilla not to cry before the funeral.

I do not usually feel old despite my frequent comment: "Getting old is not for sissies." I look forward to going to our timeshares in Wisconsin and Florida and visiting the Hotel Glavjc in Torno, Italy again.

These last 10 years, since I was inducted into the Journalism Hall of Fame, have been the "happily ever afters."

And, my dear son Laird and I perhaps have a cookbook or two to write after I get my handwriting in shape signing this book.

I will keep you posted.

Lester Brownlee died November 21, 2005, in Evanston Hospital.

A portrait of Les and Mother, by friend Brigitte Kozma.

The most lethal poison is doubt

By Les Brownlee
Chicago Defender, May 28, 1977

One of the most lethal poisons to infect the human system is doubt — energy sapping doubt.

I have seen it invade a man's mind, undermine his confidence in himself so that he was unable to function on his job, as a father, or even as a husband.

I have seen many people, well-heeled financially, who were prepared to take their lives because this poison had completely undercut their confidence in their self-image.

Evidence of how widespread this soul-sapping illness is can be found on just about every corner in the inner city – as well as in the bars and in the boozing, drug-taking culture throughout suburbia, too.

When a person begins to seriously doubt that he can achieve any worthwhile goals, he is in trouble. Athletes who have demonstrated their winning abilities have been overtaken by this sickness just before an event, and have given the poorest performance of their careers.

This same poison is undoubtedly responsible for more inmates in mental institutions, jails, welfare rolls, as well as along the nation's skid rows.

It is as contagious as the bubonic plague – and frequently just as deadly. For when you have killed a person's will to try, you have destroyed his usefulness as a person.

My great concern is not only for the great bulk of men and women who show signs of this life-taking sickness, but especially for the youth who are struggling feverishly to stay afloat in a sea of this infectious ooze.

How does one convince youth to keep trying when they are surrounded by evidences of failure – when they can't get any kind of job.

Think what an effort it must take to talk kids into getting their lessons when they have a serious doubt that the effort will give them a leg-up on a better life, especially when they are surrounded by adults who have given up on trying.

This may be the modern day replacement for slavery – a process specifically designed to keep a very large number of people in economic servitude. Remember, if they don't try, the slavemasters don't have to worry about competing with them.

Just toss enough bread to these people who are locked in slavery to keep them alive, fighting among themselves so they can't unite, and spending their little money for food, rent, clothing and whiskey.

This system can continue to work ONLY as long as it is possible to keep the vast majority of the people doubting that they can achieve, doubting that they can pull themselves up out of this life-sapping rut.

The challenge for us is to keep presenting a positive image of success in front of all who are afflicted, with special emphasis on our children, telling them over and over again that we love them, and assuring them that they can succeed.

We've got to assure them that the struggle is not going to be easy, and try to help them in every way we can – with every resource we can muster. We've got to help them build big dreams, and work to realize them.

And we can start right now by selling the idea of reading – reading for everyone, not just the youngsters in school. Let's be certain that we always carry something to read – and read it.

Let's be sure that each of our children spends some time, every day, reading. At home, let's set aside a period during which everyone reads – every day.

That one activity alone will give us a HUGE headstart.

Acknowledgements

When Les was admitted to Evanston Hospital on October 18, 2005 with pulmonary embolli, his autobiography had already been edited by the publisher, Les had reviewed every word of the edited book and made some changes and comments to some of the edits.

Everything except the acknowledgments, that is. He had saved those for the last because he was baffled as to how he could get everyone in. Walking on "a slippery slope" he called the task.

When we sat down in his hospital room to put the acknowledgments together Les started out: "How about this?"

"Following is a list of the people who threatened to sue if their names were not mentioned."

"Oh, Les," I groaned.

"OK, take this then," he said:

"Also, a list of the husbands who threatened to sue if their wives' names were not deleted!"

Although the four yellow, legal sized pages of acknowledgements we put together that afternoon got lost in the shuffle of papers from the hospital to press, those two quotes were on a separate piece of paper I had put aside, not thinking they would ever be used. But, publisher Ed Avis chuckled when he heard them and said, "put them in."

First and foremost, Les acknowledged and thanked Ed Avis, the publisher without whom this book would never have seen publication. He and Susan Stevens, his editor, to whom Les was also grateful for the hours she spent reviewing old "Ebony" and "Sepia" magazines for which he wrote in the '40s and '50s, are as fine a publisher and editor that anyone could find anywhere.

Les also acknowledged the assistance of Della Tesch, a retired Appleton Area School District teacher and dear friend. Among other feats Della somehow transferred all of Les's typewritten copy (much typed at the Hotel Glavjc in Torno, Italy, as shown on the jacket of this book), to computer and disks. She taught him how to use the computer to complete writing the manuscript.

And, he also acknowledged me, for my part in making the book a reality. And, of course, his son Laird.

Then, Les proceeded to thank people from the various parts and times of his life, in an organizational manner similar to that which I later used for his Memorial. He primarily thanked his mother, Rosa Latimer Brownlee, whose love and teaching were central to forming Les's wonderful personality and character.

I know that those four pages of names includes Les's thanks to:

His childhood siblings, particularly his brother Ray and sister June, both of whom played a mean football ("Go with the ball, June, run!" Les often reminisced), but sisters Gladys and Agnes too who taught him the joy of reading, poetry and silent films!;

All his childhood friends (his "gang," carried on in a sense by the son of one of the members, Hecky Powell, owner of the famous "Hecky's" barbecue in Evanston);

His New Trier High School friends, primarily Art Nielsen, Connie Clough Ratcliffe, Mary Frances Badger Bridewell ("Badgie"), Mary Evelyn Sundolf, Chuck Percy, Bud Riley and those who made possible the final Class of '37 Reunion a few years ago (their motto: "65 and Still Alive");

His New Trier High School principal, the late Matthew Gaffney, who made it possible for Les to enroll in New Trier High School where he could, and did, blossom and excel;

Virtually everyone in the Chicago Headline Club and Society of Professional Journalists, from Paul Davis to the newest member, but with a special thank you to Christine Tatum, current president of the national organization, for creating and continuing the annual Les Brownlee Journalism Series in 2002;

A special thank you to the one and only Helen Thomas for kicking off the first of the Les Brownlee Journalism Series in 2002 with an insightful, outstanding speech about the state and role of the media today;

The many, many journalists he worked with in his life as the original "convergence journalist," working in all areas of the media from print to movies.

Les thanked his many colleagues and supporters at Columbia, including Lya Dym Rosenblum who brought him to the college; the late president Mike Alexandroff, professor and co-teacher Robert Edmonds, and Journalism Department Chair Daryle Feldmeier; current Professors Rose Economou, John Erdman, Glenn Graham, Zafra Lerman, Pangratios "Pan" Patacosta, Louis Silverstein and Lillian Williams; the current chair of the Journalism Department, Professor Nancy Day, and the current president of the college, Warrick Carter, and many others I simply can't remember;

He also thanked the two sabbatical committees which he recalled being chaired by Caroline Latta who granted him sabbaticals in the spring of 1995 and 2002 to write this autobiography;

Les thanked our Evanston housemates Mark Staller and Edward Thatcher who have lived with us in our Evanston home since 1975 and the early '80s and been there to help Les at any time. There were only 2-3 falls, and Mark and Edward were right on the scene. Les also thanked John Brown, who has helped keep the house running since he came to Evanston from Jamaica in the early '80s when my parents were still alive;

Les also thanked all those who made the book a reality by making his last few years so happy, although he no longer did all the cooking, with Sunday night get-togethers of stimulating conversation, laughter, good food, wine and cheer, including Robert Chiarto; Nash Castaneda; Ernest and Marlene Castle; Pat Dalton; Emil Dankster; Dorothy (Dottie) and the late John Diggs; Lorraine Fishman; Danielle Haas; Fareed Haque, his wife Elizabeth Conant and their son Elihu; Lynne Heidt; Mary Jacobson; Cynthia Lee Jenner; Herb and Cathy Kraus; Blair Laden; Marletta ("Marty") Martenia (niece, daughter of sister Elizabeth); Leslie and Lauren McClellan; Louise McDowell; Joselyn Nixon;

John Otrompki; Geraldo and Cynthia Pelayo; Elaine Skorodin; Doree Stein; Judy Steinberg; Anne and Megan Sullivan; Della Tesch; Lily Venson; Ricky Wilson (nephew, son of Jennifer, granddaughter of sister Agnes), and Carl Wilson (brother-in-law) and his late girlfriend Dolores;

Les also mentioned how grateful he was to those who lived around or who came to our Door County, Wisconsin and Florida timeshares ("The Rushes" in Baileys' Harbor and "Vistana Resport" in Orlando) for the same good company, including Tom Seagard and Brigitte Kozma of the Mill Road Gallery in Sister Bay; Dale and Wendy Graf and their granddaughter Jasmine; Lynette Haleen, Bob Kaiser and Norb and Pat Lenius of Door County; Nancy Kaczmareck, her husband John Zeker and their children John Jr., Elizabeth, Emily and Sarah of Middleton, Wisconsin; Joan and Tony Haag, Nancy Webster ("Webby") and Maryann Hackel of Appleton; Della Tesch, Anne Witherell and Elaine Dinklage of Neenah, and Elaine's sister Colonel Kathleen Dinklage who came in from New Mexico to salute (literally — one of those magic and unforgettable moments) Major Brownlee; Kathy Howard and her daughter Melissa ("Missy") of Stoughton; Deb and Jerry Meylor and their daughters Erica and Brittany of Cottage Grove; Dawn Masbruch and her children Cody and Courtney, and sometimes her ex, Glenn, all of McFarland, and LaVerna Schneeberger of LaCrosse. Some of the Evanston "Sunday Nighters" also go to our timeshare gathers.

Les said he wanted all those at the Hotel Glavjc in Torno, Italy, to know how much he thanked him for giving him the writing retreat and wonderful company, food, wine and cheer he needed to write: Lena, Jean Carlo, Angelo, Valeria, Oswaldo, Maria Grazzi; Joseph, Carlo, Julia, Christian, Simone, Samantha, Miqueli and Gabrieli.

And, then, Les started on the students. "Now, here is where I am really walking a slippery slope," Les said in frustration. He started counting the dozens, dozens and dozens of students whom he thanked for letting him help them recognize their potential. He did not want to leave a single one out, but knew it was inevitable.

If those four yellow pages show up, I will print all the names! Meanwhile, Les had ended his acknowledgements with a take on his frequent quip, "Put me in the second half, Coach," when asked how he was, by signing off:

"If your name was left out, let me know and I will put you in the second edition, Friend."

I wish to add a grateful acknowledgment of my own: to Patrick Connolly, executive director of the North Shore United Educators in Wisconsin, who, for my United Staff Union, negotiated a five month sabbatical with the Wisconsin Education Association Council for me to work on getting Les's autobiography published.

04 07